THIS IS THE
BEAT GENERATION

Also by James Campbell

Invisible Country: A Journey through Scotland

Gate Fever: Voices from a Prison

Talking at the Gates: A Life of James Baldwin

Paris Interzone: Richard Wright, Lolita, Boris Vian and others
on the Left Bank, 1946–60

The Picador Book of Blues and Jazz (Ed.)

THIS IS
THE BEAT
GENERATION

New York–San Francisco–Paris

James Campbell

UNIVERSITY OF CALIFORNIA PRESS

Berkeley · Los Angeles · London

University of California Press
Berkeley and Los Angeles, California

University of California Press, Ltd.
London, England

Library of Congress Cataloging-in-Publication Data

Campbell, James, 1951–
This is the Beat Generation : New York, San Francisco, Paris / James Campbell.
        p.   cm.
Originally published: London : Secker & Warburg, 1999.
Includes bibliographical references and index.
ISBN 0-520-23033-7 (pbk : alk. paper)
1. Beat Generation.   2. American literature—20th century—History
and criticism.   3. New York (N.Y.)—Intellectual life—20th century.
        4. San Francisco (Calif.)—Intellectual life—20th century.
    5. Paris (France)—Intellectual life—20th century.   6. Authors,
American—20th century—Biography.   7. Americans—France—Paris—
Biography.   8. Burroughs, William S., 1914–1997.   9. Kerouac, Jack,
        1922–1969.   10. Ginsberg, Allen, 1926–1997.   I. Title.

PS226 B6 C36 2001

810.9'0054—dc21   2001027672

Manufactured in the United States of America
10   09   08   07   06   05
        10   9   8   7   6   5   4   3   2

The paper used in this publication is both acid-free and totally chlorine-free
(TCF). It meets the minimum requirements of ANSI/NISO Z39.48-1992
(R 1997) (*Permanence of Paper*). ♻

to Vera;
and to my friend Michael Greenberg

Contents

Illustrations follow pages 96 and 186

Foreword

In 1979, living in Edinburgh, Scotland, I set out to write the story of the Beat Generation and its descendants. I had published only a little – a few poems and articles in literary magazines – but my projected book had a grand scheme. It would be divided into two parts: the first would describe the Westward trail blazed by Jack Kerouac and his mildly criminal gang in the late 1940s, while the other would trace the journey to the East made by the proliferating Beat children – hippies, heads, freaks – in the 1960s and 70s. I was among them, and therefore felt entitled to say "I am the man, I was" etc. The book would be called "Going West, Going East". I had thumbed my way across half the globe, but had not yet set foot in the United States, so, in Edinburgh University Library, I studied maps to find the best way out of Queens, New York, where Kerouac waved goodbye to his mother on his first trip to Denver in July 1947; filleted old newspapers for current events (was there any significance in the fact that both Henry Ford and Al Capone died that year?); and tried to see the bestseller list as Kerouac the would-be novelist might have seen it. The book people were talking about was *The Plague* by Albert Camus, a carefully crafted political allegory, not his sort of thing at all. After a faltering start, Kerouac got on the road. I traveled with him all the way across a quire of foolscap before running out of steam.

Much later, in December 1994, in London, I interviewed Allen Ginsberg for a newspaper. Ginsberg was promoting his new collection of poems, *Cosmopolitan Greetings,* and we met in the deserted bar of a hotel just a few doors from the house in which Henry James had lived at the turn of the century. Ginsberg came shuffling across the floor of the lobby towards me, dressed in a suit, well-pressed blue shirt, and tie. I have always enjoyed such reversals of the popular image (Kerouac and Burroughs were also unlike many of the inventions imposed on them). The thing that impressed me most about Ginsberg had nothing to do with political subversiveness or beatness; it was his ability to memorize great chunks of English and American verse of every era. He talked more or less uninterruptedly for two hours, managing to seem self-effacing, even modest, all the while. When I asked if I might take his photograph, he composed his arms and legs and smiled ingenuously, as if for a family snap, then offered to take mine. He passed on a tip Robert Frank had given him on how to pose a sitter (keep the hands in check). Then he decorated my copy of *Cosmopolitan Greetings* with a drawing of a stern-looking Buddha floating above a skull with flower in its mouth. That evening, Ginsberg gave a reading at St James's Church, Piccadilly, where William Blake was baptized. He was exuberant and spontaneous, yet had everything under control. I learned later that his assistants would provide the organizers of every reading with a list of stipulations ("Plain chair with *flat seat,* not cushioned, not contoured. . . . Premixed camomile tea in pot or thermos. . . . Modest vase of flowers – preferably wild flowers in season. . . . Payment is due when services have been rendered . . ."). We went home full of Allen Ginsberg, daring anyone to say a word against him.

In fact, I had worried that he might accuse *me* of speaking ill of him and his Beat colleagues. A few months earlier, I had published a book, *Exiled in Paris* (issued in the UK as *Paris Interzone*), which contained a chapter on the Beats. The subject of the book is the English-language literary scene in Paris after the Second World War. It is composed of two narrative threads which run concurrently and barely intersect: one concerns the black writers who sailed from America to France in the wake of Richard Wright in the late 1940s and early 50s – James Baldwin, Chester Himes, William Gardner Smith – while the other involves the group of Europeans and white Americans who clustered around the Olympia Press, the firm which sponsored serious poets and novelists to write pornography, and at the same time published dubious works by some of the great avant-garde writers of the era: *Lolita, The Ginger Man,* Beckett's Trilogy, the first translations of Genet, and much else besides. Ginsberg and Burroughs were then in residence at the Hotel Rachou – later known as The Beat Hotel – and Ginsberg worked hard at persuading the roguish proprietor of the Olympia Press, Maurice Girodias, to take on the most dubious of all his books, *Naked Lunch.* (The Olympia edition was called *The Naked Lunch.*)

I was less than happy with the chapter on the Beats in *Exiled in Paris,* but it was through them that I came closest to weaving my two strands together. I concocted an imaginary scene in which an earlier resident of the Hotel Rachou, the black novelist Chester Himes, smart-suited, knife-carrying, as cool as life is short, met Allen Ginsberg, boyish, drug-taking, sophomorically hip, in the lobby. I called the chapter "Black and White Negroes", finished the book, and prepared to move on.

But to what? After meeting Ginsberg, I began to see this slightly unsatisfactory chapter as the foundation for another story. *Exiled in Paris* had itself been shaped from a rib taken from an earlier book, *Talking at the Gates: A Life of James Baldwin* (1991), which contains a lengthy section on Baldwin's life in Paris in the 1950s. Now, a fragment of the Paris book provided the bones for *This Is the Beat Generation.* The word "trilogy" sounds too grandiose, but I think of the three of them as a family.

During one of my research trips to New York, I rang up Ginsberg to ask for his cooperation (I had written in advance). He was friendly but wary, and – more than anything – weary. He said he might – he emphasized *might* – have some time at the weekend.

The next day, I tried to ring Gregory Corso. He was out. He had just gone out. He was expected back in an hour's time, or an hour ago, or at some hour in the unforeseeable future. Over on the West Coast, Michael McClure was similarly elusive, while the editor of a seminal Beat magazine agreed at first to meet me, then changed his mind when I declined to provide him with a list of questions from which there would be no deviation.

I couldn't blame them. They had been interviewed far too many times already. And so I decided to dispense with interviews. In any case, "personal testimony", like the tape recorder itself, can be a false friend. For example, one person I had thought of interviewing in New York was Diana Trilling, the wife of Lionel and the author of "The Other Night at Columbia", a lively account of a reading given by Ginsberg, Corso and Orlovsky at the University in 1959. When, later, I read her memoir, which contains anecdotes about Ginsberg visiting the Trillings' apartment on Riverside Drive, I found her portrait of him bedeviled by misunderstanding of his aims and motives. Had she been kind enough to agree to be interviewed, I might have included her misplaced emphases in my version of Ginsberg's relationship with the Trillings, simply because "this is how she says it was". I had discovered while writing both *Talking at the Gates* and *Exiled in Paris* that people involved in any literary history often have a piece of property for hire, the price of which is that you believe their version and not someone else's.

Freed from the entrapping spools of the cassette tape, I concentrated on reading the books, ferreting out letters and other personal scraps of paper (the most precious of all research materials), sifting through contemporary newspapers, tracking down a ton of weird and wonderful magazine articles spawned by "beatnik", the kitschification of Beat, and walking up and down the avenues of New York and the hills of San Francisco, imaginatively superimposing old landscapes, old styles of talk, old ways of seeing the world, on to the streets of today.

This account of the Beat Generation – for which the working title was my original tag "Going West, Going East" – begins in 1944, with the coming together of the three principal characters, and ends around 1960–61, with the publication of Burroughs's cut-up books and Ginsberg's travels to the East. These events seemed to me to mark the end of the "beat" part of the story.

Jack Kerouac never resolved the troubles which beset him from the mid-1950s onwards, and which are described here; he died in front of a television set in 1969, a year and a half after the death of his muse and driver, Neal Cassady. Ginsberg and Burroughs continued their remarkable exploratory careers, remained devoted friends, and died, a few months apart, in 1997. Burroughs's early partner in crime, Herbert Huncke, had expired the previous year. Many others who were associated with the Kerouac-Ginsberg-Burroughs troika, and who feature in this book, continue to thrive.

As always, my major debt is to Vera Chalidze for consistent help and advice. I wish also to thank Carolyn Cassady, Tom Clark, Paul Duguid, the late Allen Ginsberg, Michael Greenberg, Wendy Lesser and the *Threepenny Review*, where a portion of this book first appeared in different form, Antony Harwood, Gerald Mangan, Geoffrey Mulligan, Andrew O'Hagan, Kevin Ring and *Beat Scene*, the late Leopold and Bobby Ullstein, Lotte Lundell for hospitality in San Francisco, and Roger Rosen, Avery Russell and Rima Shore for the same in New York. I am also grateful to Steve Mandeville-Gamble of the Department of Special Collections at Stanford University, and to the staff of the Berg Collection, New York Public Library, and the Butler Library, Columbia University.

Many books have been used in the writing of this one. For basic information, I could not have done without *Ginsberg: A biography*, by Barry Miles; *Memory Babe: A critical biography*, by Gerald Nicosia; *Literary Outlaw: The life and times of William S. Burroughs*, by Ted Morgan. I also wish to make grateful mention of Ann Charters's edition of Kerouac's *Selected Letters*, and Oliver Harris's volume of Burroughs's letters.

The white Negro, the splendidly civilized, carelessly civilizing savage . . .

– Verlaine, on the death of Rimbaud, 1894

We decided that Salt Lake was too small for us. San Francisco was better . . . Buying tickets was throwing money away. So we 'beat it' down to Ogden and over the Southern Pacific, riding the front end of passenger trains at night . . .

– Jack Black, *You Can't Win* (1926)

PART I

I can feel myself drifting . . .

1

Crazy wisdom

During his brief career in the Navy, Jack Kerouac was regarded as a 'case'. He went to the doctor with headaches, which excused him from dull chores. He let it be known that he was writing a novel, which he liberally compared – though he had published scarcely a word in his life – to hefty American classics. He got drunk easily, often rowdily, sometimes maliciously. But his worst characteristic by far, where the Navy was concerned, was his unresponsiveness to discipline. This by itself was enough, in wartime, to have a serviceman labelled unsound of mind, paranoid, hysterical, phobic, catatonic, melancholy, monomaniacal, suicidal, or one of the other psychiatric diagnoses by which the military explained a person's failure to click his heels and snap to attention at the bark of authority.

Kerouac had no talent for authority. He was touched, almost gifted, by one of its opposites: the wanderlust. He had already made a few tightly structured journeys by road before he joined the Merchant Marine, in 1942, and then, as the war intensified, signed up for the Naval Air Force V-12 officer-training programme. But they were single-sentence journeys, usually made alone, and by Greyhound bus, hesitant with pauses, never far away from the security of the full stop: his home in Massachusetts, his mother's love and stove. As he made his way back by the same route, the same bus (a car accident in 1940 put him off driving for life), he tidied up his wandering with no notion that it could be extended to fill a page, far less a book.

It was the sea, not the road, that first inspired him to shape his travelling into a story. When he went to sea, the vastness and unexpected alienation that came off it, day after day – days of dreary expectation of more of the same – led to the conception of a novel of Melvillean scope (everything Kerouac attempted in writing, even then, was overseen by a giant literary guardian) called 'The Sea Is My Brother'. That was the exciting part of life at sea: planning his book, naming it, comparing it to its ancestors, telling his friends back home all about it in letters; everything else, including the sea itself, was grim and grey.

He did not graduate from the Merchant Marine to become a V-12 Naval Air Force pilot in the United States Navy, as he had hoped to do in mid-March 1943. He failed the mathematical part of the test and was sent to boot camp instead, at Newport, Rhode Island, to be moulded into some other, more basic fodder. This was a disappointment. Boot camp was not the source-material adventure he had anticipated when he signed up for service, and was even worse than being at sea. Kerouac found the routine unpleasant and impertinent, the people he was supposed to work for stupid. The twenty-one-year-old writer could not say 'ship-shape' with any conviction. Watch duty entailed inspection of other recruits' dress, 'to see that everyone is buttoned up, etc. Do you know what I actually do?' he asked his hometown friend Sebastian Sampas, who was to die in action within a year. 'I mind my own fucking business.'

In the military mind, indiscipline shaded into mental imbalance; it was also a quick exit from the Navy. So Kerouac began putting it on. He insisted on calling the Navy dentist – an officer in a white coat – 'doc', when 'sir' was obligatory. Smoking was forbidden before breakfast – so Kerouac smoked. When the commanding officer whipped the cigarette from his mouth, Kerouac stood up and punched him. All that was bad enough. But the unforgivable insubordination was against the integrity of the squadron. One morning, during close-order drill, Kerouac simply laid down his rifle and walked off. This was inexplicable, and the recruit was placed under observation in the mental wing of the Navy hospital. Asked for his name and rank, he replied: 'I'm only old Samuel Johnson.' The doctors took notes and made reports, and soon Kerouac was happily relaying to his friends the news that he had been diagnosed as someone subject to 'bizarre behavior'.

The second fastest escape route from the Navy was homosexuality (or 'ambisexuality', to describe the so-so), and here, too, Kerouac worked to fortify the doctors' suspicions. He might not be crazy, but he could be 'fruit'. Under examination, he shook his head when asked about girls – no, he wasn't in love with anyone. Would he like to get married? No, not at all. He mentioned some encounters with loose women, but was careful, he told a friend from his home town of Lowell, to add 'the crowning glory of being more closely attached to my male friends'. The boy-gang was more important, spiritually and emotionally, than any individual girl could ever be. It was all an act, and – he was not quite aware of this yet – it was all true.

Eventually, he succeeded in getting his discharge. The official report said 'indifferent character', but in the course of the doctors' examinations the term 'dementia praecox' – schizophrenia – was used, and Kerouac liked the sound of it. It confirmed him in his sense that, far from being 'indifferent', he was different, that he was a more complex person than anybody else, more interesting, certainly, than his friend Sebastian gave him credit for; Sebastian who had recently written a letter of censure over Kerouac's drunken and anti-social behaviour. When the doctors described to one another, and then to him, 'a complex condition of mind, split up as it were, in two parts, one normal, the other schizoid', it sounded pretty grand to an aspiring writer. Take your pick:

My schizoid side is the Raskolnikov–Dedalus–George Webber . . . side, the bent and brooding figure sneering at a world of mediocrities . . .

My normal counterpart, the one you're familiar with, is the halfback–whoremaster–alemate–scullion–jitterbug–jazzcritic side, the side in me which requires a broad, rugged America . . .

★

Before his naval fiasco, Kerouac had attended Columbia College, in uptown New York, on a football scholarship. He had walked away from that, too. But in 1941, during one of his forays downtown, who knows, he might have exchanged glances with William Burroughs as they passed on the street or stood next to one another in a bar.

Burroughs would have noticed the dark-haired, classically hand-some young football player, but would have avoided being noticed in return; his own most outstanding characteristic was his invisibility. Whereas Kerouac was boisterous, rude, sometimes inspiringly, sometimes tiringly bubbling with enthusiasm – for music, for girls, for books and the adventures they promised – Burroughs was an accumulation of negatives; he appeared to others, in his own description, as 'without context . . . perhaps a series of homo non sapiens . . . completely anonymous'.

Burroughs was not military material either, though he too was trying. He applied to join the Navy, but was turned down as a poor physical specimen. Then he attempted to become a pilot in the Glider Corps, but was refused because of his weak eyesight. In any case, he was definitely 'fruit'. He liked straight men in red-and-black wool check shirts (such as Kerouac favoured), though he himself usually dressed in a grey three-piece suit, with collar and tie, sometimes with gloves and snap-brim hat as well, just to neutralize the last, lingering trace of visibility. Beneath the armour, an immovable individualism was being shaped. Burroughs was snubbed by the military, but he did commit a heroic act during a pre-wartime visit to Europe, when he married a German Jewish woman in Yugoslavia, enabling her to come to America and escape the Nazis.

In 1941, three years out of Harvard and living in the Taft Hotel on Seventh Avenue at 50th Street, Burroughs's daytime company consisted of the great writers and thinkers of the age – all in between hard covers – while his evenings were spent in midtown saloons observing and occasionally communing with low-lifes and hustlers, palpably present in the flesh. He felt accepted in that company, by default. Times Square types, on the whole, didn't have Ivy League career assumptions about you, didn't compare membership of University clubs, or family trees. At the beginning of the war, Burroughs began the process of sloughing all that off; or, to use his own metaphor, 'shitting it out'.

Among the people he met in the subfusc bars was Jack Anderson, who had the stamp of a male model but was actually a part-time prostitute. There was a current expression about young chaps with slicked-back hair and seductive sharp cheekbones, that they 'looked like the man in the Arrow collar ad', who gazed down on passers-by from billboards around Times Square and up and down the avenues. Jack Anderson fitted the type, and Burroughs fell for him; Anderson was 'queer' but not a 'fairy'.

The Taft Hotel had its own high ideals, like the Navy, and the rules and regulations designed to protect them. After Burroughs and his handsome friend were surprised in bed by the house detective one afternoon, Burroughs had to leave. Even invisible, he failed to blend in. He followed Anderson down to Jane Street in Greenwich Village, where Anderson was boarding in a rooming house. Burroughs moved in next door to him. What could be better? Only now he discovered that the time Anderson did not spend with him was lavished on other boyfriends, girlfriends, pickups, clients. He had less time for Burroughs than before. There was less and less to see of him anyway, consumed as he was by the sounds of chinking glasses, laughter and lovemaking filtering through the wall.

Whereas Kerouac drew on fictional characters to define his attitudes (the 'Raskolnikov–Dedalus' etc figure), Burroughs found a solution to the maddening jealousy Jack Anderson provoked in him in the action of a real-life artist and sociopath. A few years later, he liked to describe what he did to friends, Kerouac among them, as his 'Van Gogh kick'.

Driven out of the house yet again by Anderson's party noises, Burroughs bought a pair of poultry shears from a Sixth Avenue store. Back at Jane Street, he placed the little finger of his left hand between the blades and cut it off. 'Waves of euphoria swept through him', he wrote in an attempt to record the incident in fictional form. The severed finger lying on the dresser was sudden, welcome proof of his corporeal reality. After cleaning up the blood and swaddling the digit in a handkerchief, he left the rooming house.

> He stopped in a bar and ordered a double brandy, meeting all eyes with a level, friendly stare. Goodwill flowed out of him for everyone he saw, for the whole world. A lifetime of defensive hostility had fallen from him.

Unlike Van Gogh, Burroughs did not offer the mutilated emblem to his beloved prostitute. Instead, he took it uptown and presented it to his analyst, who advised urgent psychiatric help. Burroughs disagreed, but allowed himself to be taken to Bellevue Hospital, for medical treatment only. Once there, he was overcome by 'a sudden faintness'. Some papers appeared before him, which he was asked to sign. His analyst disappeared.

> 'Where is my room?' he asked a nurse.
> 'Your room! I don't know what bed you've been assigned to. Anyway you can't go there before eight unless you have a special order from the doctor.' . . .
> He looked around him at the bar corridors, the men walking around in bathrobes, muttering under the cold, indifferent eyes of an attendant.
> *Why, this is the psychopathic ward . . .*

Burroughs spent a month as a 'case'. The finger joint was never seen again. In his later, anecdotal account, Jack Anderson was transformed into a she:

> 'And what about the girl?'
> 'Oh, by the time I got out of the nuthouse she'd gone to Chicago. I never saw her again.'

★

Allen Ginsberg was born in 1926, which made him four years younger than Kerouac and twelve years younger than Burroughs, but he knew about dementia praecox and suffered the smell of institutions earlier than either of those two.

The Ginsberg family lived in Paterson, New Jersey. Ginsberg's father, Louis, was a high-school teacher and a lyric poet with a modest reputation, who was often to be found occupying the poetry spot in the *New York Times*. He wrote deft, well-finished verses, in which, in his own words, he sought to express 'the glory of the commonplace'.

> This mist can make the meanest side street be
> Password and threshold for a mystery.
>
> Blest is this that muffles sense and sound;
> For, lest a cruel, heedless sun should pound
>
> Merciless deserts of a blinding light,
> Fog will bestow its gift of second sight!

Louis was stable and stolid, the son of Russian Jewish immigrants of the working class; both of Ginsberg's parents were firmly behind the Revolution, and were believers in the inevitable collapse of American capitalism. His mother Naomi, also from a Russian family, grew up speaking Yiddish. She emigrated to the United States at the age of ten. In the late 1930s, before Allen had reached his teens, she went insane, locking herself in the bathroom, hiding under the bed, screaming about Mussolini, complaining of 'three big sticks up my back' and wires in her head. One night, out of control, she was dispatched to a New Jersey 'rest home' with Allen as her escort. Within a year, she was confined in a state mental hospital – 'begging my 13-year-old mercy', Ginsberg wrote later. ' "Take me home" – . . . and I'd say, "No, you're crazy, Mama, – Trust the Drs".' She scarcely let up in her ravings until her death seventeen years later.

The close-up view of his mother's psychosis caused a severe shock to Ginsberg's system. A decade later, he committed himself to the Columbia Psychiatric Institute on West 168th Street, Manhattan, remaining there for eight months. He was twenty-three, more of a 'case' than Kerouac could hope to be. He thought that William Blake had entered his room in a Harlem tenement and was talking to him – actually in the room and reciting a poem. Ginsberg was sublimely transported; he saw the depths of the Universe; he understood the Oneness of all things. He never surrendered the validity of his vision, but not long after it he plunged into an abysmal depression.

It was the beginning, though he didn't realize it, of his lengthy struggle with the Wordsworthian maxim – 'We poets in our youth begin in gladness / But thereof comes in the end despondency and madness' – wrestling with it so that it faced the other way; madness to gladness was the Ginsbergian trajectory.

In the Psychiatric Institute, he met the man who would provide a beacon for his literary voyaging over the following decade. Carl Solomon suffered from serious mental illness, though only intermittently. He was intelligent and well read, and his reading gave him an intellectual structure for his condition. Solomon passed to Ginsberg something to read by his mentor, Antonin Artaud, who had died in a French lunatic asylum the year before, in 1948. He told Ginsberg that during a visit to Paris he had come upon Artaud reading in an

9

art gallery. He was trembling as he read, and seemed to be pointing at Solomon, as if electing him his representative across the seas.

Ginsberg was weighed down by his worrisome sexuality, his beached academic career, his mother's illness, his glimpse into eternity. The Artaud essay, 'Van Gogh: The man suicided by society', gathered together some of the threads of his unravelling brain to make a kind of redemptive sense: 'So a sick society invented psychiatry to defend itself against the investigations of certain visionaries whose faculties of divination disturbed it.'

While in the Institute, Ginsberg received a letter from a female friend who had also had a spell in 'the bin'. Nothing to worry about, she told him. Cheer up.

> I was not much surprised to hear about your hospitalization, as I've been claiming for years that anyone who doesn't blow his top once is no damn good.

2

The first cut-ups

These three, Kerouac, Burroughs, and Ginsberg, met through the agency of another man, Lucien Carr. In the fall of 1943, Carr was a student at Columbia College, the undergraduate liberal-arts division of Columbia University. As with the Navy, as with the Taft Hotel even, the University had lofty assumptions about its own integrity. Campus life, like daily life in general, like society as a whole, was rigid with law and custom. So much was not allowed that the concept of 'not allowed' was itself practically redundant. Life was stiff with propriety. The same sense of good behaviour as pervaded the student dormitories governed the classrooms and the campus itself. The College provided a forum for argument, but was itself unarguable; life, liberty, the pursuit of freedom through enlightenment – these ideals, too, were in need of protection.

Carr, nineteen years old, had visions of the other side, over the College walls, beyond the boundaries of civil order. His intellect, like his Christian name, was French. He could quote Baudelaire – '*Plonger au fond du gouffre . . . ciel ou enfer, qu'importe . . .* To cast oneself to the heart of the abyss, heaven or hell, no matter.' Carr could discuss Rimbaud's 'théorie du voyant', his insistence that 'the soul must be made monstrous', his poetics of delirium. Drug-induced? Absinthe or wine or beer-induced? – 'Qu'importe.'

Carr was himself a sort of campus Rimbaud, a teenage aesthete, slender with almond eyes and tousled blond hair. His literary aspirations involved a chemistry of poetry and violence. Or just poetry and mischief, which, given autonomy, might become violent by itself, leaving Lucien (pronounced 'Looshun') free of responsibility.

In Chicago, earlier in the year, Carr had put his head in an oven and switched on the gas. Why? asked the doctor. Carr offered the explanation that it was a work of art. This made no more sense to the doctors than Kerouac's walking away from Navy drill, but the outcome was the same: as a suicide risk, Carr was placed for a month in the psychiatric wing of Chicago's Cook County Hospital (which also got him out of military service). He too, then, had crazy credentials when he first met Ginsberg and Kerouac.

Carr had already attended the University of Chicago before coming to New York. He didn't give much for Columbia's strictly enforced decorum. He was himself a breach of the rules, a sweet-faced profanity. If the temperature dipped too low at a party, Lucien would start to chew a beer glass in front of the other guests; or open a window and urinate into the street; or start ripping the pages out of a Bible. Unfamiliar onlookers might find this behaviour revolting, but to admirers his mischief was instinctive, and had a sort of lyricism to it. 'Know these words', Ginsberg wrote in his journal, when they had been acquainted for only a few months, 'and you speak the Carr language: fruit, phallus, clitoris, cacoethes, feces, foetus, womb, Rimbaud.' The gem in the lexicon is 'cacoethes', an 'uncontrollable urge, especially for something harmful'.

Carr had another distinction: he was the object of an older man's fixation. David Kammerer had given up jobs in several states in order to follow Carr wherever he went. Each time Carr's mother moved him, in an attempt to evade the shadow, Kammerer followed. Ever since they had met when Lucien was a boy scout and Kammerer the scoutmaster, he had dogged Carr's footsteps: from St Louis, their hometown, to Phillips, Andover, to Bowdoin College in Maine, to the University of Chicago. Carr's mother, who lived on East 57th Street, had an old-fashioned, pre-psychiatric belief that the older Kammerer ('the old man', Carr called him) was spinning a web to ensnare her son, 'purely from a love of evil'. She called him a 'veritable Iago'. She had hoped that by installing Lucien at Columbia, just a short bus ride from her apartment, she could protect him. But Kammerer had quit his latest job, as a teacher in Chicago, and come creeping to New York. He was now working as a janitor at a house in Morton Street, Greenwich Village, in exchange for board. On neighbouring Bedford Street lived William Burroughs, an old friend of both the old man and the young man from St Louis days.

Kammerer was Carr's opposite: tall and clumsy, always badly dressed, with a big nose and scrubby red hair. Most of Lucien's contemporaries shared Marion Carr's feelings and regarded Kammerer as a sinister presence, but Burroughs liked him, appreciated his intellect, and found him better company, on the whole, than the magnetic but callow Carr. Lucien himself did not act as if he was being hounded. He spent a lot of time with Kammerer. His vanity was flattered by the attention. When he did something outrageous, Kammerer beamed and asked all around: 'Isn't he wonderful?' Visitors to Burroughs's Bedford Street apartment often came away having watched the two men, one overweight, the other slender but muscular, wrestling on the floor like Birkin and Crich in *Women in Love*. Kammerer would get up from these contests panting and sweating with lust, Lucien fired with adrenalin and ready for further mischief. When they went out into the street and headed uptown to the West End bar, opposite the campus, Carr might burst into song, and Kammerer would join in:

> Violate me
> in violent times
> the vilest way that you know.
> Ruin me, ravage me,
> utterly savage me,
> on me no mercy bestow.

★

Out of Lucien's Rimbaud–Baudelaire parentage came a French nickname: Claude de Maubris. It stuck, so that even in later life Lucien was Claude to certain friends. At other times, it was 'Angel Boy', or 'Lucien Midnight', or, conflating the two, 'Old Angel Midnight', an angel of darkness.

The Claude de Maubris tag was the invention of Kerouac, who really did have French ancestry. His parents were French-Canadian. He was born on 12 March 1922, Jean Louis Lebris de Kerouac – or

13

Kirouac, or Kéroack, or even Kernuk, with ancient origins spanning Celtic kingdoms from Brittany to Cornwall. The family lived on Lupine Road, Lowell, Massachusetts, and Kerouac claimed to remember the night of his birth, delivering a pun-packed *mise-en-scène* from his two tongues:

Massachusetts March
Wild howl Lupine Cold the Moony
and Loony nights.

Kerouac's father Leo had worked as a journalist on French newspapers, and the children spoke French at home, gradually changing to English once they started school. Jack's childhood name was 'Ti Pousse' (Little Thumb); 'Ti Jean', as he got older; then Jean, John, Jackie, and finally Jack. In his twenties, he was still apt to sign letters with 'Jean', to speak the *joual* dialect to his parents, and to fall back on French when moved to express pained sentiments, as when Sebastian Sampas was killed in the war: 'ayez des pensées de moi, hein? Tu m'as tant fait mal au coeur . . .'

Lowell was a working-class town on the Merrimack River, of cotton mills and shoe factories and small shops such as the printing shop which Kerouac's father ran. His hometown friends had Greek or Irish or German names – Apostolos, Ryan, Blickfeldt; all they had in common was their provincialism. Many of them would never leave Lowell, or would do so only to fight in the war or to follow work. When the intellectual set, of which Kerouac and Sebastian Sampas were the leading lights, came together, it was to discuss a politics and a poetry luminous with ideals of perfection. They called themselves the Young Prometheans, and were brimful of the 'brotherhood of man' and the residual graces of Russian socialism. The notion of a poet's soul 'made monstrous', the idea of libertinage, the literary advantages of delirium – these would have made no sense, would have seemed inhuman, to Lowell's Young Prometheans.

Oh! so long ago
Remember the mists of
early New England
the sun glaring through
the trees and chambers
of Beauty.

That was the work of Sebastian, but Kerouac wrote with a similar preciousness, in a tone balanced on inversions, abstractions – 'Tall pines standing like justice' – and facile rhymes.

As they developed, away from Lowell, his tastes became more native than classical, more American than European. He began to dream of absorbing, and ultimately expressing in terms of his own vision, 'the essential and everlasting America'. He could see it and smell it in the imagined horizons stretching beyond artificial statelines towards frontiers glowing with New World promise; and in the long, spacious sentences which strove to encompass the American landscape and seascape, of Herman Melville, Theodore Dreiser, Thomas Wolfe. 'I think Americans are much better novelists today, than the English', he wrote in a letter of September 1943 (though his choice of English reading matter was certainly quaint: John Galsworthy, Radclyffe Hall, Sir Hugh Walpole and Sir Philip Gibbs). When he mentioned the author of *Moby Dick*, it was 'our Melville'. As far as America was concerned, he was all proprietoriness. Melville had said that the whaleboats of the Pacific had been his Harvard and his Yale; in dropping out of Columbia to go to sea, Kerouac was enrolling in the school of Melville.

Three months after his discharge from the US Navy, he signed up again for the Merchant Marine, and this time succeeded in shipping out – for Liverpool, on the SS *George Weems*, with a cargo of bombs. It was the desired war service in its way, but it was also a research trip, as it always would be, wherever he went, to gather material, in this case for 'The Sea Is My Brother'. 'A hell of a lot happens', he wrote to a friend who was to die at sea before the letter was sent: 'love, the tribulations of the generations, war, the sea, foreign countries, etc, etc.' It was 'a gigantic saga'. It had to be big, like the novels of Wolfe or Melville. All the writers he admired wrote big books, including the non-Americans, Balzac, Thomas Mann, Proust; and Kerouac's individuality, strong though it was, was twinned with a wish to be just like his heroes. To the invocation of Dostoevsky, Joyce and Wolfe that he sent out from the Navy boot camp – 'My schizoid side is the Raskolnikov–Dedalus–George Webber . . . side . . .' – he had added another name, 'Duluoz', one of his fictional names for himself, possibly a high-art and down-home compound of 'Dedalus' and a Lowell Greek name, Daoulas.

In joining up and going to sea to write a big saga, he was doing more than simply apprenticing himself to his favourite novelists, in the traditional manner of young writers; rather, Kerouac was situating himself as a character in an imaginary novel by one of them. He had a strong habit of identifying himself by means of literary representation, of defining himself in terms of fictional characters, or in terms of the imagined life of real writers, and viewing his own actions this way, through the lens of literature. His intention was to substitute a novel by Jack Kerouac for the imaginary one by Wolfe or Melville, and to situate himself in that instead.

Kerouac was dark and stocky, with a patient dumbness about the jaw; sincerity blended with a hint of perversity in the eyes. His good looks were enhanced by his athletic past – before taking up his football scholarship at Columbia, he had made a name as a running back on the school team in Lowell, where the local newspapers printed his picture – and further enhanced by his literary future. If the present happened to be complicated by 'dementia praecox', well then, that too could have romantic advantages. One girlfriend recalled how, when they first met, she asked if his name was Eskimo, for it reminded her of an Eskimo friend called Inaktook. He repeated the word 'Inaktook' a few times, then put it together with 'Kerouac', and started to dance a little dance, and chant a little chant. 'And I said, Jeez, he's a little nutty. He told me he was a writer, and I must say my interest picked up a little.'

While still at Columbia, Kerouac met an art student called Edie Parker, and they began a romance which lasted three years, surviving his dropping out, his clumsy sweet-nothings – 'I miss you very much, strangely enough', he wrote from aboard ship, on his way to Liverpool – his poverty, and his all-round lack of commitment to anything except his imagination. (Was there more to life than a little dance and a little chant?) Edie came from a well-to-do family in Grosse Pointe, Detroit ('People in Grosse Pointe were not lacking in anything in those days,' she wrote, 'except enough things to spend money on'), and had a lusty eagerness about her that drew interesting people of both sexes into her orbit. When the longshoremen at the

New York Port of Embarcation began to be pressed into military service, Edie donned a set of overalls and worked in the docks, driving forklifts and electric carts with loaded trailers.

> When working at night, we would finish loading the Liberty ships, then watch the sailors board, then watch them pull out, go down the Hudson, and perhaps 'way off', see a glow on the horizon, hoping it wasn't our ship being torpedoed – knowing the German U-boats were out there; the 'Wolf Pack' even surfaced along the shore at night.

Edie rented an apartment at 421 West 118th Street, where Kerouac stayed when not at sea or at home with his family. She shared it with Joan Vollmer Adams, a student at nearby Barnard College, Columbia's sister school, and a freshman, John Kingsland. Their previous flat had been one block north, at almost the same number (420 West 119th Street), and Edie's description probably holds good for the new place as well:

> All the surrounding apartments were occupied by Juilliard students – sopranos were singing constantly along with their canaries! – they all had birds. It was like being on a Broadway stage with the cast, all included for $44 per month.

Edie's flatmate, Joan, was graceful and droll, with a taste for elegant outfits and silk stockings (nylons were just coming in). She had 'a boy's figure', wrote Edie, and 'a beautiful face, shaped a little like a heart'. Joan was a reader; she 'read slowly, savouring every moment'. She took the New York daily papers – there were six at the time – into the apartment's large bathroom, and read them in her perfumed bubble bath, receiving the occasional guest while she soaked.

Joan was slightly older than the others; she had a husband, Paul Adams, who was off fighting the war, and then all of a sudden she had a baby. She also had a big baby lover, the sixteen-year-old freshman, Kingsland, and a big Benzedrine habit. Well-meaning Edie said that Joan's idea of a good time was to 'sip Kummel liqueur at Child's on Broadway', but that elegant pastime could not have lasted very long, for by the time she met Kerouac and Co, at the age of twenty-five, Joan's idea of a good time was to wheel her daughter

Julie down to Times Square or the less salubrious parts of Broadway, or wherever was good for a score, and get stoned.

The closest many Columbia students got to the war was to brush against the V–12 Naval cadets who were occupying the campus and sleeping in the resident halls. Students had been moved out to accommodate the aspiring pilots, and were being housed in the nearby apartment blocks, or else, like Lucien Carr, in the Theological Seminary building on West 122nd Street. In the general coming and going between there and the West End bar, Lucien met Edie Parker. She found him pretty to look at and almost as fascinating to talk to as her boyfriend, who was exhausting her patience by continually deserting her, for his mother's hearth or for the sea. It was the latter that had claimed him at the time she met Lucien. He was two years younger than she, and already attached to a half-French Barnard student with the relishable name of Céline, so there was no room for romance, but a friendship started and together the francophone couple began to visit 118th Street.

When Kerouac came home on leave and was introduced to Carr, his gaze fell on him suspiciously. 'A mischievous little prick', he thought. But the presence of Céline and the renewed and sexually adventurous devotion of Edie reassured him, and soon he began to enjoy the spiciness of 'cacoethes', the plunge into heaven or hell – *qu'importe* – the visionary theories, and the talk of a soul made monstrous, that invariably emerged from an evening in Lucien's company. Standing in the aisle of a subway train, he would suddenly burst into song – 'He fucked 'em in the pantry, he fucked 'em in the hall. / By God, said the cook, he's a-going to fuck us all' – or else he would coax Kerouac into a wooden barrel found in the street and roll him down Broadway from the West End bar.

Around Lucien, the clinical severity of the terms 'schizoid' and 'dementia' melted away. Madness became play; it was madness in the soft sense, the way Kerouac himself wanted to be mad, romantically mad, but never could be for long . . . there was always someone else controlling the speed of things, and he was always in the passenger seat, taking notes: 'the only ones for me are the mad ones . . . mad to live, mad to talk' . . . Kerouac liked to experience his madness vicariously.

18

As for Lucien, he saw in the 118th Street scene the potential for obeying another Baudelairean imperative: 'One should always be drunk . . . With wine, with poetry, or with virtue, as you choose. But get drunk.' They did get drunk – with wine, with poetry – they smoked marihuana ('tea'), and sometimes they followed Joan down to the Times Square pharmacies, to indulge her dope habit, and to sample some themselves. Benzedrine could be obtained legally over the counter, in the form of an inhaler, which was cracked open to reveal a strip of paper soaked in the drug. Two or three of these, wrapped in chewing gum, gave an all-night, talk-sustained high.

Back at the flat, they listened to Leadbelly singing 'The Midnight Special', and Billie Holiday's evocation of a lynching, 'Strange Fruit'. Kerouac was a jazz enthusiast, with an unusual ability to reproduce the sounds of instruments vocally, and he could imitate the solo lines of his favourite players, such as Ben Webster and Dizzy Gillespie. There was an unstated understanding that the Negro was more earthy than anybody else, and in possession of certain secrets. Harlem, packed with blacks like the blacks in the songs, was visible, virtually stone's-throwing distance across Morningside Park, just at the foot of their street; but to Columbia students living in the strange, unofficial segregation of 1940s New York, it might as well have been in Africa.

Carr brought Burroughs up from Bedford Street. The excuse for the introduction was that Burroughs was thinking of joining the Merchant Marine, and wanted to ask able seaman Kerouac's advice; but, equally, Burroughs was curious to meet the sturdy sailor-poet whom Lucien had depicted swaggering round the apartment in his singlet, quoting Thomas Wolfe, ordering eggs and bacon from good-time girl Edie, pouring beer into his tank of a mouth.

Burroughs looked around: drugs parties, a baby, Joan mixed up with freshman Kingsland, sores beginning to break out on her body from excessive Benzedrine use, a desperate 'get drunk' gaiety motivating everyone and everything. It was Cocteau's *Les Enfants terribles* transposed to uptown Manhattan. Not a bad place.

★

Scenes from the early life of William Seward Burroughs II (warning: some contain violence).

i) He was named after his grandfather, who in 1891 invented the Arithometer, a refined version of the existing adding machine; by the time of the Depression, in 1929, all the family stock from Burroughs Adding Machine Corporation had been sold, and connections to the firm severed. Growing up in St Louis, in a wealthy family, with a name made famous in another century for a contraption which had since been superseded, Burroughs's 'invisibility' was an inherited lack. A contemporary said of his parents that they seemed 'never to be there'.

ii) Burroughs's first attempt at fiction, 'The Autobiography of a Wolf', was written when he was eight, in 1922, in the year Kerouac was born in Lupine ('wolfish') Road; also that year, a St Louis-born writer, T. S. Eliot, published 'The Waste Land', which Burroughs later described as 'the first cut-up'. In 'The Autobiography of a Wolf', the wolf is ultimately eaten by a grizzly bear. Kindly grown-ups suggested that he might have meant to call it 'The Biography . . .' No, Burroughs said, it was 'The Autobiography of a Wolf'. The title might have been inspired by a neighbour of the Burroughs family on Pershing Avenue, who described the young Burroughs as having 'a face like a sheep-killing dog'.

iii) In another juvenile story, a boy grieving over the loss of his dog is accosted by a man, 'thin and grey with pinpoint eyes', who offers him drugs. He accepts and becomes hooked. After a close shave with death, the boy turns himself in to the law. 'And if any kind stranger ever offers me some pills that will drive my blues away, I will simply call a policeman.'

iv) St Louis in the 1920s was a major river port and a centre for the chemicals industry, and Burroughs amused himself by standing on the banks of the Rivière des Pères to watch the sewage streaming out of the pipes into the water. In hot weather, the smell of shit and coal gas hung over the entire city, causing widespread disgust. 'I liked this smell myself', Burroughs recollected.

v) The first high school he attended was John Burroughs (no

relation) in St Louis, and his first published prose appeared in the *John Burroughs Review* in February 1929, on the subject of 'control'. The essay was called 'Personal Magnetism', and it offered advice on 'how to control others at a glance':

> Here is how it is done: I must look my victim squarely in the eye, say in a low, severe voice, 'I am talking and you must listen', then intensify my gaze and say, 'You cannot escape me.'

vi) After John Burroughs, he attended the Los Alamos Ranch School in New Mexico, which combined the flair of the Old West with military regimentation. In the spring of 1943, when Burroughs was on his way to New York, shortly to team up with Kerouac and others, the Los Alamos Ranch School was taken over by the US Army and became the principal site for the development of the atom bomb.

vii) At Harvard, Burroughs playfully aimed a .32 calibre revolver at a classmate. The student managed to leap sideways as Burroughs squeezed the trigger, and a bullet plugged into the wall. Burroughs said he thought the gun was empty. The student was Richard Stern, later a popular writer of crime novels. Twenty years later, another novelist with the name Richard Stern, also a Harvard graduate, was instrumental in the suppression of the issue of the *Chicago Review* which contained some of the first published instalments of *Naked Lunch*. 'If you cut into the present, the future leaks out.'

viii) After Harvard, but before the Jack Anderson / Van Gogh incident, Burroughs, in collaboration with a friend, produced a short story about a shipwreck, based on the loss of the *Titanic*, called 'Twilight's Last Gleamings'. The final paragraph was given over to a supposed account of the wreck in the *Evening News*:

> Barbara Cannon showed your reporter her souvenirs of the disaster: a life belt autographed by the crew, and a severed human finger.
>
> 'I don't know', said Miss Cannon. 'I feel sorta odd about this old finger.'

ix) His memory contained a foggy snapshot, always hovering in the mind's eye without ever becoming fully visible, of the moment when something 'evil ... something gross and improper ... something very drastic, very unpleasant' was introduced into his life.

21

It involved his nanny, Mary Evans, her boyfriend, and the four-year-old Burroughs, all together in a wood. What happened? An act of sodomy? An abortion for Mary and the concealment of the results? A miscarriage? He never knew, and he never lost the sense of evil.

★

Carr was a magnet for literary types. Literary allusions came spinning off him. A single letter might contain discussion of Spinoza, Tolstoy, Hardy, Eliot. Even his appearance was an allusion, to the bohemian hooligan poets of nineteenth-century France. 'His ego demands recognition', Ginsberg confided to his journal. 'Either he is a genius or he . . . but he can recognize no other alternative. He must prove that he is a genius.' But a genius for what? Carr tried to write, but he could not get life into his sentences. A list of exciting words (cacoethes, etc) was his greatest work so far. His short stories were as flat as his behaviour was electrically unpredictable. Even his letters choked on their own diction: "Dear Allen, I have procrastinated in writing until now. You will just have time to answer this epistle . . ." "Dear Allen, . . . You are somewhat incommunicado without a phone . . ."

They first met at the Union Theological Seminary, the relief resident hall, between Christmas and New Year, 1943–4, shortly after Carr had encountered Edie. Ginsberg was on his way to his room when the strains of a Brahms trio floating out from under a door caught his ears. He knocked, and Carr opened.

Inside, covering the walls, on the bookshelves, even in the records stacked against the gramophone, Ginsberg could see the modernist taste and style that his father's desperate need for formalism, symmetry, stability – so conspicuous in his verse, so lacking in his family life – conspired to banish from the Ginsberg home. Proceeding under the guidance of his parents, Ginsberg had decided to study law, and to serve the underprivileged masses. Although he joined Carr in his contempt for *les bourgeois*, Ginsberg looked at them from the perspective of Moscow rather than Paris. When he confided to Lucien his private pledge to serve the working classes,

Lucien replied: 'You know nothing about the working classes. You've never worked a day in your life.'

The question that linked them intellectually was the one that concerns all teenage aesthetes: What is art? Ginsberg kept notes of their discussions:

> Allen: Well, really, art should communicate.
>
> Lucien: Come now, Ginsberg, do you really think that art is communication?
>
> A (hesitatingly): No.
>
> L: If Michelangelo went over to the moon, would he be appreciated? But it would still be art. Really, Ginsberg, you ought to straighten these things out in your mind before you presume to argue with me.
>
> A: I have a right to change my mind.
>
> L: Which just about shows how light your mind is.

Ginsberg had already written poetry, and even published a little. His work regularly appeared in the *Columbia Jester-Review*, the campus magazine, but he could hardly expect Lucien to enthuse over squibs such as 'Pass the biscuits Pappy O'Daniel', or 'Songs for the tender-hearted liberal', aimed at contemporary politicians.

The pages of his journal began to bulge with Lucien, reflecting an appalled fascination. He itemized Lucien's vocabulary, as if by doing so he might draw a little black magic from the words into his own verse, which, when not too whimsical, was too gothic, or too sentimental: 'The rose that scents the summer air / Grows from my beloved's hair.' He wrote a critical 'Essay in character analysis', in which he reduced Lucien to a 'scarred ego'; his 'loud talk was 'infantilism on a high intellectual level'. He quoted Lucien's contemptuous repudiation of Allen himself – 'your little loves, your little derivative morality, your hypocritical altruism' – and yet could still kneel before him as a 'genius in his own life'.

There were other lists: for example, of Lucien's fashion and manner – 'red shirts, wild songs, drink, women, queer shoes . . . arrogance' – and of his 'fetishes'. The last included Pernod (the nearest thing a wartime New Yorker could get to Verlainean absinthe), Mahler, knives, and 'Burroughs at 48 Morton'.

Carr took Ginsberg down to Morton Street (which was actually Kammerer's place) to meet this 'fetish'. Ginsberg found a shy but self-possessed philosopher with a waxy complexion and blue eyes, who quoted Shakespeare with ease, prefacing his delivery with 'In the words of the immortal Bard . . .' When Lucien bragged about a fight in which he had bitten into another man's ear, Burroughs listened until he had heard enough, then said: 'In the words of the immortal Bard, "Tis too starved a subject for my sword." '

In Burroughs's apartment, Ginsberg found *A Vision* by Yeats, Cocteau's *Opium*, the novels of Kafka and Céline, and more abstruse works such as *Science and Sanity* by the semanticist Count Alfred Korzybski, who illuminated the concepts of political double-think, and of language as an instrument of control, rather than, in the conventional enlightened thinking, of liberation.

Poetry was not Burroughs's first choice of reading, but in him Ginsberg encountered, for the first time, the confidence to ask: why this book and not that one? Why Milton and Keats and not Whitman and William Carlos Williams? What assumptions about personal identity, social behaviour, literary excellence – ethics and aesthetics, in short – are enshrined in these texts, in their choice for study, in the methods used to expound them? To Ginsberg, Burroughs seemed just the man to solve the problem that had been preoccupying him and Lucien. 'What is art?' Ginsberg asked at one of their first meetings. Burroughs replied: 'A three-letter word.'

Burroughs, Ginsberg and Kerouac met one another within the space of two or three months. At seventeen, virtually a generation younger than Burroughs, Ginsberg was nervy, slight of stature, virginal. Kerouac felt ambivalent about him at first, partly out of a deep-lying provincial anti-Semitism, partly from an intuition that Ginsberg might be, as Kerouac would say, a 'fairy' or a 'lecher'. In contrast to Lucien, who never concealed his feelings and was an object of fascination for this alone, Ginsberg left Kerouac with the sense that he wanted to get everyone in the world into a big bathtub, so that he could feel their legs under the dirty water. Kerouac described him as a 'spindly Jewish kid with horn-rimmed glasses and tremendous ears sticking out'. Ginsberg had large, oversensitive lips; he wasn't interested in sports; he didn't make the right noises about girls' breasts and butts; he had an attitude that said 'bully me'. Still, he could talk about poetry intelligently, and he entered their Frenchified circle as 'Gillette'. Céline (also known as 'Bébé') referred to him as 'Pierre Ginsbourg'. Lucien tagged him along as 'mon ami'.

Ginsberg was already a well-read young man when he encountered Burroughs's intellect. They were a well-read group altogether. In a letter, Céline described a semester's study at Barnard in 1944:

> a history of political thought, and the late Victorian period, reading all of Carlyle with some Dickens, Thackeray, Trollope, Brontë etc. Have begun the political thought class with *The Prince* which is an amazingly lucid treatise, and which will be followed by Hobbes, Hume, Mill, Hegel, Rousseau, Montesquieu, Lenin, Marx etc. *Sartor Resartus*, on second reading, is a revelation . . . Then on the side I have been reading D. H. Lawrence's poetry.

This was the curriculum. In the way he thought and spoke and acted, Burroughs was extra-curricular. Even his life was extra-curricular. His feet rested comfortably on the cushion of a $200-a-month allowance from his family, the remnant of the large sums computed on the adding machine by his grandfather, William Burroughs. The few jobs that Burroughs had held – cockroach exterminator, private detective – also had an outsider atmosphere about them.

The English Department at Columbia College was one of the most respected in the country. The classes were small in number, allowing personal attention to students. The leading faculty members were Lionel Trilling, a critic and (about to be) novelist, and Mark Van Doren, a Pulitzer Prize-winning poet, critic and anthologist. Their approach to the study of literature was confidently elitist, based on the best that had been thought and said, and on the premiss that art was the criticism of life. The bedrock of a true understanding and appreciation of literature was the classics; a 'modern classic', in Trilling's view, might be *War and Peace*, or something by Nietzsche. His manners, literary and social (the two being, under any coherent view of culture such as his, inseparable), looked back to another time and place. Of the two books he himself had written, one was a biography of Matthew Arnold, a poet and teacher of the last century, and the other a study of E. M. Forster, an English novelist who had not published a novel for almost twenty years. There was little or no mention in Trilling's classroom of the poets who wrote in the

American grain. His belief that liberalism was 'the sole intellectual tradition' in the United States, stated in the preface to a collection of essays written mostly during the 1940s, made little impression on the self-declared libertine inheritors of the fin-de-siècle.

Trilling, in turn, was unimpressed by his English class. In 'The Mind of Youth', an article printed in the women's magazine *Harper's Bazaar* in 1944 (interleaved among the ads for 'Miss Deb's contour-molded bodice' and 'Panties of Spun-lo'), Trilling outlined the paradox that the students 'were losing their youth, because they were too young for their years'. He had found himself exclaiming, before a class of freshmen, Hotspur's line from *Henry IV*: 'O, gentlemen, the time of life is short!' He would have noticed that some members of the class, such as Ginsberg and Carr, were reading and discussing books constantly, but if they were well-read, relative to their years, it was in a scattershot way; they were 'untrained, undeveloped . . . in teaching college freshmen, it is no longer possible to assume a common body of knowledge or training. Intelligence and good will can be assumed, but not information or discipline.'

Even then, Ginsberg and Trilling were engaged in a clash of wills over what should be taught and how the mind should be 'trained' and developed. The voice Ginsberg particularly wished to hear at Columbia was that of Walt Whitman, the poet of open form, the poet against summing up, who urged '*Resist much, obey little*'; Whitman, who had a runaway slave 'sit next to me at table', who admired 'sailors young and old' ('frequent and swift flash of eyes offering me love'), and happily dwelt in the 'City of orgies', Manhattan. He was the opposite of compression, of everything recommended in the lineage stretching from Arnold, through Eliot, to Trilling and the New Critics:

> I am satisfied – I see, dance, laugh, sing:
> As the hugging bedfellow sleeps at my side through the night, and
> Withdraws at the peep of the day with stealthy tread . . .
> Shall I postpone my acceptation and realization and scream at my
>
> > eyes. . . ?

Shall I postpone? Trilling: Yes. Ginsberg: No.

Still hoping for affirmation of some kind of talent lurking within his helplessness, Ginsberg took his poems to Trilling, who cast a cold, but not altogether discouraging, eye over them. Both Trilling and his wife Diana sympathized with Ginsberg over his appalling family situation, and invited him to visit at their apartment on Riverside Drive. When Ginsberg's suppressed exhibitionism flashed momentarily in their living-room, Mrs Trilling would say to Lionel later: 'He wants you to forbid him to behave like that, he wants you to take him out of it.' She would receive the reply: 'I'm not his father.' But Ginsberg kept Trilling as a father-figure anyway, for years to come – at once seeking his mature approval, and using him as something stable to rebel against.

Under the influence of his real father, Ginsberg continued to shape his poems according to classical models. The next one lined up for publication, 'A Night in the Village', was in tetrameter couplets, though its subject matter reflected the glare of his new companions:

> In Greenwich Village, night had come.
> The darkened alleyways were dumb –
> The only voices we could hear
> Were lonely echoes, sounding clear
> From basement bars, where reddish light
> Obscenely sweated in the night,
> Where Neons called to passers-by
> 'Enter, drink, and dream a lie.
> Escape the street's reality,
> Drink gin and immortality.'

With a nod to nineteenth-century decadence, he signed the poem 'Edgar Allen Ginsberg'. Meanwhile, Carr was formulating a 'théorie du voyant' of his own – or rather, his own mixed and bottled with a strong potion of Rimbaud. It contained three basic tenets:

i) Naked self-expression is the seed of creativity;

ii) The artist's consciousness is expanded by derangement of the senses;

iii) Art eludes conventional morality.

Carr called it 'The New Vision'. There was little that was actually new about it – most of it had come and gone by the end of the previous century – but it answered a feeling in Carr, Ginsberg and Kerouac that the template of life and thought proffered by the University was too sedate for a modern existence, that it did not answer the truth insisted on by the passions, that it could not contain the whole man with his contradictory violent and erotic urges. Restraint was a folly, not a virtue.

It did not last long, this first convention of the 'libertine circle', as Ginsberg called it, comprising Burroughs, Kerouac, Ginsberg and Carr, and Joan Vollmer, Edie Parker and Céline Young. They were together as a group in the spring; by the end of August it was shattered, and each had gone in a different direction, leaving only Ginsberg and Joan and her baby in New York.

The intruder was Kammerer. He had not been welcomed into the libertine circle, or into 118th Street, for that matter. As Burroughs began to gravitate towards the bohemian set, Kammerer remained stuck in the heaven-and-hell of his obsession for Lucien. Kerouac and Ginsberg had little liking for him. They saw him only when he came uptown from his janitor's job in Morton Street, popping his head into the West End and asking, in his incongruously high voice, if anyone had seen Lucien.

Céline, who had the most reason to dislike Kammerer, wrote down her feelings. She found him personally 'charming, helpful, informative', yet she was confused as to his moral nature. Was he a ruined and distorted character who sought to bring Lucien down to his own level of degradation, 'purely for the love of evil'? This was Marion Carr's view, and Céline herself gave it consideration. However, while she agreed that the situation was unnatural – not helped by Lucien's arrogance, his assumption that the world would pay attention whenever he spoke, and take his side whenever he acted – she could not help seeing something pure in Kammerer's devotion. Céline, who was on the brink of admitting that she did not really love Lucien herself, recognized that Kammerer, her rival, 'loved him above all else'.

Three stories about Carr from the summer of 1944.

First, the raw meat. Burroughs was cooking for Carr and Kammerer one night at Bedford Street, and three steaks were sizzling in the frying pan. Before they were done, Lucien pawed one out and bit into it, growling like a wild animal as the blood ran down his face.

28

Then, the performance with his mother over the certificate pertaining to his stay in the Cook County Hospital, after his head-in-the-oven 'work of art'. His mother produced the certificate while Lucien was visiting her at 57th Street, and asked him to burn it. Lucien invited her to wrap a twenty-dollar bill in the certificate, and then – another strike against the bourgeoisie – he would burn both on the carpet. His mother refused, but the certificate was set alight in an ashtray.

Finally, there was an attempt to run away to sea with Kerouac, which, after a good deal of planning, turned into a fiasco when they got caught in the crossfire of a dispute between the bosun and the chief mate. An hour after being hired to sail for France on the *Robert Hayes*, the two runaways were fired for unruly behaviour, and found themselves back on the Brooklyn pier.

Three responses from Kammerer: entrancement at the carnal performance; shame over the episode with the certificate (in Marion Carr's mind, her son's visit to the mental ward and Kammerer were linked together); relief when he heard about the failure to enlist on the *Robert Hayes*, turning to desperation at the news that the two intended to try again.

On a Sunday night a few days after Carr and Kerouac had been thrown off the ship, Kammerer was out doing the rounds of the bars in search of his Angel Boy. Towards midnight, he met Kerouac on the deserted Columbia campus, at the Amsterdam Avenue exit. Kerouac was on his way to 118th Street, and he yielded the information that Lucien was in the West End drinking with Ginsberg. Not long after Kammerer arrived, Ginsberg also went home, leaving Kammerer alone with Carr. Eventually, they left the bar and walked one block west to the half-wild strip of park that slopes down to the Hudson river. Carr's version of what happened next was set out in detail for readers of the *New York Times*:

On Monday morning between 3 and 4 A.M. the two were sitting on the grassy bank below Riverside Drive, at the foot of 115th Street, enjoying a breath of the cool morning air, according to Carr, when Kammerer once more made an offensive proposal.

Carr said that he rejected it indignantly and that a fight ensued. Carr, a slight youth, 5 feet 9 inches tall and weighing 140 pounds was no match for the burly former physical education instructor, who was 6 feet tall and weighed about 185 pounds. He was rapidly getting the worst of it, he said. In desperation, Carr pulled out of his pocket his boy scout knife, a relic of his boyhood, and plunged the blade twice in rapid succession into Kammerer's chest, according to the story he told at the District Attorney's office. The bigger man fell heavily to the ground.

Not knowing whether he was alive or dead, young Carr rolled the fallen man down the grassy embankment to the water's edge. There he took the laces from Kammerer's shoes and used them to tie his hands and feet. He took off Kammerer's shirt and tore it into strips and tied them about the body also, and then fastened Kammerer's belt about his arms.

Working with frantic haste in the darkness, unaware of whether anyone had seen him, the college student gathered together as many small rocks and stones as he could find and quickly shoved them into Kammerer's pockets and inside his clothing. Then he pushed the body into the swift-flowing water.

After he had left the area he toyed with the notion of running away and joining the Merchant Marine, Carr said, but further reflection convinced him that this was not the wisest course. Unable to make up his mind what to do, he eventually confided in his mother. She immediately communicated with a lawyer, who, after hearing young Carr's story, took him to the District Attorney's office.

The first person in whom Carr confided was not his mother, as stated in the press report, but Burroughs. Carr knocked on the door of 69 Bedford Street at dawn, and, when Burroughs answered, handed him Kammerer's packet of Lucky Strikes, with the remark: 'Have the last cigarette.' As if willingly accepting his part in a French operetta, featuring Rimbaud, Verlaine, Baudelaire and Van Gogh, Burroughs uttered a final summing up: 'So this is how David Kammerer ends.'

Burroughs flushed the cigarettes down the toilet and advised Lucien to tell his family, get a good lawyer, and make a case for self-defence based on an unwanted homosexual advance. The jury would sympathize, he said. Carr then travelled back uptown to wake up Kerouac, who was in bed with Edie. Kerouac recorded their initial exchange:

'I disposed of the old man.'

'What in hell didja go and do that for?'

Lucien said he intended to take Burroughs's advice and tell his family, but first he wanted to have a last drink with Kerouac. If only events had taken a different turn, they would now have been safely at sea. They crossed Morningside Park and went up to Harlem.

In front of a bar on 125th Street I said 'There, look, a good subway grate, that's where money keeps falling down and little kids put bubblegum on the ends of long sticks and gum it up. Drop the knife down there and let's go in this cool zebra-striped lounge and have a cold beer.' Which he did, but instead of hiding now, in full view of everybody, he dramatically knelt at the grate and let the knife drop from his stiff fingers . . . as tho this was one thing he really didnt want to hide . . . The knife, the boy scout knife I s'pose he had when he was fourteen and joined the boy scouts to learn woodcraft but only ran into the Marquis de Sade scoutmaster, lay there now probably among a trash of dropped heroin, marihuana, other knives, cundroms, what-all. We went into the air-conditioned bar and sat at cool swivel stools and ordered cold beers.

The operetta continued, with different characters now, though still in French. The situation in which he found himself recalled to Lucien's mind Renoir's film *La Grande Illusion*, in which the soldier played by Jean Gabin escapes from a prison camp with another man. 'You're Gabin,' Carr–Claude–Rimbaud told Kerouac–Duluoz–George Webber, 'and me' – alluding to a scene in the film – 'my white gloves are starting to chafe.'

They did go to see a movie, not Renoir but Zoltan Korda's *Four Feathers*, a tale of espionage set in the First World War. Then they went to the Museum of Modern Art to look at paintings. In the afternoon, Carr went to his mother's place, and, finally, accompanied by a lawyer, walked into the DA's office to confess.

But to what? No one had been reported missing. No one had seen or heard a crime being committed, such as Lucien described. So far, there had been no body drifting in the Hudson, tied up with shoelaces. It was now three days since the struggle on the riverbank had taken place.

Puzzled as to what to do with Carr, the police temporarily averted action by keeping him in [assistant DA Jacob] Grumet's office. Mr

Grumet was the authority for the information that Carr spent most of the night reading poetry. Unfortunately for connoisseurs of crime, however, the prosecutor told enquiring reporters that he 'didn't pay any attention' to what the poetry was.

It was Rimbaud – of course – *A Season in Hell*.

On the Wednesday after the crime, the body was found, and Carr was charged with second-degree murder. When he appeared in court the next day, he was clasping a volume of Yeats. The journalists again went for the story of the poetry-reading killer, though the book was actually a copy of *A Vision* – borrowed from Burroughs – Yeats's 300-page mystico-philosophical work which expounds his theories of *Will* and *Mask* and *Creative Mind* and *Body of Fate*. In it, Yeats divulged his automatic-writing techniques (to be given an American tune, in time, by Kerouac), referred to his 'instructors', and claimed that what they instructed, he was bound to do.

Kerouac was arrested as a material witness and held in the Bronx jail – known as 'The Opera House'. He was offered his freedom if he could raise bail of $500. His father said he would not pay even a dollar. When Kerouac had been discharged from the Navy, Leo Kerouac was delighted: 'Good boy', he wrote to his son; the war was for 'the Marxist-Communist Jews and you are a victim of the whole plot'. Now, however, his good boy was a bad boy in bad company. 'No son of mine ever got mixed up in a murder', he railed at Jack, his only surviving son.

The New York daily papers followed every stage of the case with relish. The *Times* reported that Kammerer came from a 'socially prominent' family, from Clayton, Mo. Alfred Kammerer told a reporter that he had just received a letter from his son, 'in which he wrote of a pleasant meeting with Lucien Carr'. The police revealed that they had 'uncovered a second material witness, William Seward Borroughs [*sic*], 30, of 69 Bedford Street'. He had heard Carr's story, 'and had done nothing'. Bail was set at half of Kerouac's price (Kerouac had, after all, done more than just nothing), but before Burroughs could be shipped off to the Bronx, his father came in with the money, got his son released, and took him home to St Louis – as had happened when Burroughs found himself in Bellevue following the finger incident.

In the Opera House, Kerouac doodled in his notebook and wrote bad poetry of confinement, which continued to meddle in the old-new philosophy: 'The bottled mortals, / like flies, buzz about within, glimpsing new visions.' His thoughts and his notebooks were full of Raskolnikov, Gide, the *acte gratuite*. With the murder of Kammerer, life had hardened into the desired shape of fiction. Kerouac's devotion to Lucien was undimmed. The more experienced prisoners in the Opera House wanted to know about the homosexual overtones of the drama, but Kerouac had been forewarned by Carr (who had probably been warned by his lawyer) to keep quiet about that, or anything else about the relationship between assailant and victim. A wrong use of the word 'queer' or 'fairy' could lead to a long sentence, possibly the chair. Where the judge was concerned, two homosexuals fighting on a riverbank in the early hours was an entirely different proposition to the one being presented by the press, of a morally upright young student fighting off the advances of a thirty-five-year-old pederast. (The undercurrents in the relationship between Kerouac himself and Carr are well expressed in Kerouac's recollection of the event more than twenty years later: Kerouac introduces 'Claude' by stating his resemblance to Oscar Wilde's 'model male heroes'. But this 'Angel Boy' is 'no fairy'. He stresses: 'I'm not queer and neither is Claude.' None the less, it was not only 'old queens' in Village bars who were devoted to Claude, but 'even this old dreamy hard-hearted seaman and footballer, Jack'.) The police drove Kerouac downtown to the City Morgue, at Bellevue Hospital on First Avenue, to identify the body. He could not help but notice that, even after three days in the water, Kammerer's penis was erect. Lucien, Kerouac suggested, had dispatched his suitor to 'an older lover, the river'.

The bail money to get Kerouac out of jail was finally put up by Edie's family. It came with the condition that she and Jack had to be married first.

It was, no doubt, their way of injecting a dose of respectability into their daughter's life, but it was a strange stipulation on the face of it. The intended was a college dropout, a Navy discharge, an unpublished writer, from a poor family, impecunious himself, and implicated in a murder. On top of all that, it would have to be a jailhouse wedding.

The *Times* reported the event, which took place on 22 August:

> The police escorted Kerouac to the Municipal Building on Tuesday to witness his marriage to Miss Edie Parker and then took him back to Bronx Prison.

Céline acted as Edie's bridesmaid, while Kerouac's best man was Detective Shea of the NYPD. Within a few days, the money had been paid in, the formalities completed, and Kerouac was a free man. He wrote to Ginsberg that their wedding 'fell on the day of the liberation of Paris. I suppose this news Lucien views morosely – he who always wanted to be in Paris among the first.'

Carr accepted the option to plead guilty to manslaughter in the first degree, thereby sparing himself a jury trial and the risk of being convicted of a more serious charge. The severity of the punishment hinged on the question of homosexuality, and the extent to which Carr had wielded his knife in self-defence. Burroughs had been correct in predicting that that would win the public's sympathy. The *Daily News* referred to Carr's action as an 'honor slaying'. Marion Carr testified that she had found desperate letters written by Kammerer to her son. She repeated her 'Iago' reference for the benefit of the court. In her letters to Kerouac and Ginsberg, Céline, who had already made up her mind to end their relationship, wrote disapprovingly of Carr's attitude: he seemed to think he had done a great service, she told Ginsberg, in ridding the world of Kammerer.

In October, Carr was given a sentence of one to twenty years. He was released after two, having spent the same period of time in prison that Verlaine served after being convicted of shooting Rimbaud.

After the wedding, the Kerouacs went to live with Edie's family in Grosse Pointe. Jack got a job in a factory as an inspector of ball-bearings, while Edie worked as a riveter, once more eager to help the war effort. Left alone in New York, Ginsberg wrote in his journal: 'The libertine circle is destroyed with the death of Kammerer.'

But two months later, Kerouac had separated from Edie (to the list of impossible disciplines could now be added 'marriage') and had come back East to live with his mother and father, who had moved to Ozone Park, in Queens. One night, he lit a candle in his room, and on a piece of card wrote 'The Blood of the Poet', after the title of the film by Jean Cocteau (1931). Then, as Burroughs had done before him, he took a blade to his finger. He only cut it open, though, holding back from Burroughsian severance. With his blood, he wrote the word 'BLOOD' on the card, which he then hung over his desk as a notice of his vocation.

Behind the beat

Hipikats

'I have him on the hip – Hipshot'
– Rimbaud, after Shakespeare, in his 'Notes in English'

Among the first cargoes of Africans delivered to the Virginia shore in the early seventeenth century, there must have been a few who were regarded by their fellow slaves as *hipikats*. The word belongs to the Wolof language, still spoken in parts of West Africa. *Hipikat* means a sage or intelligent fellow, one who is in the know, and the same all-round alertness is supposed to characterize his descendants, the hep-cat, the hip cat, the hipster.

Wolof speakers also used the word *bugal*, to annoy or worry, which was retained more or less in that form until 200 years or so later somebody said: 'Don't bug me.' Wolof *deg* or *dega* means to understand or appreciate. You dig? *Gay* is an ordinary guy, while *honq* – literally 'pink' – was used to describe a white guy, especially one who was bugging a hep black cat. The hep-cats of the 1920s and 30s kept the word as 'honkie'.

Other words associated with jive talk have been traced to Mandingo and Bantu languages; yet others may have been cross-fertilized by the idioms of Southerners of British descent. The origins of the blues, for example, is rooted as much in Scottish and Irish ballads as in African rhythm, and the use of 'man' as an insistent form of address is universal among Scottish highlanders, many of whom left their own poverty-stricken territory to become prosperous plantation owners, overseeing African slaves in the American South.

36

During the 1930s, jive talk moved out of black society, as swing bands became popular, and jazz was more widely broadcast on radio, and heard on records. The vocabulary percolated down to white musicians, and became known in mainstream jazz journals as 'swing talk'. They ran glossaries as features, partly as a form of entertainment, but also as a way of emphasizing the jazz musician's special attitude to life, denoted in his music by altered chords, and in his speech by the set of alterations known as 'jive', the hip cat's seven types of ambiguity; for blacks a way of keeping one step ahead of the listener-in, for whites a way of stealing a little of the outlaw glamour of blacks.

Mezz Mezzrow's *Really the Blues*, the first book by a white man to exploit the speech of blacks at length and without condescension, came out in 1946. Mezzrow, a clarinet player, was Jewish, but spent his days and nights in Harlem, where he was as well known for pushing drugs as for playing his clarinet, or liquorice stick. In the 1930s, he had twice attempted the radical experiment of combining black and white musicians in the same ensemble, though he failed on both occasions. As the magazine *Down Beat* reported of the second attempt, in 1938, 'Nobody showed'.

When Mezzrow went to prison for drug-dealing, he was housed in the Negro section, presumably so that people could make out what he was saying. To give the reader of his autobiography an idea of how this sounded, a playlet set on a Harlem street-corner was included:

First Cat: Hey there Poppa Mezz, is you anywhere?

Me: Man I'm down with it, stickin' like a honky.

First Cat: Lay a trey on me, ole man.

Me: Got to do it, slot. (Pointing to a man.) Gun the snatcher on your left raise – the head mixer laid a bundle his ways, he's posin' back like crime sure pays.

First Cat: Father grab him, I ain't payin' him no rabbit. Jim, this jive you got is a gasser, I'm goin' up to my dommy and dig that new mess Pops laid down for Okeh. I hear he riffed back on *Zackly*. Pick you up at The Track when the kitchen mechanics romp.

Second Cat: Hey Mezzie, lay some of that hard-cuttin' mess on me. I'm short of a deuce of blips but I'll straighten you later.

Mezzrow appended a glossary to *Really the Blues* (and a translation of the playlet: '*First Cat*: Hello Mezz, have you got any marihuana? *Me*: Plenty, old man . . .'). The glossary included '*kick*: good feeling', '*junkie*: dope fiend', '*skin-beater*: drummer', and many other words which had been given in the vocabularies printed in music magazines before the war. And a new word, postwar: '*beat*: exhausted, broke'.

3

The muses: Huncke-junkie and Neo-Cassady

Burroughs first heard the word 'beat' used as a desirable piece of argot in the same year as *Really the Blues* was published; but in his case, it came with criminal, rather than musical, overtones. Burroughs had no friends in the jazz world, and no ear for the music, but he was developing a taste for the rascally and picaresque, with the end in view of finding a resting place for his misfit soul, and he liked the sound of 'beat' and the concept of 'underside', 'at odds', that it contained.

It wasn't the first time that he had felt the gravitational pull of low life. It had been tugging since his boyhood. The tone of the 'beat' world, as Burroughs first perceived it, chimed with the world of Jack Black, a hobo-crook whose memoir of larceny and fugitiveness, *You Can't Win* (1926), had encouraged young, wolfish Burroughs in his search for a replacement for the imperturbable gentility of his family in St Louis. The society of burglars, jewel-thieves, travellin'-men, dope-users, safe-crackers, D and D men (who beg under the pretence of being deaf and dumb), brothel-keepers and the rest suggested a rosy alternative to a hearth and home constructed on the profits of a machine used for doing sums.

Recuperating at home, following his brush with the law in the Carr–Kammerer affair, Burroughs might have had time to take down his copy of *You Can't Win* and read again about the sub-crust where all the bums carried razors, 'for shaving, fighting, or cutting through a sleeper's clothing to get into his pocket'; where 'if he is feeling bad, a fiend takes a jolt so he will feel good. If he is feeling good, he takes one to make him feel better'; where strangers asked: 'How long you been on the road?', and where jewel-thieves such as the Sanctimonious Kid would coo over the spoils of a heist with a quotation from Shakespeare: 'There's a stone, kid, that "A Jew would kiss and an Infidel adore." '

It was this world, the 'carny' world, the beat, off-beat world, that Burroughs began to seek out when he returned from St Louis to New York City in 1945. And he found it in the Lower East Side apartment of Herbert Huncke, which appeared to Burroughs as an updating of the Jack Black realm to which his boy's imagination had sneaked off to escape the dreariness of social clubs and pruned gardens and conversations about flower-arranging (on which Mrs Burroughs was an expert). It was from the mouth of Huncke that Burroughs first heard 'beat' and other bits of jive talk close up. Huncke was well beat, a committed reject, a hustler *engagé*.

He was a small, faintly Arabic-looking man, with heavily lidded eyes and a countenance which Kerouac was later to characterize as 'sincerely miserable'. Not yet thirty when Burroughs encountered him, Huncke had seen the insides of half-a-dozen prisons, and was familiar with outlaws of every type, including sexual outlaws. One of his friends from a spell in Chicago before he came to New York was Elsie-John:

> His mouth was large and held at all times a slight idiot smile and was always painted bright red. He shaded his eyelids green or blue and beaded the lashes with mascara until they were a good three-quarters of an inch long. He exhibited himself among freaks in sideshows as the only true hermaphrodite.

When Huncke was not in prison, or doing something which was likely to lead to prison, he was on the road, 'beating it' – travelling in freight trains – criss-crossing America with other hoboes, black and white and red, just as Jack Black was doing half a century before. Here is Huncke:

> Through the whole period of the 30s and after '34 for six years I didn't do anything but float around the country. If I've hit New Orleans once,

I've hit it four or five times. Same with California. A favourite of mine was Route 66, because I could make it straight across the country.

Here is Jack Black:

> It was springtime. Sundown found me miles away on a country road, walking westward. Darkness was coming on, but it did not strike me as unusual that I had no supper or room for the night.
>
> I came to a bridge and stopped when I heard voices below ...
>
> 'Where you from, kid?'
>
> 'The city,' I answered.
>
> 'Where you goin'?'
>
> 'Oh, just west, anywhere, everywhere.'

Drifting to New York, Huncke began to haunt Times Square and 42nd Street, the basin of cheap urban outlawry. There were to be found the single-room hotels and shabby cafeterias which housed a population of prostitutes, sailors and slummers, and the thieves, such as Huncke, who were at once their companions and who preyed on them. When he couldn't afford a room, Huncke stayed in one of the all-night movie theatres, or packed himself into a toilet cubicle in Penn Station.

Huncke is pronounced to rhyme with 'junkie', which was his principal occupation. Jack Black could write of the Western boom towns that 'morphine and opium were almost as cheap as tobacco', but in mid-century New York a drug habit was expensive and, therefore, time-consuming. Huncke would get double satisfaction when he succeeded in locating a croaker – a crooked doctor – who was willing to write out prescriptions for morphine. From the supply, he could keep himself straight, and sell the remainder to prostitutes crawling around Times Square in search of a 'john' who would pay them enough for a 'jolt'. If the croaker was willing to write out the prescriptions liberally, then the junkie could restrict himself – much as the prostitute might hope to do – to a few regular customers.

Huncke was also known in his circle as a good story-teller, and occasionally, while shifting from 'doorway to doorway, to restaurant and subway entrances, and along the side of graystone buildings seeking shelter from the cold', or in the scented privacy of his toilet cell, he would write one of his stories down. He carried his worldly

41

goods with him in a cigar box, a beat Dick Whittington. They amounted to little more than a toothbrush, a shaving razor, a handkerchief, and maybe a syringe. Without self-consciousness, he was an archetype in letters: the queer, drug-addicted poet-thief. A muse for the behatted, begloved, besuited William S. Burroughs II.

At the turn of the year, in obedience to his natural downward urge, Burroughs came into possession of a strange cargo. It consisted of a Thompson submachine-gun – a tommy gun – the cartridge-clip for an automatic pistol, and several boxes of the disposable, ready-to-fix capsule called the 'morphine syrette', a small tube, like a toothpaste tube, with a needle sticking out the end. Like the weaponry, the syrettes had been stolen from a Navy store by a casual acquaintance. He had asked Burroughs if he knew of anyone who would like to buy them, and, just to see what it felt like to buy narcotics, which he had never used, to snap the firing-pin on a real tommy gun, to place himself definitively among the shady and the shifty, Burroughs offered to find someone.

An acquaintance called Bob Brandenburg, who worked in a drugstore in the vicinity of Columbus Circle, said he might have a buyer. He led Burroughs downtown to an apartment on Henry Street, overlooking the Brooklyn Bridge, and here Burroughs found what he had been looking for: Jack Black's *You Can't Win* come to life.

Herbert Huncke was among the occupants. But he thought Burroughs was a policeman, or, as he said (in another bit of jive talk), 'heat': the hat, the coat, one hand in glove, the other glove in hand, the altogether grey look. Then, on second thoughts, maybe not; heat would have taken trouble to disguise the grey look. No heat looked this much like heat. Also in the apartment were Phil White, a professional pickpocket and 'lush worker' (specializing in mugging drunks on the subway), who had once killed a man in the course of a robbery; Little Jack Melody, a safecracker, and Little Jack's lover, Vicki Russell, the daughter of a Philadelphia judge. She was described as amazonian; she was a full foot taller than Little Jack, and kept herself in drugs – and sometimes the others, too – by working in a related industry, as a middle-rank, non-street-walking, prostitute.

The walls of the living-room were black, with yellow panels, and matching black-and-yellow drapes kept out natural light at all times. The ceiling was painted red, and, to give an oriental effect, the medallion in the centre of it had been coloured plum, green, orange and yellow. A china Buddha with a votive candle placed before it was conspicuous among the exotic bric-à-brac. Every day, they got high in front of the Buddha and gossiped about crime and other criminals.

Huncke wanted nothing to do with Burroughs, even after he was persuaded that the stranger with the guns and drugs was not from the FBI. 'He obviously didn't know any of the underground language', Huncke recollected. 'He appeared like a fish out of water to me.' But Phil White bought the stuff, and Burroughs returned to Henry Street a second and then a third time. While Kerouac worked at a soda fountain next door to his mother's house in Queens, and Ginsberg continued to go to classes at Columbia, Burroughs was with Vicki Russell as she shared her trade secrets – how to keep a john happy: 'Build him up. If he has any sort of body at all, say "Oh please don't hurt me" ' – and with Phil White talking about dead drunks coming alive on subway trains while he was rummaging through their pockets.

Eventually Huncke became less wary, and on one of his visits Burroughs asked to be included when the others started preparing their injections. Huncke advised him what to expect:

Morphine can be pretty frightening the first time you shoot it up mainline, because it gives a terrific pins and needles sensation. You can literally feel the drug travelling through the system, and it usually hits the back of the neck. You get this flush feeling, a sort of heatwave, and if you're not prepared for it, it's pretty frightening.

After Huncke and Phil White had had their regular shot, Huncke indicated to Burroughs that there was enough left over for him.

So Bill said, 'Well, what do you think? How should I go about this? . . .

We tied him with a very effective tourniquet. He rubbed a little alcohol on, then turned his head the other way. I got the needle in and drew up a little blood. I said, 'Loosen the tourniquet.' He loosened it, peering down at his arm, and began to feel the sensation as I shot the morphine into him. All of a sudden, he said, 'Well – that's quite a sensation . . . that's very interesting.' He gave the impression of being scientific-minded about everything. He hadn't given me any indication of where his intentions lay, but he was so methodical about everything that I felt his approach came from a purely scientific standpoint. As I discovered later, it was. He became a drug addict principally as a result of research.

★

By this time, the circle that had broken up in the autumn of 1944 had reformed. Joan Vollmer had found another large apartment, a few blocks down from the last one, at 419 115th Street, at the back of Barnard College. Edie Parker Kerouac came and went from Grosse Pointe, Céline began to hang around, and one by one the members of the boy-gang drifted back.

Kerouac had asked Edie for a divorce less than six months after they had pledged themselves to one another eternally under the watchful eye of Detective Shea, but he still wrote to friends and family about how wonderful she was, even though his sexual instinct was sniffing around elsewhere (around Céline, for example). The real problem for any wife or girlfriend was the other woman, the one Jack could never leave: Gabrielle Kerouac – known as Mémère – nursing her concern in Ozone Park, forever in the act of preparing the bedroom-study for her son's next visit. When Leo Kerouac died in 1946, their need for one another grew stronger than ever.

By this time, too, Ginsberg had had his first face-to-face meeting with a psychiatrist – a meeting to talk about him, that is, and not his mother. Still only nineteen in 1945, Ginsberg was sometimes patronized by Kerouac. Everything about Ginsberg was 'little' or dumb: he was 'little Allen' and 'little friend' and 'jeune singe' (young monkey). 'I shall answer all your questions, as there is nothing else to do', Kerouac might write; or 'Your little letter moved me'. Should Ginsberg have been wondering why that might be so, Kerouac provided the answer: 'because you'd been and still are sick'.

That was the way others saw him, too, including the Associate Dean of Columbia, N. M. McKnight. In March, Dean McKnight had written to Louis Ginsberg:

> I regret exceedingly to be obliged to send you a copy of a letter which I have just written to your son ... The two principal elements are obscene writings on his window, and giving over-night housing to a

person who is not a member of the College and whose presence on the Campus is unwelcome.

The unwelcome guest was Kerouac, who had been declared persona non grata on campus following the Carr affair and his part in it. Attention was drawn to his presence in Ginsberg's dormitory in Livingston Hall by the cleaner one early morning (they had slept in the same bed, without sexual contact). Having Kerouac in bed was bad enough (though it was a common enough thing for two men to sleep in one bed, and homosexual love was probably far from the thoughts of the Dean), but the primary objection concerned the 'obscene writings' Ginsberg had fingered in the grime which coated the window. The intention was to shame the cleaner into washing it. Ginsberg took the extreme route. 'Butler has no balls', he wrote – referring to Nicholas Murray Butler, President of Columbia – and 'Fuck the Jews'. Underneath, he made a crude drawing of a prick, and another of a skull and crossbones.

The result was suspension from the College. Ginsberg was told that he would not be permitted to re-enroll until he had seen a psychiatrist. Even that might not be enough, as Dean McKnight told Louis in a further letter; he wished to correct Louis's misunderstanding 'that Allen's opportunity to resume his work in Columbia College will rest upon the presentation of a letter from a psychiatrist stating that he is well enough to do so'. Medical opinion would have a bearing on the question, but the final decision rested with the College. McKnight suggested that Ginsberg work at a job for a year. What he needed was 'a dose of reality'.

A diversionary expedition into Ginsberg's sexuality of the time takes the traveller through 'Mountains of homosexuality, Matterhorns of cock, Grand Canyons of asshole'. It was not a land of content. The Matterhorns and Grand Canyons, Ginsberg told Burroughs, who was participating with him in an ad hoc form of psychoanalysis, posed 'a great weight on my melancholy head'. He was not ready to admit his homosexuality fully – if he should burst out with his desires to a friend, such as Burroughs or Kerouac, it had the immediate kickback of a depression and inward withdrawal – and for many years to come he would keep on hoping that a woman, or a psychoanalyst, would cure it.

45

In the meantime, cast out from college, he enrolled in the Maritime Service Training Centre, to become a merchant seaman. (The sea, as much as literature, gave the boy-gang cohesion; Huncke had just returned from the Caribbean and Pacific islands when Burroughs first met him, and Burroughs himself would make several unsuccessful efforts to gain seaman's papers. On the final occasion, in August 1945, it was the dropping of the atom bomb on Hiroshima – expertly developed at his old school – that kept the Los Alamos old boy out; VJ Day was declared, and the training centre where Burroughs had intended to join Ginsberg was closed down.) Sailors, the traditional partners for secretive homosexuals, provided Ginsberg with momentary respite, but the aftershock from those encounters would push him down into the depressing valleys between the mountains and Matterhorns. 'I feel more guilty and inferior for reasons of faggishness than intellectualization will admit is proper', he wrote to Burroughs.

It was Kerouac, the seaman–poet, who particularly inflamed him. One night, while they were walking in Greenwich Village, Ginsberg made a pass, and to his surprise Kerouac responded sympathetically. Standing between two trucks where the elevated West Side highway passes over Christopher Street – 'Oh, just west, anywhere, every-where' – Ginsberg masturbated his friend. (It was doubtless an act of kindness more than desire on Kerouac's part, but he had had sex with men before – rudimentary, sometimes oral, usually out of doors or aboard ship; when he mentioned a 'sexual problem' to friends from Lowell, as he had done, they probably didn't imagine that he meant this, rather than paralysing stage fright or the imagined smallness of his penis. From first to last, when drunk and belligerent in a bar, Kerouac was apt to throw out the invitation: 'Come on, I'll fuck you.')

Jewishness was another area of self-consciousness for Ginsberg, and he was, of course, continually worried about his mother's madness and its effects – long-term, short-term, psychic, domestic – on the rest of the family. And while he was not happy about the teaching he received at Columbia, he had been unable to bring himself to quit. So his scrawled collection of messages on the dormitory window at Livingston Hall seems to have drawn all the strands of his unhappy mind together in a convocation to demand a solution.

Evicted from Livingston Hall, he went in search of his dose of reality at 115th Street.

Where there was now a new member of the fraternity.

Joan had let out one of the spare rooms to a Columbia student from Denver, Hal Chase, 'a hero of the snowy West', as Ginsberg saw him. Like the incarcerated Lucien, he was intellectual and impetuous; like Lucien, he was blond and good-looking; like Lucien, he was attracted to Céline, who became his lover. (She recognized in him 'that feeling of futility . . . that reminds me of Lucien'.)

Hal Chase made two contributions to boy-gang life, a minor intellectual one and a major social one. First, he came up with the concept of 'Wolfeans' and 'non-Wolfeans' – that is, those who were in the rugged American tradition, expansive, encompassing, healthily panting for the future; and those who were rooted in European sensibility and tended towards the degenerate and the effete – and, by implication, faggishness.

The distinction was based on two types of contemporary American writer. Thomas Wolfe was one sort, an all-embracing melting pot of a writer, a 'putter-inner', as Kerouac said. The other kind was personified by F. Scott Fitzgerald, refined, old-world, a 'leaver-outer'. Hal Chase made a division among the 115th Street boys: he and Kerouac were the life-loving Wolfeans, he declared, while Burroughs and Ginsberg were non-Wolfeans. (Ginsberg took it as yet another rejection.) The girls, not being writers, did not qualify for a reckoning.

Out West, Chase had done some work with Native American artefacts in the Denver Museum; he had served in the ski troops, training in the Rockies; and he was influenced, in his conception of the essential American spirit as an open-hearted, on-the-move, creaturely thing, by one of his Denver acquaintances, Neal Cassady. He told the others about Cassady. Neal was a 'cocksman', so keep an eye on your women; he had made a living before the war as a poolhall shark and done a little time inside; and he had read his way through the Denver Public Library, from A to Z. There was no one like Neal. They would see for themselves: he was coming to town.

The 'prize room' in Joan's apartment – according to Huncke, who had begun to visit – was reserved for Burroughs: 'a beautiful room, in which he kept his books and a desk and a bed for himself'. His other bed was in Joan's room. They had become lovers. Although Burroughs was primarily attracted to men, homosexuality was not a fixed state, and he was not without experience of women; on the whole, Burroughs appreciated feminine smoothness in young men, while responding to strong intelligence in women. In Joan, slightly older than the others, Burroughs found the maturity that had been lacking in his friendships since the death of Kammerer. Like him, she was interested in ideas, and could answer his talk of Freud and Korzybski, his theories of hypnotism and mind-control, of multiple personalities concealed in the unconscious, with ideas of her own. Burroughs enjoyed her sharp city wit.

The other flourishing aspect of their lives was the use of drugs. As Burroughs continued his narcotics research, Joan stepped up her doses of Benzedrine. It was a punishing habit, and had completely overcome the 'soft and dewy' side of Joan that Edie had liked so much. In addition to causing body sores, the amphetamine addiction brought difficulties of blood circulation, so that by the age of twenty-five Joan was walking with a limp, occasionally assisting herself with a cane. As well as having to put up with Burroughs's strange routines, she had her baby daughter to care for. Once Kerouac – who made raids on 115th Street from his mother's hearth when in need of his own dose of reality – caught sight of her in Times Square on her way to buy in a stock of inhalers, hobbling along with little Julie in tow, one arm swinging loosely at her side.

Some time around the end of 1945, she began telling Ginsberg and the others that she was able to hear the voices of the people in the apartment below. Allen replied that he couldn't hear a thing, but Joan explained this by saying that the drugs she was taking had heightened her auditory faculty. She would elaborate: they were an elderly couple; they had fights; they said vile things about her and her friends. They also knew that everyone upstairs was a dope fiend (as they would say, not yet having the hip word, 'junkie'), and they wanted to call the police. Joan listened to everything they said with great attention, sometimes conveying it on down the line as it was happening. No one else could hear a thing.

One night, she announced that the couple were having a dreadful brawl. The old man was threatening his wife. He had a kitchen knife. Now he was chasing her round the apartment with it. Kerouac and Ginsberg rushed downstairs and banged on the door, but there was no answer. No one lived there.

Paul Adams, Joan's lawful husband, returned from military service to find that the pretty Barnard student he had left behind to look after their baby daughter had become the leading lady in an avant-garde expressionist drama, which, to him, was incomprehensible. He went away and didn't come back. Gradually, unceremoniously, Joan Vollmer, Joan Adams, began to call herself Joan Burroughs. She told her new man that he made love like a pimp. In the theatre of 115th Street, it was considered a compliment.

Under the tutelage of Phil White, who had probably pimped in his time, Burroughs learned a new trade, a Jack Black trade: he became a lush-worker. His monthly $200 allowance from his parents was not enough to feed a growing drug habit. Phil White showed him how to rob drunks in the subway, and how to talk the lingo at the same time: rolling lushes like this was 'working the hole'.

The natural, Huncke, watched as Burroughs studied the ways of the street. By now, he had overcome his suspicions that Burroughs might be a lawman, but with the true deadbeat's respect for proper learning, he could not help but be sceptical about Burroughs's latest enterprise:

> They informed me they were making the hole together as partners with Burroughs learning to act as a shill and cover-up man for Phil – helping to pick pockets by standing near, holding a newspaper open, spread wide – Phil reaching behind Bill, fingers feeling the inside breast pocket of the mark's suit jacket or perhaps the overcoat pockets searching for the wallet – or poke, as Phil referred to it. Somehow there was something ludicrous about a man of Bill's obvious educational background becoming a business partner with knock-around, knock-down, hard hustling Phil.

Burroughs's anthropological studies – which would later be

ploughed into his first book, an autobiography thinly disguised as fiction, a lost chapter from *You Can't Win* – were terminated in April 1946.

It began with Huncke, who was fingered by a boy who had agreed to cooperate with the police in exchange for lenient treatment. By this time, Burroughs had rented a place on Henry Street next to the apartment where he had taken his original morphine shot, and Huncke was living there and using it as a storehouse for stolen goods. Following a trail, the police began to pick up Huncke's associates one by one, eventually arriving at 115th Street to arrest Burroughs on a charge of forging a doctor's signature on stolen blank prescriptions. They took him to the Tombs.

His new life had got him into trouble, but his old life could be relied on to get him out of it. Long-suffering Mortimer Burroughs made the journey to New York again to bail his son out of prison for the second time in eighteen months. In June, the case came before the courts, and Burroughs, technically a first offender (and a Harvard graduate), was sternly ordered by the judge to spend the summer at his parents' home in St Louis. Huncke, a graduate of the school of vagabondage, got four months in prison. When he was released, he found a room at 115th Street.

Joan liked Huncke, but did not welcome the criminal flotsam and jetsam that drifted in his wake. Whoever took pity on Huncke found themselves in trouble sooner or later. One story in his later recollections involves a Polish guy, a black queen, a stolen car, and a missing valise; then the police at Joan's apartment, with 'this black queen looking very righteous' and accusing Huncke of taking the valise:

> They knocked on the door and just came in. Joan was absolutely horrified. This was the first experience with the law she'd ever had. Of course, they couldn't touch her. They were primarily interested in me . . . The queen pointed out the car downstairs in front of the house. She was really very spiteful. Sure enough, all three of us ended up in the Bronx jail with this case on our hands. Well, I beat it . . . they couldn't do anything to me.

For Joan, it was a further twist in the downward spiral. Her beauty had gone, and her mind was following. She cleaned the apartment obsessively. She was apt to strip naked in front of visitors. In the several accounts of her state at this time, her Benzedrine habit is mentioned frequently, her daughter Julie scarcely ever.

At the beginning of October, John Kingsland, the teenage student who for a term had been her lover but who had since been reclaimed for respectability by his parents, paid a call at 115th Street. When he left the apartment, he wrote a letter to Ginsberg: 'I saw Joan last weekend. She seems to be losing her mind.' Two weeks later, she was picked up off the street and taken to the Bellevue psychiatric ward. 'It's a shame, don't you think?' asked Kingsland.

As Joan entered her brief confinement, Lucien Carr emerged from his. The conditions of his parole made it unwise for him to socialize too often with his old libertine friends, especially as he could not help but notice the addition of hard criminality to what had been (until his own notorious deed, as it happened) a prankish bohemianism.

Ginsberg met him and confessed, for the first time, his desire for men (including Carr). Carr seemed shocked. The words 'homosexual', 'queer', 'fairy', 'faggot', conjured up a dingy picture of stinking toilets and restless shame. Carr had gone to prison for killing a homosexual, in what many onlookers at the trial had regarded as an honour slaying. He told Ginsberg that it was a 'sorry life'. Ginsberg, suitably sorry, replied that he was planning to see a psychiatrist and seek a cure.

Kerouac, who had been so deeply involved in the events of August–September 1944, saw little of Carr. He was too wary, and too deeply involved in his writing. He came and went at 115th Street, but his year had been taken up with a novel, *The Town and the City* ('The Sea Is My Brother' had been abandoned). It told the story of a family growing up in a mill town on a river, very much like Lowell. It was very Wolfean and very long, and Kerouac discovered in writing it the deep capacity of his memory, its fine net for detail, and its ability to fetch up a great amount of story in the course of a single day. Kerouac was memory's servant. Sometimes he would write up to 4,500 words in a night. By the end of 1946, the manuscript of *The Town and the City* was approaching 1,000 pages.

While storms blew about him – as Burroughs willingly went

51

down to a life of drugs and crime, as Ginsberg got lost in Grand Canyons of asshole, as Carr knifed his pursuer and Joan went mad – Kerouac was gifted with the ability to take one step back, to take the passenger seat, to take notes, and to think of shaping them into a book. By Christmas, there was a new chapter.

★

A brief tour of Huncke's New York.

Start at Bryant Park, behind the New York Public Library at 42nd Street, originally a potter's field, or pauper's graveyard, latterly the resting place (in life) of every sort of human detritus New York's famous tide of energy throws up. In the 1940s, Bryant Park was hustler Huncke's base of operations. On one occasion, he used a 'Keep Off the Grass' sign to smash a car window, intending to steal the contents and sell them for drug money. He was caught, and spent six months in Rikers Island, his first visit to that prison.

Walk west along 42nd Street, towards Eighth Avenue. At no. 210 42nd Street was Chase's Cafeteria, a notoriously lowdown place, which Kerouac fictionalized as Ritzy's Bar: 'You don't see a single girl', he wrote.

Next door to Chase's stood Grant's Cafeteria, housed in the Chandler building (named after the Coca-Cola magnate).

Across the street, at no. 225, was Bickford's, an all-night place where Huncke was often in residence, when not in a movie theatre or a station toilet. He could spend up to eighteen hours a day in Bickford's, reliably stationed at the window in view of pushers, ponces, and friends such as amazonian Vicki and Little Jack Melody. The place had the novelty of a jukebox. The light was described by Ginsberg as 'submarine'. The food was said to be good and cheap.

Cross the street again, and stop at no. 250. Here stood the Horn and Hardart Automat. Automats were an experiment in food dispensing, in which diners used a nickel to open a little window on to their choice of dish. Macaroni and cheese was a favourite. The absence of disapproving waiters was a welcome feature to idlers, such as

Huncke, and to other thieves who used the automats as 'meets' where they could discuss the sale of overcoats and what–not, and the corresponding purchase of drugs. The automats were also open all night, making them a top attraction to the submarine community.

Turn right into Eighth Avenue, and walk one block north. On the corner of 43rd Street stood the Angler Bar (also known in books as the Angle Bar), a favourite of Burroughs and an overcoat thief he had befriended called Bill Garver. Burroughs recalled Huncke at the Angler, 'always high on something – weed, benzedrine, or knocked out of his mind on "goof balls" . . . his head kept falling down onto the bar'. Burroughs also provided a snapshot of the typical clientele:

> Roy and I were standing at the end of the Angle Bar. Subway Mike was there, and Frankie Dolan. Dolan was an Irish boy with a cast in one eye. He specialized in crummy scores, beating up defenceless drunks, and holding out on his confederates. 'I got no honor', he would say. 'I'm a rat.'

It was at the Angler that Huncke met Alfred Kinsey, and related details of his sex life for honest cash, details later integrated into Kinsey's *Sexual Behaviour in the Human Male*. 'The one thing I could not supply him with was the size to my penis', Huncke wrote later. 'He finally gave me a card and asked me to fill it out and send it to him . . . I never did.'

Walk east to Broadway, then turn north in the direction of 44th Street. At 1506 Broadway, between 43rd and 44th, was Hector's, one of a chain of Jewish cafeterias in New York. Kerouac loved its 'glittering counter', its 'decorative walls', and above all its 'noble old ceiling . . . almost baroque, plaster now browned a smoky rich tanned color'. Hector's was the first stop in New York City for Neal Cassady and his child bride LuAnne, after they stepped down at the Greyhound Terminal on 50th Street, in December 1946. They ate, according to Kerouac's memory, glazed cakes and creampuffs.

★

'Travelling?' he asked.
'Yes.'
'Which way?'
'Denver.'
'Beating it?'
'Yes.'

– Jack Black, *You Can't Win*

Neal Cassady had a beautiful voice. He *was* his voice. It charmed, seduced and conned for him; it expounded his ideas, often all at the same time, sending them haring along the course of a sentence in a competitive spirit. The voice did his thinking on the mind's behalf, for Cassady was not reflective, and could not long endure an atmosphere of solitude and silence. He cultivated the natural richness and maturity of his voice. When he read Proust and Shakespeare into a tape-recorder, it came out sounding like a trained actor.

Cassady esteemed literature and book-learning above all else, but his grammar and spelling, his use of capital letters, his placing of punctuation, were all to pot, which made him self-conscious when it came to writing down an anecdote, a thought, a flash from his early life, that had sounded so good, so multi-layered, when spoken. It came out all formal, bedecked with big words, stiff with inversions, and, cripplingly, drained of confidence. In speech, however, his latinate diction added to the overall surprise that was the general reaction to the Cassady monologue. Imagine him talking about Huncke, whom he dubbed 'an incongruity': 'He who would wind up spectralized the color of blue cheese under the main drag lights from LA to Chicago to Rikers Island, saw the light of life for the first time in the smoky raw woods of West Massachusetts . . .'

Neal was equally an incongruity. At his friends' urging, he did eventually write his story, which, in its early stages, reads like a tale of the Old West, describing a semi-lawless world of cowpokes, family feuds leading to shootouts, farms where an ever-increasing brood of children made up the labour force. Neal's grandfather William killed his brother Ned with a pitchfork during a battle in a hayloft in 1880, and, after burying him – here's the badlands detail – took over Ned's wife and children. William then added four of his own, including Neal senior, the father of our Neal.

The Cassadys were frequently in transit. Neal was born on the road. When his mother, Maude, signalled that she was ready to deliver her latest, on 8 February 1926, the family was near Salt Lake City on the way to Los Angeles, where Neal senior hoped to open a barber's shop. He merely pulled the Ford truck over to the side long enough for his wife to give birth to junior, before continuing to LA. It was frequently observed about Cassady's driving that he never liked to break the journey.

The elder Cassady boys were Negro-haters and wife-beaters, and took to the habit of battering their father once a week:

> When, in 1932, the family situation was resolved by my parents' parting, I was not sorry to accompany my father in his retreat to Larimer Street. Most especially, I was not sorry to bid what proved to be a year's farewell to my terrifying bully-brother Jimmy and even to my little-thought-about mother and younger sister. The prospect of adventure filled my six-year-old head; besides, I would now be spared the sight of violence every Sunday. With my father gone for good, my older half-brothers, Jack and Ralph, would not be able to pound his face bloody when he returned home from his Saturday-night binges.

Larimer Street was Denver's red-light district and Skid Row. Jack Black mentions it as a street lined with gambling dens, where card-sharps won fortunes and were sometimes relieved of them by hold-up men waiting outside the door (the hold-up men included Jack Black's partner, the Sanctimonious Kid). Having failed to establish himself in Los Angeles, as everywhere else, Old Neal had returned to cut hair in one or other of Larimer Street's saloons. But he was always what his son called 'third chair', in other words, the spare man, last in and first out, and spent more time drinking than hairdressing. When Neal's mother Maude abandoned them, drifting into the rough life, Neal and Old Neal slept in Larimer's flophouses, among snoring drunks, some of whom were kept awake only by boy-hunger.

'Weakened bodies of shattered souls' was Cassady's phrase to describe the men of this community, and only his impulse to move, genetically implanted, prevented the muck from sticking. He became expert at sloughing off stale skins. Love: trouble: flight. These were the stages of every Cassady adventure. In his writings, the dominant motif is 'move'; the prose is getaway prose.

In a flash of memory, too suddenly bright to be revelatory, he recalls an early experience in which 'a funny older boy kissed then put his mouth over it to drink my pee-pee.' The emotional and psychological repercussions of what was a first homosexual experience go unremarked, just as the thing to which 'it' refers is left unspecified. Neal is already off somewhere else, doing in response to this first affair what he basically did later in response to every affair: 'We ran through the ramshackle rickety of the hole-covered house together . . .'

The sentences run fastest when the storyline combines the two great loves of his life, existing side by side in strictly equal partnership: sex and cars. In a fragment entitled 'Adventures in Autoeroticism', Cassady described the theft, in 1940 when he was fourteen, of a current-model Mercury; no sooner did he have the car, than he had a girl on the front seat:

> Anyhow, the erotic nature of the Mercury experience happily included exploring the anatomy of the schoolgirl picked up in it, and therefore has no further, sharper, stronger, more meaningful remembrance than the one of its get-away moments, which included wading thru a three-phase traffic signal in the first block . . .

(The sentence, and the fragment itself, end here, in mid-traffic.)

Between the ages of fourteen and twenty-one, Cassady claimed, he stole 500 automobiles, and if his psyche were made visible it would sport 500 dented fenders. Sometimes his thefts were more like borrowings. He could take five or six cars from a parking-lot in a single evening, driving each one around central Denver before zooming back and parking it again. On one occasion, when the police were called to investigate reports of someone stealing cars from the lot, Cassady jumped into another vehicle while they were taking down details from the attendant, passing the empty-handed policemen on their way out as he darted back to his starting-point. Even his appearance was shaped by an automobile, the 'crooked Grecian curve of his nose', his salient feature, having been caused by a minor car accident two years before he arrived in New York.

Speed was also the element of his seduction technique, and he employed a vocabulary of relentless motion in order to describe it.

He would boast of meeting a waitress during a coffee break, charming her from her cafeteria, and making love to her 'in nothing flat' during the lunch hour. On a bus, having plotted for two hours how to accomplish a similar conquest, he suddenly, 'without the slightest preliminaries . . . plunged into knowing, completely subjective, personal and so to speak "penetrating her core" way of speech'. On the same bus, after this woman had departed (interested but intact), Cassady fixed on another, and

> from 10.30 am to 2.30 pm I talked. When I was done, she (confused, her entire life upset, metaphysically amazed at me . . .) called her folks in Kansas City and went with me to a park . . . and I banged her; I screwed her as never before; all my pent-up emotion finding release in this young virgin . . .

Neal's women remember him as piston-like in sex, a steam-hammer at full pelt. Often he 'banged' three or more women in a day, sometimes mixed them with a man, and masturbated as a stopgap.

Delicate and dismal faces were tucked away behind a picture of a grinning boy jangling the happy keys to a Mercury or a Packard; outwardly, his problems compressed themselves into one emotion, fear of the law, the mention of which could spin him into a panic. By the age of twenty, Cassady had been arrested ten times and had served a total of fifteen months in reformatories, boys' homes and prisons. Sex and a new car (owner not relevant) added up to bliss. Prison (often the outcome of seeking that bliss) was Hell. He had nightmares of future arrests, and an active dread that a cell would be his family home, and convicts his only relatives.

In December 1946, his family amounted to his wife LuAnne, née Henderson, a sixteen-year-old with blonde ringlets and local-beauty-queen looks, who had (illegally) become Mrs Cassady the year before; and, drifting God-knew-where in the mid-Western spaces, old broken-face, Neal senior, his pa.

Neal and LuAnne started out for New York in December. In a stolen car, of course. It belonged to her uncle and aunt, with whom the couple had been living in Nebraska, but they had to abandon it in a snowdrift halfway through the journey. There is something poignant, with more than a hint of destiny, about the way in which Neal's stolen fire was blocked and snuffed out by snow and ice on this first road adventure. Fortunately, LuAnne's purse held $300 (also the aunt and uncle's) which enabled them to complete the trip and think of setting themselves up in Manhattan.

After Times Square and Hector's Cafeteria, where they marvelled like children – LuAnne *was* a child – at the glittering counter and the scale of everything compared to hick Denver luncheonettes, they found Hal Chase, who took them to the West End to meet his friends. Ginsberg and Kerouac were there, but also Chase's Denver friend, Alan Temko, who could see nothing in Cassady but a criminal, and the atmosphere was subdued. Kerouac was more taken with LuAnne, the walking pin-up, than with Cassady, whom Chase had so badly wanted him to meet.

The second meeting between Kerouac and Cassady was more stimulating, and so aptly established the subliminal erotic link that was to clasp them together on their journeys across the continent, that when he began the task of shaping and recording their legend – recognizing the legendary status of Cassady from the start – Kerouac restructured events and put the significant second meeting first.

It took place up in Harlem, where Cassady and LuAnne were staying. Kerouac and Hal Chase went to visit, and when they knocked, Cassady came to the door in the nude. He and LuAnne were in the middle of lovemaking. Above all, Kerouac was amazed and touched by the lack of self-consciousness in Cassady's actions and manners; he saw, as he had not on the previous evening, Neal's 'amorous soul', fetchingly set off by the pose, as he stood in the doorway, of 'a young boxer', his trim, 'thin-hipped' physique, and his circumstantially large penis (well attested by other sources, but particularly impressive to Kerouac, who had a complex about his own). Behind him, LuAnne scrambled about, trying to cover herself. Neal asked the guys to wait until he was 'through'.

In the amorous soul, Kerouac glimpsed the possibility of romance, not directly with Cassady or with LuAnne – although, in a different way, there was potential for each of these, too – but with something mystical, which, in a shaft of insight akin to a vision, he recognized in Cassady. He held the keys to America. Rough plans which had been scuffing against one another for years in Kerouac's head were miraculously crafted and finished by the naked Neal. He was a hero in search of a context, while Kerouac was a scene-painter, a memory-sifter, in search of a hero. Kerouac's present 'Niagara of a novel', *The Town and the City*, was faulty, he knew, because it lacked a strong centre; and it may have been in compensation for this absence that the flow of words continued, as they did, unendingly.

Standing in the doorway before he returned to LuAnne, Neal kept nodding, saying 'That's right' in reply to whatever one of the other two said, and repeated 'Ye-es' over and over – 'a thousand manifold yesses', as Kerouac joyfully wrote.

By March, the Cassadys were back in Denver. Weary, guilty, homesick in New York, tired of working long hours in a bakery while Neal had occupied himself with odd jobs in parking-lots, LuAnne reported one day when he returned from work that the police had been at the door and were looking for him. It was a lie. But although there was no factual truth in it, Neal recognized in LuAnne's story a spiritual truth, the kind that says, you may not have sinned today but you are still a sinner. Convinced that the law was on to him, he left the apartment that night. LuAnne returned to Denver, possibly with the feeling that this was her own form of justice for what she and Neal had done to her relatives. Before long, Cassady was on his way back West, too.

Soon Kerouac would set out to find him. He scented a trail that went from craziness, through bumdom and criminality, to modern saintliness. Kerouac's word for this was 'mad', by which he meant an old-fashioned happy-go-lucky temperament, fired up with inventive mischief, and tinged with religiosity. Of the 'mad ones', Neal was the maddest yet, the maddest it was going to get. Kerouac's encounters with Cassady during the early part of 1947 began the process of a profound change in his attitude towards his own experience. His new passion was for 'things rather than ideas', as he wrote in a letter to Hal Chase, not a month after Neal's departure. His recent reading was all of a 'practical nature', he said, and he provided a list: Francis Parkman's *Oregon Trail*, a history of the United States, a biography of George Washington, and last but not least I have begun a huge study of the face of America itself, acquiring maps (roadmaps) of every state in the USA, and before long not a river or a mountain peak or bay or town or city will escape my attention.

It was an affirmation of his commitment to Wolfeanism to the founder of Wolfeanism (Chase), a vote for the purposeful, poetic America over the 'vague and prosy' Europe. Goodbye, then, to 'the Raskolnikovs and the Julien Sorels of Europe'; welcome, the new American hero, Neal Cassady, delinquent and hungry for purpose.

★

Far from a bitter world of toil
  They led, these roads of long ago:
They climbed the skies to fairy soil,
  They glittered like a line of snow.
> – *On the Road: A book of travel songs,*
> Douglas Goldring, 1910

Workman: You're a stranger here, happen . . .
Tramp: I'm on t'road.
Workman: Ay. (Politely) Well, so might many a one o'us be if things had happen been a little different.
> – *On the Road*, Gwen John, 1920

'Where you goin'?' Sargeant said, stopping by the tracks. He looked at Christ. Sargeant said, 'I'm just a bum on the road. How about you? Where you goin'?'
  'God knows,' said Christ, 'but I'm leavin' here.'
> – 'On the Road', Langston Hughes, 1935

Jane: That car plays too big a part in your life.
Lucille: Well, it's a very big car.
> – *On the Road: A play for women,* Cyril Campion, 1954

★

In the third week of July, Kerouac left his mother's place in Queens and lighted out. He was, at last, a participant in the most compelling of New World idylls, life on the open road. 'Where you from?' – the quintessential American question. 'Where you goin'?' Riding boxcars, blazing the trail, scouting the West, the frontier hero blends with the mythical anti-hero, the Indian, inhabitant of a pre-America, land of instinct. Kerouac, the dropout and discharge, who had begun to feel he couldn't stick at anything, was now looking out of the window at 'the face of America itself'.

The journey began on public transport. Kerouac took a train north of the city, to the road which runs up the Hudson, where he could begin hitch-hiking to Bear Mountain Ridge. Once there, he would follow the road west, Route 6, leading from the tip of Cape Cod to Ely, Nevada. It was an itinerary scattered with the names of old frontier trails; it was the Territory.

But no one had told him: Route 6 was no longer the main artery westward; it had fallen into disuse years before. Five rides on from where he had started hitch-hiking, Kerouac had covered only forty miles. The rain came down heavily, and, because of a roundabout close to where he was standing, catching lifts was difficult. A more experienced cross-country traveller could have told him that the best route west from NYC was to go through the Holland Tunnel and head for Chicago via Pittsburgh. Denver was 2,000 miles away, and the rain looked as though it would never stop. Eventually, he turned around and went back to the city. There, he caught a bus to Chicago.

Twenty-four hours later, more than half his money gone, Kerouac got a lift across the Mississippi River and arrived in Des Moines, Iowa. Sitting at his desk in Ozone Park, he had envisaged himself jumping a freight train, hobo-style. But, at the moment of decision, he had no way of making out the directions of the trains. This one with the open freight cars might chug him all the way back to New York. So he boarded another bus and hitched some more lifts. Along the way, he wrote home to his mother: on 24 July, in the morning, from Nebraska ('You ought to see the Cowboys out here'), in the afternoon from Wyoming ('they're having "Wild West Week" '), on the 28th from Denver ('Just arrived'), and the next day again to tell her that he was broke and needed her to wire him money.

Cowboys, but few Indians; so Kerouac's rhapsodies-in-the-making were inspired and directed by surrogate natives: Mexicans and Negroes. And, 'somewhere along the way I knew there'd be girls,

61

visions, everything; somewhere along the line the pearl would be handed to me.' But first he had to find Neal Cassady, who would be his guide. 'I keep losing track of him', Kerouac had written to Burroughs on the eve of departure, 'like his landladies'.

Ginsberg, openly smitten with Cassady, had preceded Kerouac to Denver. When Kerouac arrived and finally found Cassady, following clues provided by Hal Chase and Alan Temko, he discovered that he and Ginsberg were emotionally engaged in a way that excluded him . . . he who had seen in naked Neal a 'long-lost brother', who aspired to form with him (as he put it to Cassady himself) an 'animal relationship'. Instead, he found himself hanging around and watching while Ginsberg and Cassady stared into each other's eyes for twenty minutes at a time, or tagging along silently on Denver's Logan Street while they continued their 'long rapport', using a private language which left him mute.

As Neal talked about three things at once, so he was usually involved with at least three people at once. To complement the ambiguous relationship with Ginsberg, there was a new attachment to a woman: Carolyn Robinson, a middle-class art student, who thrilled him not only with her blonde hair and good looks, but with her respectability, her natural tendency to order and stability. Somewhere, not far away, posing and pouting, was LuAnne.

The set-up confused Kerouac, who reflected later that, in all the time he spent in Denver, not once did he and Neal have the opportunity to talk. 'I knew there'd be girls . . .' – but when there *were* girls, Kerouac felt that they got in the way of the romance he wished he was having with Neal. 'The night we picked up the Columbian girl and the Scott Fitzgerald decadent flapper from Dallas (with the languid eyes), I really would have preferred eating that pork chop alone with you . . .'

It was not the only appeal to Cassady's amorous soul in the long letter Kerouac wrote from California in August, to which state he had decamped and taken a job in Marin City as a special policeman ('I can hardly wait to tell Burroughs'). He also wrote: 'I am dying to have you here with me . . . I wish you would really understand me and yet not require that I constantly lay myself before you . . .' It is the pang of the sorely neglected lover. But he ended on an optimistic note, guessing that by now Neal would have left Carolyn. 'A nice girl. But hardly your type.'

'Thank you for your information in regard to Joan', Burroughs wrote back to Ginsberg in October, from his parents' home in St Louis; he had spent the summer there, sitting out his suspended sentence from the Huncke affair. In a letter to Edie Parker in the spring, Joan herself summed up what had happened at 115th Street after the second break-up of the libertine circle:

> After a while we began taking in desperate characters as boarders so before long I was running quite a pad. Everything in the damn place was hot, as were of course a couple of cars outside. Inevitably, people kept going to jail, until finally, due to that and the ever-present back rent we got tossed out . . . I'd been taking so much benzedrine that I got way off beam, with the result that I finally landed in the Bellevue psycho ward . . . It took me a week to convince these stupid doctors that I wasn't completely mad. Everything was nicely timed though, because just before I got out at last Bill got back in town.

Once he had picked her up from the ward, Burroughs drove down to Texas, where he had purchased a 99-acre spread in a small town called New Waverley, north of Houston. His family had put up the capital. They must have seen hope for the future in their wayward son's plans to quit the corrupting city and grow grapefruit and tomatoes. There was money to be made, 'like picking fruit off the trees', Burroughs told Ginsberg, and he probably told his father the same thing. To Ginsberg (though probably not to his father), he went on to say that he intended to raise marihuana, using his legal crop as a cover, with a posy of opium poppies interleaved.

The flight to Texas was the beginning of an exile from New York that was to last, with minor interruptions, almost thirty years. New York was so fast and demanding that it seemed to hold the power of identity over people; with Burroughs, it was his drug-addict identity. He had found it interesting, but not conducive to useful endeavour. His relocation was the first of several attempts to make money out of farming and – although he was far from forswearing drugs – to make himself stop using heroin and morphine. 'I have given up junk entirely', he would soon write to Ginsberg, a boast that was to be repeated over and over again in letters written through the years.

Huncke had done the same thing, going to sea with Phil White (nicknamed 'the Sailor') in an effort to escape the addict-shaping pressures of the metropolis; now Huncke joined Burroughs and Joan, and Joan's daughter Julie, on the road to New Waverley, an innocent town of just a few blocks. To friends, Joan took a sanguine, didn't-do-me-any-harm attitude to her mental crash, and Burroughs sent news of life down on the farm: 'The house is overrun with huge rats . . . I shot one who was too fat and got wedged in his hole.'

Behind the beat

Naked Neal

To Kerouac and Ginsberg, Neal Cassady was the embodiment of an artistic manifesto. Its essence was apprehended by Kerouac on the threshold of the Harlem apartment the previous winter: a thousand manifold *yesses*; and *nakedness*. These were to become the basis of the literary aesthetic of both writers. And nakedness not just metaphorically: in the years to come, Ginsberg would incorporate the act of stripping into his poetic practice.

It is notable how often Cassady appears naked in other people's recollections, often having had, or about to have, sex. The first person from outside the Larimer Street flophouse world to take an interest in Cassady was a Denver lawyer and high-school counsellor named Justin Brierly. He was involved in trying to help bright boys from dark backgrounds on to better things, especially if, like Neal, they had 'piercing blue eyes, chiseled features and [a] hard, well-muscled body'.

There is more than one version of Brierly's first encounter with Cassady – either the lawyer was inspecting a rent-house where Cassady was a tenant, or he was paying a call on his uncle – but, anyway, having let himself in with a key, he met, in the hallway or on the stairs, the fifteen-year-old, chiseled, muscled Neal, who in all variations of the story is naked. Taking it up later, Kerouac added the refinement that Neal had 'been upstairs with the maid'.

When the errant boy landed in the Colorado State Reformatory at Buena Vista, for stealing cars, Brierly made attempts to secure an early release – efforts which, however well-meaning they might have been, were not entirely disinterested. Cassady told Kerouac later that he had been 'flirting' with Brierly for years, and it turned out that the expected reward for helping Neal out of a tight spot was sex with the helper. Neal compromised by offering Brierly the opportunity to watch him make love (while naked, presumably) to his current girlfriend.

The Harlem introduction of Kerouac to Cassady was the principal statement of a theme. When, after much searching, Kerouac finally caught up with Cassady on his first trip West, the theme was repeated: Kerouac knocked on the door of the Denver back-alley rooming-house where he had been told Neal was staying, and Neal opened the door 'stark naked'. In New York, LuAnne had busied herself in the background trying to cover her nakedness; this time, Kerouac glimpsed 'a creamy thigh covered with black lace'. On the wall behind was a drawing of Neal, naked, with 'enormous dangle and all'.

Both thigh and drawing belonged to Carolyn Robinson, Neal's new girlfriend. But LuAnne was still in the frame, even if Carolyn had been led to believe that she was not. One morning, in the dawn of their love affair, having been boarding elsewhere for reasons to do with work, Carolyn tiptoed up the stairs to the room she and Neal shared, intending to give him a nice surprise. But it was she who was surprised: 'There, in *our* bed, sleeping nude, were LuAnne, Neal and Allen, in that order.' The scene was re-enacted years later, in California, sans LuAnne.

When the long-haul drives from coast to coast began, LuAnne accompanied Kerouac and Cassady on one of them. During a stretch in the middle of winter, Cassady enjoined his two passengers to 'do as I'm doing, disburden yourself of all that clothes – now what's the sense of clothes?' Unable, or unwilling, to rebut the argument, they complied. When they pulled over to the side of the road in order to examine a monument, Neal stepped out of the car 'stark naked' (Kerouac and LuAnne opted for overcoats).

Herbert Huncke, who did not know Cassady well, made only a few observations about him, one being that 'his success as a lover was actually the warmth of his body. He generated such a terrific warmth that one couldn't lie next to him without feeling the energy coming from him.'

Naked Neal

It is with a sense of inevitability that we find ourselves with Kerouac some time later in San Francisco, once again in search of Cassady, once again knocking on doors, this time in the dead of night. We wait with him, until – at last – 'he came to the door stark naked'.

4

The little auto

We understood, my friend and I,
That the little auto had taken us into an epoch that was New
And that although we were mature men
We had nevertheless just been born

– Apollinaire, 'La petite auto' (1918)

Special police constable Kerouac wrote enthusiastically to Cassady from Marin City about a reunion in New York in the autumn: 'I feel like writing a huge novel about *all* of it. Just think' – and he reeled off the names of his characters: Ginsberg, Burroughs and Joan, Lucien and Céline, Huncke, Vicki Russell, 'and us'. New York was the great city, and they were living at the great New York moment: 'Johnson and his London, Balzac and his Paris, Socrates and his Athens'; and now, 'the same thing again' – Kerouac and his New York, or, at any rate, his 'great and everlasting America'.

After a month policing the barracks at Marin, he quit the job and thumbed down to Los Angeles, where he met a Mexican girl who told him they could make money by harvesting grapes and picking cotton together. Her name was Bea Franco, later adjusted, for book use, to 'Terry'. Kerouac fell briefly in love with her, and (a longer lasting affair) with the deliciously subversive thought of her being Mexican – dark and closer to the colour of the soil, and therefore closer to the aboriginal Americas. When an Okie family on the farm where they were working started to behave belligerently towards

Bea and her compatriots, Kerouac experienced the thrill of racial masquerade, of passing oneself off as another kind: 'They thought I was a Mexican, of course; and in a way I am.' He relished it as only one who can step safely back across the dividing line can do.

Soon he had to leave Bea and be off again to keep the rendezvous with Neal in New York. He mixed buses with hitch-hiking, all the way back across the continent, bypassing Denver, upwards and eastwards by Greyhound beyond Chicago to Pittsburgh, taking the final stretch into New York by thumb. He was a proven 'beating it' man now, a new type of hobo, pre-industrial and post-atom bomb at once, criss-crossing the nation not for work, not because he was on the run, or on the lookout for a jeweller's shop, like Jack Black, but for kicks, the pure poetry of moving on. Kerouac, the Atomic Bum.

Or at least he liked to think he was doing it only for kicks. In truth, it was always research.

In all his movements, Kerouac cannot stop watching himself move; he cannot help seeing himself having a great time; when he joins in, a part of him detaches itself and watches him joining in. When he tells the Navy psychiatrist: 'I'm only old Samuel Johnson', it is so that he may write a letter and record himself saying it. 'I hid in the grapevines, digging it all . . .', he wrote about one tricky escapade with Bea Franco out West. 'I was adventuring in the crazy American night.'

Cassady understood this aspect of Kerouac at once, understood it better than Kerouac himself did. And he understood, too, that it defined a crucial difference between them. He called it Kerouac's 'constructive involvement' with the world, a type of involvement which he himself never had. Cassady could see that Kerouac, as he was running, was reading – reading the landscape, the 'American night', or 'America itself' – and, while reading, composing. Whatever Kerouac did in the day, he caught himself doing it, and made a note of his perception at night, which would come in useful for writing in the morning.

Cassady had grown up in a world deprived of the concept of usefulness – and he raced around his universe filling the gap with 'kicks'. Living for the moment was his gift – and he cursed it. He had the Midas touch, envied by everyone but lamented by the King.

When Ginsberg wrote a letter praising his 'vast realistic vision', Cassady was not flattered but exasperated. He snapped back:

> Bullshit. I spoke of no realistic 'vision'. What possibilities? I'm ill, man. Why, why, do you speak of realization, of expression? I wrote for a month straight – what came out? terrible, awful, stupid, stupid trash – it grew worse each day . . .

While Kerouac on the road scribbled down images for a book, or just for the pleasure of watching words become things under his hand – or took a job as a policeman, so that he might include that in the 'huge novel', too – Neal's eyes blinked at a different set of facts: the flophouse world, a no-hope father, the policeman at the door.

Carolyn Robinson was not hip, and did not want to be. She had been raised, in her own words, 'in fear and reverence of existing social codes', and she carried the reverence with her to Denver. Before continuing her studies at the University there, she had attended the smart East Coast ladies' college, Bennington. Although she enjoyed the company of men, she was not sexually experienced, as the girls in the New York crowd were. Goodness and simplicity shone in her face and hung in her wavy blonde hair. While she had begun to fulfil her ambition to work in the theatre – occasionally as an actress, mainly as a set-designer – her major goal was to graduate to homeliness. She wanted to be wife to her amazing new boyfriend Neal, and mother to his children.

The prospect inspired Neal to utter a thousand manifold yesses. And then he might ask Carolyn to wait in the car outside a strange house, saying he had to visit a friend there and would be back in twenty minutes. Only later did Carolyn realize that the friend was a girlfriend, and that the twenty minutes had been spent in bed.

For Neal, the sexual message could not be refused or rejected. Sex, all sex, any sex, his or hers, duets, trios, quartets and solos, made life quiver with meaning, as nothing else did. His natural tendency was heterosexual, but the amorous soul perceived by Kerouac found it hard to say no to a man, if the man impressed him with his needs; or, to flip the pathology over, if Neal thought he might gain by the exchange.

While working as a parking-lot attendant at the New Yorker

Hotel and trying to console the troublesome, homesick LuAnne, Cassady had drawn Ginsberg into a sexual drama. In the affair, there was both the desire to please and the desire to profit. He was moved by Ginsberg's need for him, and, at the same time, was interested in making an investment in Ginsberg's literary talent. Ten days after his flight back to Denver in early March, he wrote to say that his need for Allen strove to match Allen's longing for him: 'I am almost free enough to be a real help to you, but my love can't flurish [*sic*] in my present position. By God, though, every day I miss you more and more.' The sign-off magically sealed the pledge, compounding the amorous with the spiritual: 'Your other self'. The encounters with Cassady gave certainty to something Ginsberg felt, but had feared to believe, that the homosexual problem would disperse in the solvent of love. And, unlike his furtive infatuations with Kerouac and Carr, it seemed to be joyfully reciprocated.

Yet in the phrase about being a 'real help', Ginsberg surely felt the pressure of brakes being applied. By the end of the month, Neal had gone into reverse:

> I really don't know how much I can be satisfied to love you, I mean bodily, you know I, somehow, dislike pricks & men & before you, had consciously forced myself to be homosexual . . .

The Denver pleasure-ground failed to live up to his hopes, and Ginsberg headed home with a suitcase full of familiar sadness. The affair with Neal had been a holiday affair, a brief respite from sexual disgust and from fears about his mental instability. Now he was back from Denver, 'back to reality', or to the maddening appearance of reality which he knew to be illusion – back in the East and mired in the conundrum that the promise of first love, and freedom, were unattainable, in the West.

As he approached his twenty-first birthday in the middle of the year, Ginsberg wrote to Kerouac of the discernible and highly unwelcome spectre of his 'true nature': 'I am one of those people who goes around showing his cock to juvenile delinquents . . .' In a letter to the psychiatrist Wilhelm Reich – recommended by Burroughs, who believed that most psychiatrists were 'jerks' who felt that 'anyone with-it at all belongs in a nut house' – Ginsberg outlined his psychic geography, just as he had done to Burroughs

71

earlier: 'conscious masochism ... depression, guilt feelings ... sordidness ... melancholy ... the whole gamut, I suppose'.

He could only be cast down further on receiving word from his mother, in Pilgrim State Hospital, Long Island, that the doctors had discovered kerosene in her system. She reiterated her complaints, as she would continue to do for years to come: there were wires in her head; there were sticks up her back. Mixed in with these diagnoses were pitiful pleas to be taken home: 'Allen, please take me out. I'll make such lovely meals for you! ... Please ... I was a good woman! Hurry, Naomi.'

In the middle of November, Ginsberg started twice-weekly sessions with an analyst suggested by Reich. In the same month, he received grisly confirmation of his fears about what manner of family inheritance awaited him, in the form of a letter signed by the Senior Director of Pilgrim State:

> Please be advised that your mother Naomi Ginsberg was seen in consultation with the Assistant Director and it was decided that her mental condition is serious enough to warrant a prefrontal lobotomy ... we are enclosing a permit for the operation which you can sign and return to us if you so desire.

In the hope that a neurological cut might succeed in relieving the pain of wires and sticks, where reason, therapy and filial love had failed, Ginsberg signed and returned.

Then, more confusion, as Cassady once again made a U-turn. Cassady strewed a confetti of contradictions before Ginsberg. He was living with Carolyn, who was pregnant, but he still saw LuAnne, even as he set about having their marriage dissolved. And now he spoke of integrating Ginsberg into the set-up. He suggested an arrangement whereby he and Allen would 'have an apt, a girl, go to college', with the idea that they would try to live as friends, becoming 'truly straight (through analysis ...)'.

Then that seemed not to be enough, and, as suddenly as he had pushed Ginsberg away in the letters of March 1947, now he pulled him towards him. The 'truly straight' condition was dropped, and Neal was back to serenading again:

> I love skinny women & strong-chinned (queer's ideal) men. I love all – sex – yes all, all sex. anyway I can get it. I need it, I want it, shall *have* it –

now. I wanta fuck – In despair I cry 'Allen, Allen will you let me spatter my come at you.'

It was 7 September. Earlier in the day, Carolyn had given birth to a daughter. 'If it is a boy', Cassady had written to Ginsberg two weeks before, 'I shall name it Allen Jack Cassady.'

Two months before, in July, Ginsberg had received a peremptory note from his father:

Dear Allen,
　　Exorcise Neal.
　　　　Louis.

In his correspondence with his father, Ginsberg often included his latest poems. Louis Ginsberg, whose letters were as sane as Naomi's were mad (the parents were now divorced), welcomed his son's efforts. The advice he sent back was intended to impel him towards greater discipline, in poetry and in life. Louis equated poetic practice with moral practice:

Your verse is at times a bit amorphous . . . not focussed enough . . . use concrete images . . . watch the grammar . . . you don't seem to me to be searching for moral and political values.

Lacking in such values or not, Ginsberg's poetry still aspired to a high degree of formalism; he employed archaisms to attain a poetical longing, no more so than when describing his desire for Cassady:

Most dear, and dearest at this moment most,
Since this my love for thee is thus more free
Than that I cherished more dear and lost . . .

Kerouac warned him against passing off his sadness as art, and tried to steer him clear of 'musing and wondering and frantic intellectual chasing after vague submerged truths'. He understood that Ginsberg was piqued over the outcome of his early hopes for Neal, but, he urged: 'Don't pull your head back into the shell, never.'

And, indeed, in Denver in the spring of 1947, Ginsberg had begun to experiment with a freer, more colloquial verse, which anticipated sage Kerouac's theoretical advice, and attempted to act on Neal's bodily example – a verse which would act and speak more like the real Allen Ginsberg. If he could hear his own voice, maybe he could find his own self.

'In Society' is a dream poem, a medium Ginsberg was to favour increasingly in the future, as he endeavoured to locate, then express and purge the taboos in his subconscious. It is an important poem therapeutically, if not poetically, notable for the first use of taboo words in anything written by Ginsberg or his friends; for a metaphorical acceptance of homosexuality; and for the boldness – inspired by the poet's love of another man – to speak back to a woman 'who looked like / a princess' and who has spoken harshly to him. Most notable of all, though, it is the earliest sounding of a voice which is 'violent / messianic' but 'inspired' as well, and shows the poet confidently inside the role of outsider.

> I walked into the cocktail party
> room and found three or four queers
> talking together in queertalk.
> I tried to be friendly but heard
> myself talking to one in hiptalk.
> 'I'm glad to see you', he said, and
> looked away . . .
> I ate a sandwich of pure meat; an
> enormous sandwich of human flesh,
> I noticed, while I was chewing on it,
> it also included a dirty asshole.

More people arrive at the party, including 'a fluffy female' who glares at the poet and says, 'I don't like you'.

> 'Why you narcissistic bitch! How
> can you decide when you don't even
> know me,' I continued in a violent
> and messianic voice, inspired at
> last, dominating the whole room.

★

In the middle of 1948, Kerouac stationed himself in his mother's corner house on Cross Bay Boulevard in Ozone Park, in order to complete *The Town and the City*, the fat, Wolfean novel which chronicled the movement of the Martin family from the Massachusetts town of Galloway, where they were born, to the big city, at the beginning of the Second World War.

The saga demanded a more traditional novelistic form than Kerouac was ever to use again. He made the Martin family Irish-American, and put a little of himself into each of the five brothers, emphasizing his identification with Peter Martin, who shares the author's year of birth, his athletic ability, and his difficult relationship with his father. In the second half of the book, Peter encounters the libertine circle in New York. Kerouac found places for Ginsberg, as Leon Levinsky, Burroughs, as Will Dennison, Lucien Carr and David Kammerer as Kenneth Wood and Waldo Meister (though he spared Waldo's life), and he gave a cameo appearance to Huncke as 'Junky'. The manuscript topped 1,800 pages. It was signed with a name which would in future look like someone else's: 'John Kerouac'.

> The town is Galloway. The Merrimac River, broad and placid, flows down to it from the New Hampshire hills, broken at the falls to make frothy havoc on the rocks, foaming on over ancient stone towards a place where the river suddenly swings about in a wide and peaceful basin, moving on now around the flank of the town, on to places known as Lawrence and Haverhill, through a wooded valley, and on to the sea at Plum Island, where the river enters an infinity of waters and is gone.

It was the first completed work by a beat writer, but it wasn't a beat book. Kerouac believed that it would make him a lot of money, as he confidently stated in letters to friends and family, but the expected rush to publish the novel and film it did not happen. Then, after a number of rejections, Robert Giroux, of the firm Harcourt, Brace, showed a serious interest in it. He offered Kerouac a $1,000 advance. Kerouac's response was to take Giroux out to Cross Bay Boulevard to meet his mother, who immediately registered his French–Canadian background and approved his manners.

> She said, 'You don't look like a publisher', and I said, 'Well, what do I look like?' She said, 'You look like a banker.' Then she turned to Jack and said, 'You stick with him and give up those bums you're running out with.'

75

The professional author signed a letter to a friend, 'BET-A-THOUSAND KEROUAC'.

Already, though, his travels to Denver and California had ignited his imagination, and a new story was ticking over. He wrote in his journal that it was to be about two friends hitching lifts in cars and trucks out West, 'in search of something they don't *really* find'. It was no more than kindling for a novel. But he had a title in mind: ' "On the Road" . . . More later.'

Six months on, at the beginning of 1949, he set off on the cross-country trip in Cassady's majestic big Hudson, all shine and chrome, that was to provide the raw material for half the projected book. On a Wednesday night in December, Kerouac had received a phone call, long-distance, and immediately danced a minuet of joy:

Dear Allen,
    Neal is coming to New York.
    Neal is coming to New York for New Year's Eve.
    Neal is coming to New York for New Year's Eve.
    Neal is coming to New York for New Year's Eve.

The Hudson, he added, with studied casualness, seeking perhaps a mite of reflected witchery, was probably stolen.

In fact, it had been procured legally. To get it, Cassady had pledged a $1,000 down-payment – money he and Carolyn had been saving to buy a ranch. He did not tell Carolyn in advance that he planned to withdraw it and spend it on a car, but how could she resist? It was a gorgeous machine: two-toned metallic, maroon and grey, sporting a radio, a dashboard like an aeroplane, and the fashionable feature of a floor sunk below the door frame.

Neal drove home and showed it off proudly to Carolyn. Take a look at this! She burst into tears.

'Now, now, Carolyn, look here, don't you understand . . . Jack wants to come out, but, he hasn't any money to get here. So, ol' Cass to everybody's rescue . . . Well, our savings, yes, but look I can make that much back in two months when I'm on the railroad again next spring . . . easy. The monthly payments are practically nothing. You know we need the car with the baby and all . . .'

Carolyn – baby and all – was not to be placated. So – what else to do but turn the key and be off? 'And what a trip it turned out to be!' marvelled Kerouac. 'I only went along for the ride' – the ride being the fun of seeing what Neal would do next. They spent Christmas in North Carolina with Kerouac's sister's family, and New Year in New York with the gang. Then it was back in the car and on the road for a month. Where go? What do? No answers needed – just move. And who should turn up but LuAnne? She sat in the middle as they rushed through the days and nights, joining in on the freezing-cold day when Neal said they must all take off their clothes. And Neal made it clear, as he did with Carolyn later, that he would have no objection if Jack and LuAnne became lovers.

They powered down through Maryland, Virginia, Georgia, eventually reaching the Burroughs household, which had flitted from Texas to another farm at Algiers, straight across the Mississippi River from New Orleans. The visit was not a success. Burroughs didn't like Cassady. He couldn't see the point of 'this voyage into pure, abstract, meaningless motion'. When Neal tried to touch Burroughs for gas money, he got the brush-off. Soon he and Jack were behind the wheel again, picking up hitch-hikers and charging them fares, and cheating in gas stations with Neal's trick of winding back the petrol meter. Jack was fascinated by this kind of street knowledge. They drove south and west through Texas and Arizona, the car swallowing up fabled names such as Laredo, El Paso, Tucson, until they cleared LA and continued north for San Francisco. Neal sent a postcard to Carolyn and the baby. 'Great car. Doing 800 miles a day.'

After they had completed a great big circle, Cassady hurtled back to San Francisco, and announced that the adventure was over. Or at least this chapter of it. He put down Kerouac and LuAnne on a street in North Beach, and drove off in the now dented and unshiny Hudson, in search of his wife and baby. 'You see what a bastard he is', LuAnne almost proudly told Kerouac. 'Neal will leave you out in the cold any time it's in his interest.'

They found a cheap hotel, where they performed Cassady's bidding by becoming lovers. Then LuAnne – 'what a whore' – went off with a nightclub owner in a Cadillac, without saying goodbye. Kerouac began the long road home to his own domestic peace, with mother. Travelling alone through Washington State and Montana, then curving north-eastwards back to New York, he gathered the names and flavours of rivers and mountains and roads into his notebook for his possible novel about a journey made with an impossible character like Neal. He sent a postcard to Ginsberg, giving 'The Bitterroot Mountains – Root of Rivers & Rainy Nights' as his return address.

Sometime around the turn of the year 1948–9, the word 'beat' acquired glamour. From being a despised, Huncke-like condition, a fugitive shifting at best, *beat* became something someone might want to be. As used by lowdown blacks, in the spaces btween drug-highs and sex-highs and music-highs, *beat* packed into its abrupt syllable the experience of no–money, sadness, rejection. In its altering usage, however, the sense changed from passive to active – you weren't rejected, you did the rejecting. As part of the process, the black word *beat* turned white.

In February 1947, Burroughs could use 'beat' in a letter to Ginsberg to mean tame or submissive: 'what they want is some beat clerk who feels with some reason that other people don't like him', he wrote, circling round his obsession with the analyst and the patient. This is far from what Kerouac had in mind when, in the middle of a conversation two years later, he tagged his group, and all the Benzedrine-suckers and tea-heads and jazz fans and mad ones everywhere, a 'beat generation'.

Kerouac was talking to a new friend, John Clellon Holmes, also a tyro writer. In a letter to Ed White in Denver at the end of 1948, Kerouac announced that he had met 'another fine couple', Holmes and his wife Marian. Typically, Holmes made a note of what Kerouac said about a beat generation. It was his habit to make notes about the people he met, the conversations they had, the way they spoke. He had it in mind to dramatize their various relationships in a novel structured around a central idea which would mark them out as distinctly 'postwar', and would act as a central organizing principle for the story.

Holmes, like Kerouac, was from Massachusetts. He had attended Columbia College, though without making contact with the libertines. Like Kerouac, he had married young, but had stayed married. At twenty-three, he was among the youngest, and certainly the most stable, of the group he now found himself in, settled into a domestic regime which the others, buffeting from side to side in the shallower reaches of madness and crime, seemed already unsuited for.

No sexual ambiguity troubled Holmes's sleep. The unexpected knock at the door could only signal a friend, never 'heat', though 'heat' was a word he liked to use. Holmes also liked to smoke tea, but his wife, Marian, who didn't care for his new friends, or for words such as 'heat' or 'beat', wouldn't let him smoke tea in the apartment. Neal Cassady was the litmus test. Where Kerouac and Ginsberg saw a saviour, or a saint, in Cassady, Holmes could only see a psychopath.

Holmes listened as Kerouac talked late into the night in Holmes's living-room in Lexington Avenue, drinking and reeling off stories about 115th and 118th Streets, about Kammerer, about hitch-hiking in California and being mistaken for a Mexican, about mourning 'the Negroes' lot' in North Carolina, about

> all the junkies, musicians, collegians, sailors, con men, teenage Raskolni-kovs, parking-lot hipsters, and their rootless willing girls . . . stories rich and chaotic with life's improvisations; stories that seemed to be describing a new sort of stance toward reality.

Holmes recognized the people Kerouac talked about, or, if not the people, the mood. It was his mood, his search, even if he'd never crossed a junkie's path or had a rootless, willing girl. Holmes noted that he 'kept goading Jack to characterize this new attitude', and that Kerouac called it 'a sort of furtiveness . . . a kind of beatness' –

> 'I mean, being right down to it, to ourselves, because we all *really* know who we are – and a weariness with all the forms, all the conventions of the world . . . It's something like that. So I guess you might say we're a *beat* generation.'

To Holmes, it was akin to the existentialist mist seeping across the ocean from Paris, but at street level; with a jazz rhythm; and hinting at the superior yet subterranean knowledge of that enigmatic but ever-present jazz figure, the Negro. Here was the idea that Holmes had been searching for, the state of being beat.

The trouble was, Kerouac had the idea of doing something

similar. He hadn't presented his definition of 'beat' and the beat generation to Holmes as the basis for a book, but when he realized that Holmes was writing his own beat novel, the conflict of interest became apparent, and became a problem.

If Kerouac actually said 'we all *really* know who we are', he must have been drunker than Holmes realized: Ginsberg heading for the asylum on the heels of his mother, Burroughs scuttling among pickpockets in the subways, Joan soaking in Benzedrine, Cassady twisting from marriage-bed to stolen car to man's bed . . . The anecdote in which Kerouac defines the beat generation was patented by Holmes, and bore his genial trademark; it is neatly wrapped and ribboned with the romance of the outsider-writer that the steady Holmes longed to be.

Holmes couldn't help putting things in a larger context. He dipped everything in *Angst* – a dope fiend's trip to the pharmacy, a tenor player's solo – then brought it out to see how it looked in fresh daylight. You couldn't say 'kicks' without him starting to talk about Sartre; he couldn't hear 'hip' without making a reference to Hiroshima. To Cassady, kicks were just kicks, a filling-in of the gaps. To Kerouac, they were source material. But to Holmes they were symptoms.

Holmes was not wrong. The moment calls out for definition – the end of a decade, the closing of the first postwar chapter, the dawning of a new era of imperialist stand-off, crowned by bigger, better, quite invisible yet omnipresent bombs. In the sociological surgery, the juvenile delinquent is operated on to reveal organs infected by meaningless liberty. It was the moment to start growing up absurd. It was the Beat Generation.

In jazz, Holmes wrote, the beat youngsters heard

> something rebel and nameless that spoke for them, and their lives knew a gospel for the first time. It was more than a music; it became an attitude toward life, a way of walking, a costume . . .

It was a sense of rhythm, a sense of style, a cool attitude, intended to shield the vulnerable self from a hostile world. Rhythm and cool are the essential elements of hip, which, as one writer wrote at the time, involved 'the frequent use of metonymous gestures, for example, brushing hands for handshaking, extending an index finger, without raising the arm, as a form of greeting', all connoting prior understanding – 'there is no need to elaborate, I dig you, man, etc'.

The writer is describing old hip, black hip, while Holmes is seeking to define the new, white hipsterism. The 'something rebel and nameless' that Holmes refers to was the aspect of black life that had hitherto been concealed from whites, and which was now revealed through jazz. Black music seemed to young white people 'to express all sorts of inexpressible exuberance and energy'. The secret was out, and on the way to becoming *beat*. The new attitudes were as much as anything a new set of rhythms; jive talk made it possible to be rhythmic whenever you opened your mouth.

Kerouac did not always see eye to eye with Holmes – he disliked Holmes's intellectualism, for one thing – but they combined in their love of jazz, and in the feeling that New York's black wastelands were themselves a kind of urban Territory, reservoirs of primitive yet present rhythm. In company with Cassady, when he was in the city, they drove up to Harlem, through 'miserably squalid tenements' (Holmes) lining 'god-awful streets' (Kerouac), to a black rent-party where you could hear some grass-roots jazz and blues. In one place, from among the sounds of an impromptu black combo, Kerouac heard 'the pit and prune-juice of pure beat life itself'. The first Beat saw the face of his first ancestor; and it was a black face. 'You ain't known the new hipness in America', Kerouac told Holmes, 'until you've dug the younger Negroes who call New York the Apple.'

But it was the rhythm of the purring car engine that set not just the spirit but the body free – and here the white hipster takes leave of his Negro forebear. While music and talk opened up a territory once exclusive to the multi-marginalized black, the automobile promised kicks to the white boy which, to the black, remained out of bounds.

Imagine: two black buddies cruising across state lines at the close of the 1940s, in a car which may or may not be stolen, may or may not be paid for, making stops for beer and hamburgers at any old roadside eaterie, flirting with the waitress, cutting the breeze with the local cowpokes, nudging one another at the sight of a shapely behind, going in search of music at the local joint come evening. The reality factor in that commercial for the American Dream is precisely zero. History united the beat and the black; geography (so essential to beat rhythm) separated them.

As he glided across the country, Kerouac met more blacks face to face than he ever had in Lowell or New York, but the vocabulary he uses to describe them is more reminiscent of a patrician abolitionist than a postwar would-be hip kid. Kerouac's blacks are 'wise and tired', 'laughing', 'joyous', 'kindly', 'patient', 'sensuous', 'sullen', 'sad'. If not muttering a prayer, as they walk along a road or work in the fields, they are likely to be moaning a spiritual or an old blues. At nights, they revert to character and sing and dance and get violent and make love – which is where the young beats would like to come in and share their sense of style: 'old-fashioned spade kicks', wrote Kerouac, 'what other kicks are there?'

When regarding the Negro, Kerouac – as in his escapade with the Mexican girl, Bea Franco – is enchanted by the thought of passing through the veil into a zone of sensual enhancement, a place where the inhabitants, in Holmes's words, 'knew something that we didn't know'. Walking around Denver one night in the middle of 1949 – 'the Mexican-Nigger Denver', as he called it in a letter to Ginsberg – Kerouac surrendered to the temptation to lose 'whiteness' altogether, and plunged headlong into kitsch:

> At lilac evening I walked with every muscle among the lights of 27th and Welton in the Denver colored section, wishing I were a Negro, feeling that the best the white world had offered was not enough ecstasy for me, not enough life, joy, kicks, darkness, music, not enough night . . . I wished I were a Denver Mexican, or even a poor overworked Jap, anything but what I was so drearily, a 'white man', disillusioned . . . I passed the dark porches of Mexican and Negro homes; soft voices were there, occasionally the dusky knee of some mysterious sensual gal; and dark faces of the men behind rose arbours. Little children sat like sages in ancient rocking chairs.

★

The anatomy of hip was a rare science in 1948–9. Black writers by and large ignored the subject; the predominant theme of black literature at the turn of the decade was improvement, and its uppity twin, protest; the tone was leavened by an ironic humour. The most successful black American writer of the day was Richard Wright, whose books were all about social justice for the Negro. Of the obtuse reactions of a hostile world to the hep cat or hipikat or hipster, little was revealed in black writing, or in writing in which blacks featured.

On the white side of the fence, no writer could get close enough to the hip in, say, Harlem to be able to describe it in true psychological detail. And although there were black faces in Greenwich Village bars, the banal perils of just walking the streets downtown, never mind negotiating civil rights with waiters and landladies, kept most away. Even in the Village, there were bars and restaurants which refused to serve blacks. In 1948, James Baldwin, a young black writer who was often to be found at the bar of the San Remo in MacDougal Street (which operated a 'no Negroes' policy in its restaurant next door), published a short story in which the routine awfulness of being black when all around are white is vividly shown. Through the intervention of a white friend, the narrator secures a room in a house downtown. One day, he hears a knock:

> When I opened the door the landlady stood there, red-and-white faced and hysterical.
>
> 'Who are you? I didn't rent this room to you.'
>
> My mouth was dry. I started to say something.
>
> 'I can't have no colored people here,' she said. 'All my tenants are complainin'. Women afraid to come home nights.'

Kerouac and Holmes were not intimate enough with this sort of experience, or the code which existed to enable those involved to transcend it – *hip* – to be able to write about it. Kerouac was in the grip of a baleful romance about being 'so drearily, a "white man" '; Holmes, after a night at a Harlem jukejoint with Cassady, would return home to scribble down a triumphant description of Neal climbing on to the stage with the black singer and crying: 'Blow! . . . You know who you are!'

Faced with this degree of trespass, well-meaning though it was, the hep cat had no choice but to move on, leaving his effects behind, jive talk and all.

Just as Kerouac and Holmes were smithing late into the night to forge shapes for the new feelings and new attitudes, the black hipster was declared *passé*. He wrote his own obituary. It appeared in the radical monthly, *Partisan Review*, as an essay by a young writer from Brooklyn who had become part of the Village scene, Anatole Broyard, he of the elegant 'metonymous gestures' etc. 'Portrait of the Hipster' presented a picture of an 'oracle':

> He was asked to read things, look at things, feel things, taste things, and report. What was it? Was it *in there*? Was it *gone*? Was it *fine*? He was an interpreter for the blind, the deaf, the dumb, the insensible, the impotent . . . His old subversiveness, his ferocity, was now so manifestly rhetorical as to be obviously harmless. He was bought and placed in the zoo. He was *somewhere* at last − comfortably ensconced in the 52nd Street clip joints, in Carnegie Hall, and *Life*.

The biographical note to another article on a similar theme, published shortly afterwards, described Broyard as 'an anatomist of the Negro personality in the white world'. Actually, he was more than that: he was himself a 'Negro personality'. But, shortly before his appearance in the Village, where he came to know Kerouac and Holmes and where he would soon be considered a part of their movement, Broyard dropped his race and depended on his light skin to pass as white, rather like an item of jive talk that had crossed over.

Holmes and Kerouac were now tugging at opposite ends of the same subject. Kerouac described it as 'the new American generation known as the "Hip" (The Knowing), with an emphasis on their problems in the mid-century'. Holmes thought of it as being a drama of ' "postwar kids", or our own displaced persons'. For Kerouac, the accumulation of material involved 'many restless travellings'; for Holmes, who seldom ventured far from his desk in Lexington Avenue, the story presented itself ready-made and fit for a novel in the shape of his new circle of friends. As the boy-gang came and went, to and from his apartment, Holmes made notes on their conversations, their characteristics, funny habits of speech, anything that rendered them 'displaced' or set them apart as 'the "Hip" (The Knowing)'.

Holmes planned a central role in the novel he was writing for Ginsberg as 'Stofsky', a highly strung, talkative character who took delight in shocking other people with insights into their own characters that were 'disturbing as well as perceptive'. It was a notion drawn from psychoanalysis, one which allowed the patient to assume temporarily the role of the therapist. 'Everyone has his monster', Ginsberg explained to Holmes (who noted it down, and put it straight into his novel, in the mouth of Stofsky), 'the personification of everything he really fears'. Ginsberg hooted at, for example, the idea of dressing down and going in search of Kerouac's mother, who already despised him as 'unclean': 'Well, for her I'd get all made up in filthy rags and paint huge running sores and pimples on my face, and then knock on the door and groan pitifully when she opened it!' In order to offend Holmes himself – the decorous rebel – 'You know what I'd do? I'd simply walk into your place one quiet afternoon with no clothes on! . . . which would shock your sense of decorum even more!' What else is analysis, the manic Stofsky-Ginsberg demanded to know, 'but the patient coming to that moment of self-truth where he can embrace his monster?'

What would be the monster in Ginsberg's own life? Rapping on his psyche in the middle of 1949 was his mother's madness. He made an entry in his journal, in which any amateur analyst might spot a direct reflection of his mother's operation eighteen months before. And no psychiatrist would overlook the significance of the date of the entry, 3 June, his birthday:

> What a terrible future. I am 23 . . . I am ill. I have become spiritually or practically impotent in my madness this last month. I suddenly realized that my head is severed from my body.

In the subway, one day, he asked Kerouac to hit him. Kerouac demurred, but wrote and told Burroughs, who replied in astonishment: 'Has he flipped his lid?' A few days later, at the end of June, Ginsberg committed himself to the Columbia Presbyterian Psychiatric Institute on 168th Street, which was to be his home for the next eight months.

The alternative was prison. Two events contributed to his admission to the Psychiatric Institute (PI), one spiritual, the other material, one benign, the other malign.

The first, a religious visitation, occurred in the spring of the previous year, in Ginsberg's sublet apartment in East Harlem. Sitting on the bed, dipping into William Blake's *Songs of Innocence and Experience*, Ginsberg heard a voice in the room which he knew, without having to ask how he knew, was the voice of Blake himself. The book was open at the 'Experience' poem, 'Ah, Sun-flower', and the voice intoned:

> Ah, Sun-flower! weary of time,
>   Who countest the steps of the sun;
> Seeking after that sweet golden clime,
>   Where the traveller's journey is done.
>
> Where the youth pined away with desire,
>   And the pale virgin shrouded in snow,
> Arise from their graves and aspire
>   Where my Sun-flower wishes to go!

Ginsberg heard the voice recite another poem, 'The Sick Rose' – 'O Rose, thou art sick!' – and then a third, 'The Little Girl Lost' – 'Do father, mother weep? / Where can Lyca sleep?' The voice of Blake became the voice of God, and – like many seers of visions before him – Ginsberg had no doubt that God was speaking directly to him and about him.

And my eye on the page, simultaneously the auditory hallucination, or whatever terminology here used, the apparitional voice, in the room, woke me further deep in my understanding of the poem, because the voice was completely tender and . . . ancient. Like the voice of the Ancient Days. But the peculiar quality of the voice was something unforgettable because it was like God had a human voice, with all the infinite tenderness and anciency and mortal gravity of a living Creator speaking to his son . . . and simultaneous to the voice there was also an emotion, risen in my soul in response to the voice, and a sudden *visual* realization of the same awesome phenomena . . . I suddenly realized that this existence was *it*! And that I was born in order to experience up to this very moment that I was having this experience, to realize what this was all about.

Naomi Ginsberg had also had a vision of God. She had cooked him a nice supper – 'lentil soup, vegetables, bread & butter' – and asked why he didn't put a stop to war. 'I try, he said', Naomi told her son. 'That's all he could do. He looked tired.'

Allen's God, speaking in the voice of Blake, was everything a believer in visions and revelations of the Truth could hope for. Ginsberg held to the validity of the experience, as the moment when his spiritual and poetic selves fused into the man and poet he would become. He claimed Blake as a spiritual teacher, guiding him towards his mission, the commitment of self to poetry, the commitment of poetry to immediate experience, to the 'perceptions of the moment . . . a memento [composed] during the time of ecstasy'.

A contingent apprehension, immediately following this commitment, was that such poetry was necessarily subversive; that society – the outside world of jobs, bad marriages, bomb-making factories – would always be suspicious of and opposed to 'ecstasy', because the insights gained in the ecstatic experience threatened it.

> Never deny the voice – no, never *forget* it, don't get lost mentally wandering in other spirit worlds or American job worlds or war worlds or earth worlds. But the spirit of the universe was what I was born to realize.

As Kerouac was directed on to his poetic path by the example of Neal Cassady, so Ginsberg's vision in Harlem led him into divinely revealed 'creative freedom of the will'. It made him realize the largeness of the soul. It had the potential to change the world.

He had an irrepressible urge to tell someone else what he had seen. The most convenient recipients of the news were two girls living in the apartment next door. To get to them, he had to crawl out of his apartment on to the fire-escape and announce himself by tapping on their window. They opened it – 'I've seen God', Ginsberg said – and immediately banged the window shut in his face again. ('Oh what tales I could have told them if they'd let me in!')

He walked to the University, where he had resumed his studies following the suspension over the obscene etchings on the window-pane. In the campus bookstore, he had a further vision, of the 'tormented soul' of the shop assistant. And yet, 'I realized that *he* knew also, just like I knew'. Everybody knew the truth that had just been revealed, but 'they were all hiding it'. He looked hard at the other students on the campus: they were all reading books by Santayana and Martin Buber and other thinkers and mystics, and yet they carefully kept themselves closed off from what those books contained:

> the position that everyone was in was *ridiculous*, everybody running around peddling books to each other. Here in the universe! Passing money over the counter, wrapping books in bags and guarding the door ... They all looked like horrible grotesque masks, grotesque because *hiding* the knowledge from each other.

Eventually, Ginsberg made for the English Department, where he found his professors, Mark Van Doren and Lionel Trilling, his *bêtes noires*, propounders of the academic approach to literature, and – it suddenly made perfect sense to say so – the academic approach to life, keeper-downers, suppressors of the gospel that literature really contained.

And what did *they* see, coming through the door? The scruffy boy who didn't know how lucky he was to have a scholarship; who was too close to a trio of misfits who'd got mixed up in a killing; a Jew who wrote 'Fuck the Jews' on the dormitory window.

Trilling and Van Doren would have been immediately sceptical of Ginsberg's, or anyone else's, vision-thing. Is it possible that, as they listened to the story of Blake appearing in Harlem to recite his poems to their student, they were reminded of some lines of another of his favourite poets, Whitman? Was it possible that those lines had been a spur to Ginsberg's excitable imagination?

> As I ponder'd in silence,
> Returning upon my poems . . .
> A phantom arose before me with distrustful aspect,
> Terrible in beauty, age, and power,
> The genius of poets of old lands,
> As to be directing like flames its eyes . . .

Trilling or Van Doren, both of whom had encouraged Ginsberg in his attempts to write poetry, may even have recalled at that moment two lines from a poem by Ginsberg published in the *Jester-Review* back in 1944, which encapsulated to a remarkable degree the experience he was attempting to describe, at length, now:

The little auto

I looked up horrified to see
Eternity glaring down at me!

They already knew him as a boy with a mentally disordered mother, who feared for his own sanity in times of distress. How much more exciting and consoling to turn, unconsciously, that fear into a unique communion with William Blake.

The incident which led directly to the PI took place a year after the vision, and landed him, briefly, in prison. It was the old story, bad company, and Huncke the poet-thief (with the emphasis on thief) was at the centre of it.

The previous fall, Ginsberg had moved out of East Harlem and had sublet an apartment from a theology student at Columbia who had an expensive collection of books. Ginsberg allowed Huncke to move in, and very soon he was stripping down the place, first removing the books, a few at a time, then continuing on to the record collection, from there into the wardrobes, through the kitchen drawers for silverware, making the place lighter by the minute. When Ginsberg roused himself sufficiently from his preoccupations to notice that he was practically living in an unfurnished flat, Huncke moved out.

Now Ginsberg was in another apartment, on York Avenue, and Huncke, Vicki Russell and Vicki's boyfriend, Little Jack Melody, asked to be allowed to use it to store their stolen goods. Vicki, 'a remarkable, beautiful, good-hearted, tender girl', according to Ginsberg, had persuasion. Kerouac had had an affair with her. She had also slept with Ginsberg, in an attempt to allay his consuming fear of homosexuality; he kept a photograph of her on his mantelpiece. In addition, he had a romantic attachment to her and Huncke as underworld figures, and finally, sneakily, an expectation that he might get paid back, out of their rackets, for past thefts. Maybe the smell of crime in the rooms of the apartment also reminded him of Neal Cassady. He wrote nervously to Neal of his hopes for a share of the ill-gotten gains, though he could not help adding: 'perhaps I shall find I have been self-destructively greedy on this score'.

One day, he accepted a lift from Vicki and Little Jack out to Long Island, where Jack's mother lived. The car was full of stolen goods.

The car itself was stolen goods. As they drove through Queens, Little Jack committed a minor traffic offence, turning the wrong way up a one-way street. When a policeman tried to wave them over, Little Jack made such a frantic swerve in the attempt to escape that he overturned the car. Ginsberg was struck by

> the very distinct sensation, slightly mystical, that all my mistakes of the past year – my moral indecisions and my slight acquisitive interest in the loot that was coming into the house – had led in a chain to this one retribution moment where I was now going to have to pay for it.

He began singing as the car rolled over, 'Lord God of Israel, Isaac and Abraham', from the *Messiah*, as if 'evoking the Hebraic father-figure authority divinity to come and get me'.

He and Vicki crawled out and managed to get away before the police caught up with them. They went back to the apartment to warn Huncke, but there were papers belonging to Ginsberg in the car, with his name on them, and no sooner did the pair arrive home than the police swooped, arrested all three, and carted them off to the Long Island precinct house. There they were held with Little Jack, who had been picked up on the spot.

At the police station, Huncke, who was as much at home there as anywhere else, noticed Ginsberg peering at his surroundings

> with a woebegone expression. It was the first time he'd come so close to anything of this nature. He was saying Jewish prayers. I felt so sorry for him ... It was a turning point for him.

As in the Carr–Kammerer case, the newspapers enjoyed the coalition of high and low worlds. Ginsberg was portrayed as the clever youth who was used as the 'brains' by a gang of desperadoes to plot their cunning thefts. Then he was a writer in search of material. The *Daily News* carried a picture of Huncke, Jack and Vicki – 'a six-feet marijuana-smoking redhead' – climbing down from a car on their way to the court hearing on 22 April, while the *Times* faithfully reported Ginsberg's alibi:

> One of the accused, Allen Ginsberg, 21 years old [*sic*] of 1401 York Avenue, told the police that he was a copy boy for a news service who had 'tied in' with the gang, all with police records, to obtain 'realism' he needed to write a story.

At a subsequent hearing, Lionel Trilling, his wife Diana, Mark Van Doren, and Ginsberg's analyst Dr Cott turned up and spoke on his behalf. Ginsberg, who had not known of this in advance, wrote to Kerouac that it was 'mightily cricket' of them to have done so. He was cleared of any criminal involvement, the understanding being that he would commit himself to the Columbia PI. Trilling urged him to recognize the fact that he was sick, and took him to a psychiatrist called Dr Fagin, who told Ginsberg that he was sicker than he knew. Van Doren confronted him with a choice between life in a healthy society and the half-life of the criminal underworld, with its connecting passages to prison. Dr Fagin assured him that in the PI he would, as Ginsberg put it to Holmes, 'be given the works psychoanalytically'. His father could only urge him, once more, to keep away from Neal Cassady and William Burroughs.

As for Burroughs himself, who took the view that the madhouse was nothing but a con to stamp out nonconformism, he was not at all impressed by Ginsberg's so-called luck in evading prison. As far as Burroughs was concerned, it was Trilling and Van Doren who were bad company. 'If I was in Al's place', Burroughs wrote to Kerouac,

> I would say 'Go ahead and place your charges, if any.' His present position is insufferable. Imagine being herded around by a lot of old women like Louis Ginsberg and Van Doren . . . Snivelling old Liberal Fruit.

Vicki was removed to the Women's House of Detention in Greenwich Village, and at the trial received a suspended sentence of five years. Little Jack Melody avoided prison by being sent to Pilgrim State Hospital, but Huncke was eventually charged with fifty-two other burglaries – only 'a small portion' of the true number, he admitted – and served four years of a five-year sentence. 'Somebody had to do it', was the way he looked at it.

Unhappy and facing a terrible future, Ginsberg came across Carl Solomon the moment he walked into the Psychiatric Institute (PI). Solomon dwelt on the border where art and insanity are kin. He was fat and mad. Heavy consumption of glucose had rendered him obese; repeated insulin convulsion therapy (then an accepted treatment for schizophrenia) had cast him into a state of 'atomized amnesia', a 'concrete void': 'Upon consulting a mirror, I was confronted with the dual inability to recognize myself or to remember what I had looked like prior to treatment . . .'

When Ginsberg first set eyes on him, as he waited in the reception room for his bed to be prepared, Solomon was dressed in a bathrobe, with a towel wrapped around his head. His walk was a waddle. As Solomon peered at the new arrival through thick spectacles, Ginsberg began nervously to talk about his recent visionary experiences, as if by recounting them, rosary-fashion, he might regain the faith in a second reality and a Blakean fellowship that they had originally inspired. The fat young man made a comment about 'repentant mystics' – the point being that the place was full of them and he was not impressed.

'Who are you?' he asked, after he had dismissed the vision talk. Ginsberg replied: 'I'm Prince Myshkin' – the gentle holy fool of Dostoevsky's novel, *The Idiot*. 'Who are you?'

'I'm Kirillov', replied Solomon, invoking the cynical nihilist of *The Possessed*, and introducing himself as Ginsberg's muse.

Behind the beat

Neurotica

The Beat Generation writers are unusual among literary gangs in never having had a little magazine of their own, through which to distribute their early work. At the beginning of 1950, Ginsberg had still to publish in anything other than a student journal; Kerouac, though he had a novel waiting to come out, had to date published nothing of a literary nature at all, while Burroughs, age thirty-five, did not even consider himself a writer.

The closest there was to a beat magazine (though it could only be seen that way in retrospect) in the late 1940s and early 50s was a slim, eccentric journal whose contributors moved among the bases of art, sex and neuroticism. *Neurotica* was owned and edited by a young gallery owner from St Louis, like Burroughs, called Jay Landesman. In the first issue, Spring 1948, he set out the magazine's aims:

> *Neurotica* is a literary exposition, defense and correlation of the problems and personalities that in our culture are defined as 'neurotic'.
>
> It is said that if you tie a piece of red cloth to a gull's leg its fellow-gulls will peck it to pieces: and *Neurotica* wishes to draw an analog to this observation and the plight of today's creative 'anxious' man.
>
> We are interested in exploring the creativeness of this man who has been forced to live underground . . .

The magazine's most prolific contributor was a maverick psychologist called Gershon Legman, described by John Clellon Holmes, who was a friend of Landesman and provided the conduit for beatness, as a 'small belligerent facsimile of Balzac'. The general

93

theme of Legman's articles for *Neurotica* was that the American public's increasing appetite for violence and sadism in fiction (Legman did not condescend to study film) stemmed directly from the puritanical suppression of the libido in everyday life.

Legman made his debut in *Neurotica* 3, with 'The Psychopathology of the Comics', which examined the aggressive nature of children's comic-books. In the next issue he published 'Institutionalized Lynch: The anatomy of a murder-mystery'. In three separate columns, he listed the instances of 'Sadism', 'Sadism and Sex' and 'Sex' as they occurred in the action of a bestselling novel, *The Strange Woman* (1941), by Ben Ames Williams. Legman worked on the principle that, as the law tolerated no general description of sex, the result was the 'mundane substitute for sex' − i.e., sadism.

> Murder having replaced sex in the popular arts, the glorification of one requires the degradation of the other . . . so that we are faced in our culture by the insurmountable schizophrenic contradiction that sex, which is legal in fact, is a crime on paper, while murder − a crime, in fact − is, on paper, the bestseller of all time.

Taking a fifty-page sample of *The Strange Woman*, Legman found ten examples of 'Sadism' ('Woman listens "with pent breath" to details of whipping a man . . . "Did he bleed?" ' etc), ten examples of 'Sadism and Sex' ('her knotted fists beat at him in passionate ecstasies'), and a single evocation of 'Sex', that being a 'nebulous description of a coitus'.

The early issues of *Neurotica* contained articles which combined a serious intellectual tone with a tendency to titillate, such as a piece on prostitution as a force for social good, by Rudolph Friedmann (in the way that books on spanking and bondage were often written by someone with a medical practitioner's initials after his or her name, Friedmann was said to have 'worked in connection with educational activities in London'), another on homosexuals who marry, by Nathaniel Thornton ('Professor Thornton teaches abnormal psychology'), and others on fetishists such as 'Jack the Snipper', who secretly cuts off locks of ladies' hair in cinemas, and on the bar as a pick-up place. In *Neurotica* 2, there was a very short story, 'Tea for Two', by Holmes (signed simply 'Clellon Holmes'), a limbering-up exercise for the novel he was planning to write about the scene, and the first appearance in the pages of the magazine of a writer defined (even self-defined) as 'beat':

> This is a local fable and the boy is Beeker. This guy was a Pekoe-man, and he blew himself out of the coils of a trumpet every night. He came on for culture, not for loot; so he passed the marihuana to his cohorts when the need was near. This tea-dispensing on the cuff brought in enough for bills, and the lad was living in a new era.

There were few journals in 1948 which were willing to publish a sympathetic portrait of a drug-pusher, and there were even fewer editors who would risk confrontation with the law by printing the word 'fuck', which appeared in *Neurotica* 5 (Autumn 1949) and led to the banning of the issue by the Post Office. The same issue included an article by Marshall McLuhan, in which he wrote that '*Time*, *Life* and *Fortune* (the *New Yorker* can be thrown in with them) are the American Bloomsbury, our psychological bureaucracy, inhabited by well-paid artist-apes'.

Ginsberg's first contribution to a magazine with a nationwide circulation appeared in *Neurotica* 6, Spring 1950, by which time the magazine had adopted a furtive beat identity. Ginsberg's brief 'Song: Fie My Fum' was not likely to advance by much the editor's avowed cause of describing 'a neurotic society from the inside'; nevertheless, it was the right kind of verse for the venue, with its playful sexual content:

> Say my oops,
> Ope my shell,
> Roll my bones,
> Ring my bell . . .

The contributor's note informed readers that 'Allen Ginsberg recently recovered from a serious illness'. There was also an article on homosexuality and art, a dissertation on 'Afro-Cuban rumba' by the white Negro Anatole Broyard, and a short piece on literary parties by the up-and-coming novelist Chandler Brossard, who was soon to set himself up as Broyard's nemesis, exposing him as a black man passing for white. The longest and most serious contribution to *Neurotica* 6 was 'Report from the Asylum: Afterthoughts of a shock patient' by Carl Goy, the pseudonym of Ginsberg's new friend in the Columbia PI, Carl Solomon:

> The testimony that follows is that of an eye-witness, one who has undergone insulin shock treatment and has slept through fifty comas . . .
>
> Upon being strapped into my insulin bed, I would at once break off my usual stream of puns and hysterical chatter. I would stare at the bulge I made beneath the canvas restraining sheet, and my body, insulin-packed, would become to me an enormous concrete pun with infinite levels of association, and thereby a means of surmounting association with things, much as the verbal puns had surmounted the meaning of words . . .
>
> Each coma is utterly incomparable to that of the previous day. Lacking a time-sense and inhabiting all of these universes at one and the same time, my condition was one of omnipresence, of being everywhere at no time.

Neurotica published only three more issues, before coming to an end in another battle with the law, over an article by Legman on – what could be more fitting? – the castration complex.

The house where Jack Kerouac was born in 1922, in Lupine Road, Lowell, Massachusetts

Kerouac's first wife, Edie Parker

The front of Edie's apartment on 118th Street New York, where Kerouac first met Allen Ginsberg and William Burroughs in 1944

Newspaper accounts of the Kammerer slaying, 1944

Kerouac, the merchant seaman

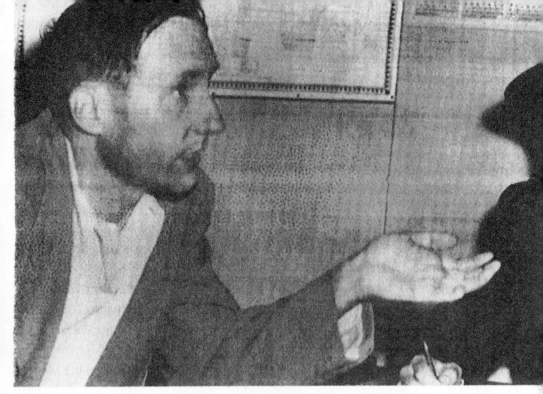

Burroughs being interrogated after the Mexico City shooting, 6 September, 1951

New York Daily News,
8 September, 1951

Heir's Pistol Kills His Wife; He Denies Playing Wm. Tell

Mexico City, Sept. 7 (AP).—William Seward Burroughs, 37, first admitted, then denied today that he was playing William Tell when his gun killed his pretty, young wife during a drinking party last night.

Police said that Burroughs, grandson of the adding machine inventor, first told them that, wanting to show off his marksmanship, he placed a glass of gin on her head and fired, but was so drunk that he missed and shot her in the forehead.

After talking with a lawyer, police said, Burroughs, who is a wealthy cotton planter from Pharr, Tex., changed his story and insisted that his wife was shot accidentally when he dropped his newly-purchased .38 caliber pistol.

Husband in Jail.

Mrs. Burroughs, 27, the former Joan Vollmer, died in the Red Cross Hospital.

The shooting occurred during a party in the apartment of John Healy of Minneapolis. Burroughs said two other American tourists whom he knew only slightly were present.

Burroughs, hair disheveled and clothes wrinkled, was in jail today. A hearing on a charge of homicide is scheduled for tomorrow morning.

No Arguments, He Says.

"It was purely accidental," he said. "I did not put any glass on her head. If she did, it was a joke. I certainly did not intend to shoot at it."

He said there had been no arguments or discussion before the "accident."

"The party was quiet," he said. "We had a few drinks. Everything is very hazy."

Burroughs and his wife had been here about two years. He said he was studying native dialects at the University of Mexico. He explained his long absence from his ranch by saying that he was unsuited for business.

Wife From Albany.

He said he was born in St. Louis and that his wife was from Albany, N. Y. They have two children, William Burroughs Jr., 3, and

William Seward Burroughs in Mexico City prison.

(Associated Press Wirefotos)
The late Mrs. Joan Burroughs—killed at party.

Julie Adams, 7, who he said was his wife's daughter by a previous marriage. The couple had been married five years.

She had attended journalism school at Columbia University before her marriage to Burroughs. Burroughs, who also had been married before, formerly lived in St. Louis in 1886.

Loudonville, a swank suburb of Albany. He is a graduate of Harvard University and worked for two weeks in 1942 as a reporter for the St. Louis Post-Dispatch.

His paternal grandfather laid the foundation of a fortune when he built his first adding machine

Lucien Carr

Herbert Huncke,
Burroughs's muse

Gary Snyder, 1956

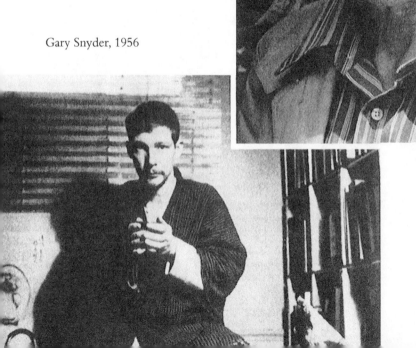

Kerouac in his football-playing days

Carl Solomon,
Ginsberg's "Kirillov"

Lawrence Ferlinghetti
at City Lights Bookstore,
San Francisco

The cover of Corso's
novel *American Express*,
showing the author

Allen Ginsberg in Berkeley, California, at the time of "Howl"

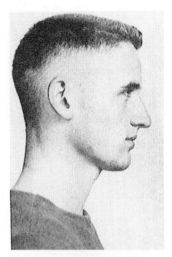

Neal and Carolyn Cassady at the time
of their wedding

Mug shots of
Cassady, taken in
1944, following his
arrest for car theft

Neal Cassady, right,
with colleagues
from the Southern
Pacific railroad

5

The place of dead roads

As for the severed ear, that was direct logic.
— Artaud, 'Van Gogh'

Carl Solomon re-established the French connection. Honour demanded the belief that society held 'no room for an honest man'. The postwar politics of conformity had vacuumed the creative matter from original minds. In the view of the twenty-one-year-old New Yorker, American intellectual life was made up, in equal parts, of 'charlatanry, propaganda and corruption'. Solomon, who couldn't recognize himself when he looked in the mirror, had an extreme reaction to the American-dream version of society: he made himself a piece of protest art; he adopted insanity as a form of revolt.

Solomon was raised in Brooklyn, but, like Carr, like Ginsberg, Kerouac, and Burroughs to a degree, he grew up intellectually in Paris. The defining moment of his education in the strategy of surrealist revolt, as he releated it, came on the Left Bank in 1947, when, by accident, he stumbled on a public reading in a St-Germain gallery by the French dramatist and director Antonin Artaud, propagandist for, and exemplar of, the artist as lunatic-saint, as a man mad (i.e., sane) in a sane (i.e., mad) society. The reader was declaiming the essay 'Van Gogh: The man suicided by society', in which Artaud affirms his belief that the lunatic is someone who has 'preferred to become what is socially understood as mad, rather than forfeit a certain superior idea of human honour'.

Solomon was an instant devotee. He returned to the United States with a will to 'give up the flesh and become a professional lunatic-saint'. (It must have come as a severe disappointment to him to discover, as he did later, that the reader in the Left Bank gallery was not Artaud himself, but someone else reading from his work.) He was released from the Columbia PI shortly before Ginsberg, in early 1950, but was to spend his life afterwards in and out of mental hospitals.

The little game of 'I'm Myshkin', 'I'm Kirillov' might have sounded an echo in Ginsberg's head of the 'You be Rimbaud, I'll be Verlaine' drama of earlier years. To Solomon, the exchange signalled the entry of a fellow spirit into the House of the Dead. Delighting in puns, he demonstrated to Ginsberg the kinship of the two French poet-seers simply by the application of brackets: Art(hur Rimb)aud. In every aspect of his voluntary non-existence, Solomon claimed fellowship with his hero. Artaud was with Solomon as he was strapped down on to his insulin bed for the umpteenth time; with Artaud, he said, 'I died . . . under electric shock'; when he emerged from the thirtieth, fortieth, fiftieth insulin coma, following a hefty dose of glucose, 'bawling like an infant and flapping my arms crazily (once they had been unfastened), screaming "EAT!" or "HELP!" ', Solomon was visualizing himself 'inhabiting that Void of which Antonin Artaud had screamed'.

More than any of the poets and novelists with whom, through Ginsberg, he was to come into contact, Solomon had abandoned the practical manoeuvres of 'reality' for the madness of art. Yet, on the outside, there was no *art* at all – or, if there was, it was a performance art, a distorted body, a surrealist life.

Artaud was not the only writer to whom Solomon introduced Ginsberg. He also spoke of Gérard de Nerval, telling Ginsberg, in Artaud's words, that de Nerval 'was not mad, but he was accused of being so, in order to discredit the vital revelations he was about to make'. Besides being so accused, Artaud continued in his essay,

> de Nerval was hit on the head, physically hit on the head one night, to make him forget the monstrous facts which he was going to reveal . . . all of society, secretly united against his consciousness, was at that moment strong enough to make him forget its reality.

What sense these remarks must have made to the seer of East

Harlem, as he himself gradually evolved into the epitome of beat surrealism, rooted in clinical insanity. In the first exchanges between them, Solomon heard 'the cadence of the superreal', which was never challenged:

S: I'm Kirillov.

G: I'm Prince Myshkin.

S: I'm Carl Goy.

G: I'm Edgar Allen Ginsberg.

S: I have been conditioned in illness by classic surrealism.

G: All the doctors think I'm crazy; / The truth is that I'm really lazy.

★

Solomon's acts of rebellion were trivial disruptions, brief subversive messages, literary footnotes to social revolt. He wished to test out Dada on the streets of New York, offering himself up as the experiment. Once, he threw potato salad at the novelist Wallace Markham during a lecture on Mallarmé. On another occasion, he pretended to be W. H. Auden, and autographed some books. The incident that got him turned over to a psychiatrist early in 1949, the first step on his path to the PI and insulin shock treatment, seems unbelievably petty: in the cafeteria of Brooklyn College, Solomon stole a sandwich in front of a policeman, inviting arrest. When apprehended and admitted to the PI, he regarded himself as having successfully broken into the laboratory, and his experimentation became more intense. He demanded a lobotomy. Once again, his mentor was Artaud, who wrote that the fate of the 'mad' rebel was to be 'suicided' by the psychiatric authorities, standard-bearers of social control. Van Gogh cut off his ear; Solomon, following almost to the end the 'direct logic' cited by Artaud in his essay on the painter's sociopathology, asked his medical guardians to cut out his 'mad' mind.

These admissions, and further gestures yoking together absurdity and normality, naturally fascinated Ginsberg. He had been told by Dr Fagin that he was sicker than he knew, and was attempting to respond to the beckoning of Trilling, Van Doren and his father, to return to the fold. As Solomon threw off aphorisms, Ginsberg took notes, thinking that some of what his new friend said might come in useful later in the making of a poem.

The Burroughs household, which had been farming outside New Orleans, had moved again, this time across the border, beyond the reach of US law enforcement. Here are some topics of conversation around the family dinner table in Mexico City, *circa* 1950.

Burroughs suggests to Joan that, once out of the bin, Ginsberg would benefit from coming down to visit them. He has lapsed into that bad habit of talking socialism again. Mexico's the remedy. Later, he writes to Allen: 'I fear you have become infected . . . socialism and communism are synonymous, and both unmitigated evil.'

Joan reminds him of what he has often said, in this context, about the Welfare State. In a follow-up note to Ginsberg, Burroughs adds: 'The Welfare State is on the way to be a Communist State, and that means a *bureaucratic police state.*'

Joan complains about not being able to get her Benzedrine inhalers in Mexico City. She is enduring painful withdrawal symptoms. (She writes to Ginsberg that thyroid tablets help.) Wilhelm Reich's invention, the orgone accumulator box, helps, too. Burroughs has made one himself – a box lined with metal on the inside and organic matter (leaves, fur etc) on the outside – and sits in it for hours at a time. Joan is 'hitting the lush' pretty hard. She is drunk from eight in the morning onwards.

Burroughs brings up an item of news just received from the US, a country he constantly compares unfavourably with Mexico, concerning civil rights legislation in favour of blacks. It convinces him that he has done the right thing by jumping ship. Later, he writes to Kerouac, jazz-lover and seeker-out of 'spade kicks', with (perhaps) the hint of a tease: 'Nigra laws, eh? That really is the pay off.'

The prices in Mexico appeal to him greatly – about one-third of what they are in the States. Income tax is 3 per cent. You can buy a good house in Mexico City for $4,000. 'Mexico is my place', he says. 'I would not go back to the US under any circumstances.'

Joan raises her theory that low-level radiation from testing the atomic bomb is not so much a physical threat as an invisible weapon of psychic control. Burroughs writes to Ginsberg: 'She has convinced me that her kick contains a solid core of reality.'

Burroughs says he is pleased, finally, to have discovered a 'fine free country' to live in. Down here, he can pack a gun without interference from the law. A policeman in Mexico City ranks with a bus conductor. Mexicans mind their own business. He writes to Kerouac: 'I don't have to take nothing off of nobody.'

★

> Mexico – the land of flowers, color, and life in
> a pleasant tempo . . . For those who love
> open spaces, wild horses and roundups.
> – Laura Lee Burroughs, *Flower Arranging: A fascinating hobby*, 1942

The flight from Louisiana, first to Texas then down to Mexico City, was sparked by a raid on Burroughs's house, in which the police uncovered no drugs but some correspondence with Ginsberg and others in which drugs were mentioned. The action was prompted by Burroughs having been stopped by traffic police in the centre of New Orleans with a friend known to them, who, it turned out, was driving a stolen car. The case did not look good. If convicted,

> I am subject to 2–5 years in Angola, which is definitely not a Country Club. While the case is pending, of course, I have to avoid any contact. One stick, one cap now could send me away for seven years . . . So I am back on lush. I kicked a good part of my habit in a Precinct Cell. (It shouldn't happen to anyone but a Narcotic agent.)

Mexico was also a refuge from Mortimer Burroughs, still the distant superintendent of his wayward son. After being released from police custody on bail, Burroughs checked into a sanatorium in order to kick what remained of his addiction. As Joan explained to Ginsberg, the cure was a practical necessity if they were to avoid having Mortimer Burroughs 'swoop down upon [us] from St Louis with the intention of hospitalizing Bill elsewhere for at least six months'. Psychic control, even at thirty-six, still began at home.

In the jumps and jitters of her own withdrawal (their son, Billy, had been born an addict), Joan wrote to Ginsberg about his confinement, a letter which manages to combine sympathy, affection, scepticism, and a clear view of her own fractured psyche:

101

I was not much surprised to hear about your hospitalization . . . I'd feared at one time that you'd never see the light, but when I saw you at Atlantic Beach I had some hope for you. When you asked Bill once in a letter to refer me back to Blake's sick rose, whose worm I'd been sharing for months, I had more hopes and lately they've been amply justified. When I refer to it as top-blowing I'm sure you know what I mean. No percentage in talking about visions or any super-reality or any such lay-terms. Either you know what I know (and don't ask me just what that is) or else I'm mistaken about you and off-beam somewhere – in which case you're just a dime-a-dozen neurotic and *I'm* nuts.

As for her husband, he was equally sceptical of visions of Blake and of mental hospitals. 'I wouldn't let them croakers up there treat my corn let alone my psyche', he told Kerouac. He would also have shrugged a mighty So-What if anyone had started chucking potato salad at minor novelists, or signing Auden's name and calling it an act of surrealist revolt.

The escape to Mexico, and the shaking-off of his junk habit, had freed Burroughs to work on his book. The first reference to it is made in a letter to Kerouac dated 10 March 1950: 'I have been writing a novel about junk.' Working title: 'Junk'. The hard-boiled phrases of his letters to his friends – 'don't have to take nothing off of nobody' – were peeled off and combined with jive talk – '*Are you anywhere* . . . Do you have any junk or weed on you?' – and used to form the basis of a style which resides at sub-zero temperature. The expression '*Hep or hip*', Burroughs noted in the glossary he was compiling, to be appended to his novel once it was finished, 'is not subject to definition because, if you don't "dig" what it means, no one can ever tell you'.

'Convey my congratulations to Jack', Burroughs requested of Ginsberg in the midst of his own trouble. 'I would have written to him except I haven't been able.'

The Town and the City was published in March 1950, a hulk of a novel, anchored in traditional story-telling. Its strong tidal paragraphs drew the reader in, and left him to drown. The dust-jacket portrait of the author, 'John Kerouac', showed a well-groomed fellow in a white shirt, suit and tie; Kerouac, expressing a recurring fear, thought it made him look like 'a fag'. In a letter to Cassady, he compared his book to the work of Faulkner and 'young Tolstoy'; he also referred to 'the curse of Melville' – meaning his 'shitluck' in getting mixed reviews in the spring of the year, culminating in neglect by the end of it, disappointing sales, and a failure to sell the film rights. It was anything but an uncommon experience for a first novelist, but it made him sick of 'John Kerouac'.

The novel was begun before Kerouac met Cassady, before he understood that he was being gifted a new aesthetic of speed and spontaneity, a talk aesthetic, a buddy prose: 'The car swayed as [we] both swayed to the rhythm of the IT of our final excited joy in talking and living . . .' He also took lessons from modern jazz. In most writing, Kerouac felt, there was a gap between happening and reporting, into which the unique emotional nature of the moment sank and disappeared. Jazz improvisation showed him how to close the gap. Kerouac wanted a style which would record thoughts, emotions, memories, images, freely and instantaneously. The reader, like the listener, would share the vibrating response of the recording instrument, the writer, as the musical prose passed through him and on to the page.

The rudiments of this theory came from Cassady himself, who had written to Kerouac back in 1947:

> I have always held that when one writes, one should forget all rules, literary styles, and other such pretensions as large words, lordly clauses . . . Rather I think one should write, as nearly as possible, as if he were the first person on earth and was humbly and sincerely putting on paper that which he saw and experienced and loved and lost, what his passing thoughts were and his sorrows and desires . . .

Neal knew that he lacked the ability to make his vision cohere; but he realized he had found the missing element, the writer in the passenger seat, in Jack – not John – Kerouac. And Kerouac repaid the compliment, for a style needs a subject, and in this case style and subject were one: Neal. Neal and the road. Neal and the road and speed. Neal and the road and speed and talk. And sex. If a proper job were made of catching Neal's runaway soul on the wing, then the new beat spirit would be caught, too.

★

Kerouac got married again in the fall of 1950: another snap proposal, the consequence of another death (and soon to be another divorce).

Joan Haverty had been the girlfriend of a likeable fellow called Bill Cannastra, something of a hell-raiser who had met a terrible end when his body got jammed in the window of a moving subway train. Cannastra had been entertaining some friends by pretending that he wanted to climb out of the window to get back to a barmaid in a Bleecker Street tavern, when the train left the station. With his head jutting out, he found he was stuck. People tried to help pull him back, but his shirt ripped in their hands and his head hit a post.

The accident happened in mid-October. Within three weeks Kerouac had taken over Joan; within a few days of their meeting, he had proposed; a fortnight later they were man and wife.

At the age of twenty-eight, Kerouac was beset by medical problems, chiefly thrombophlebitis, which resulted in a chronic swelling of the legs and which, if not regularly checked, could be fatal – as he told friends, 'anytime'. He was now of the belief that marihuana was bad for the muscles, especially for one whose occupation kept him sitting down for hours at a time. Not long after the wedding, he signed a letter to Neal ('My Dear Neal') as 'Your pale pal'.

Joan was a dressmaker, the sort of domestic and feminine vocation that lit a candle in Kerouac. Their marriage made him feel 'healthy and living again', after the season of parties on the cusp of the decade (Holmes, toastmaster to the new mood and attitude, was an especially lusty party-giver). He told Joan all about Neal ('From the very start we were brothers . . .'), gave her Neal's letters to read – in particular, the letter dated 23 December 1950, which contained Neal's theory of spontaneous prose, and which Kerouac called his 'great work' (only part of it survives). He told her about his own dreams of a ranch where they could all live together – he and Joan, Neal and Carolyn (or whoever Neal chose to bring along), and Mémère. Joan and Neal and he would make long trips down the coast to visit Burroughs. Joan said she had a girlfriend out West who would be sure to dig Neal, and Kerouac relayed the news. 'Here we go, we're off.' But for the next five months ('Hate to leave you now. Love you so'), he and 'Dear Buddy Neal' did not go anywhere, and neither did he and Joan, except to Kerouac's favourite destination, his mother's place.

Ostensibly to save money, they moved in with Mémère immediately after the wedding, at her new house in the Richmond Hill district of Queens. He had never felt comfortable in the 21st Street loft, in which resided the headless ghost of Cannastra. People who had not caught up with events would drop by looking for Bill, and would be puzzled at seeing Joan with a strange man, her husband. In Richmond Hill, Joan designed, made and mended dresses, while Mémère watched to see if she would dare to try to make and mend her Jackie. She and Jack spoke French, which Joan did not understand. Jack had always been an erratic eater and sleeper – pork chops at midnight after a mid-evening snooze – and where Joan's making-and-mending instinct was to regularize his habits, Mémère wished only to cater for them. When Joan insisted privately that they spend the money to find an apartment in Manhattan, he was offended.

Through the final days of December and the month of January, Kerouac wrote long letters to Cassady, full of passionate detail, instalments of personal history, mostly about his childhood. He referred to this series as 'a full confession of my life', and could discern in it his future path as a writer. The commercial failure of *The Town and the City* had sickened him; now he regarded it as an artistic failure as well. He made a pledge to 'renounce all fiction', and to make his stories 'less literary'. From now on (in response to Neal's beckoning), it was 'the actual truth of my life' that would form his subject matter. And what was truer in life than Dear Buddy Neal? Eventually, at the beginning of 1951, Joan persuaded him to move back to New York; she had found a place in a brownstone at 454 West 20th Street, near Tenth Avenue, in view of the elevated railroad tracks. Kerouac had the perfect reason for complying with her wishes: Neal was in town.

At the dawn of the new decade, *Life* identified something novel, which it called the 'teen-idol'. The magazine did a survey, and produced a list of the ten most popular figures among the youth of America: it included Louisa May Alcott, Florence Nightingale, F. D.

Roosevelt, Abraham Lincoln, Roy Rogers, Joe di Maggio, Doris Day and General Douglas MacArthur.

At the same time, Kerouac was drawing preliminary sketches for the portrayal of a different kind of hero, one possessed by 'madness', by which he meant displaying the inner man, wearing the soul on the outside. According to Joan's recollections, she returned home to 20th Street night after night from the waitressing job she had taken to help them make ends meet, to find Kerouac locked in a stale struggle with his road book. 'I started asking questions. Questions about Neal, about traveling, cities, trains, New York, Mexico, cars, roads, friends, Neal, Neal, Neal, and Neal. The questions, after a time, seemed to ignite some spark in Jack. He went back to his typewriter, and now he typed with accelerating speed.'

Whether it was Joan's questions or something else that made him do it, Kerouac sat down in the Chelsea apartment at the beginning of April and began a marathon typing session, using coffee for mental kicks – the best stimulant for writers, in his opinion – resulting, less than three weeks later, in 'the story of my life on the road'. It was 125,000 words long, typed on one continuous stretch of paper. Years of chopping and shaping lay ahead; but the foundations of what began as 'On the Road', then changed to 'The Beat Generation', then to 'Anywhere Road', before at last becoming *On the Road*, were laid between 2 and 22 April. Speed of composition was an essential part of the scheme. 'Story deals with you and me and road . . .', he told Cassady. 'Went fast because road is fast.'

The numbers of highways, the makes and years of cars, the names of fishing streams and wide rivers, mountain ranges and cities, accumulate to form the ground beneath the narrator's feet. 'I had a book with me', he wrote, 'but I preferred reading the American landscape as we went along.' The road was the story; *On the Road* was his rendition of it.

He did not even pause to break it down into paragraphs, indicating a more emphatic gap than a full stop by using the three-dot ellipsis . . . He kept the real names of his characters, not only of himself and Neal, but of Ginsberg, Burroughs, Huncke, Chase, Temko, and the three Cassady wives: to LuAnne and Carolyn was now added Diana Hansen, whom Neal had married bigamously in New York, and who had just presented him with a son. He employed space as a form as well as a subject: spread out along the floor, the single strip of paper rolled on like a road.

★

From the three-week *On the Road*:

> I first met Neal not long after my father died . . . I had just gotten over a serious illness that I won't bother to talk about except that it really had something to do with my father's death and my awful feeling that everything was dead. With the coming of Neal there really began for me that period of my life that I could call my life on the road. Prior to that I'd always dreamed of the West, seeing the country, always vaguely planning and never specifically taking off and so on. Neal is the perfect guy for the road . . .

From a revised version, one year later:

> I first met Neal Pomeray in 1947 but I didn't travel on the road with him until 1948, just the tail end of that year, at Xmas time, North Carolina to New York City 450 miles, and back to NC, and back to New York City again, in 36 hours, with washing dishes in Philadelphia, a teahead ball in Ozone Park, and a southern drawl evening drive in Rocky Mount in between. And in all that time Neal just talked and talked and talked.

From the published version of *On the Road*:

> I first met Dean not long after my wife and I split up. I had just gotten over a serious illness that I won't bother to talk about, except that it had something to do with the miserably weary split-up and my feeling that everything was dead. With the coming of Dean Moriarty began a part of my life you could call my life on the road. Before that I'd often dreamed of going West to see the country, always vaguely planning and never taking off. Dean is the perfect guy for the road because he actually was born on the road . . .

★

The three-week *On the Road* was not to be the final version, but nor was it the first attempt at a road book. The earliest conception of it, sketched out as notes and half-scenes in his journal, involved a hero called Ray Smith. Kerouac began to construct this in the fall of 1948, when, though still at work on *The Town and the City*, he told Hal Chase that he was writing 'three new novels', entitled 'Doctor Sax', 'The Imbecile's Christmas', and finally, 'an American-scene picaresque, "On the Road" '.

A year later, having at last got *The Town and the City* off his desk, Kerouac returned to *On the Road*, filling his notebooks with plot outlines and character sketches. In this incarnation (*On the Road* II), Kerouac introduced Red Moultrie, an ex-baseball player, drummer, seaman and truck-driver, an oblique composite of everything the author had ever wanted to be, the Kerouac ideal, an 'artist in his own life'. He was also a criminal, and therefore enjoyed another of Kerouac's imagined adventures. In *On the Road* II, Ray Smith became 'Smitty' and assumed the Boswell role which Jack Kerouac would take in the three-week *On the Road*, and which would be given to Sal Paradise in the final version. In *On the Road* II, Red and Smitty are about to head out West to join up with Red's old friend Vern Pomeray, the Cassady figure who was eventually recast, closer to the life again, as 'Neal' in the three-week version, and Dean Moriarty in the finished book.

Kerouac planned to open the story with Red enduring the final night of a prison sentence handed down for his part in a robbery. Inside, he reads the Bible and *Pilgrim's Progress*, and undertakes a private pledge that, once released in the physical sense, he will seek a spiritual release, 'an inheritance', like Bunyan's Pilgrim, 'incorruptible, undefiled, and that fadeth not away'.

Red's soul was to move through five stages, which Kerouac listed: first, in prison and then on the road, his soul will be pure; second, he will experience apathy, linked to drug-taking and contact with Vern Pomeray; third, there will be a crisis, precipitated by winning a large sum of money; fourth, derangement, leading to Red attempting to regain his equilibrium and sanity; and fifth, repentance, and the recovery of 'joy'.

Red Moultrie's progress was only one of several projects Kerouac was working on (it appears to have remained confined to his notebooks). The 'three new novels' projected in the fall of 1948 had been joined by a few more by late 1950, the happy season of his marriage to Joan and his preparation for the real work on *On the*

Road. Writing to Cassady, at the end of 1950, he ran through his plans: 'one book in nigger dialect, another in bum dialect, another in hip-musician dialect, another in American-Mexican dialect, another in Indian dialect, another in cool dialect . . .' Not much of it got further than this, but he did begin a novella called *Pic*, a mini-road story about a black orphan boy who runs away from his relatives' care in the South and makes for New York with his brother. Once they hit the city, they decide to move on to California. In one version of the tale, told in the first person by Pic, a little black Huck Finn character, the two boys are offered a lift by Dean Moriarty and Sal Paradise, criss-crossing the country in their car in search of another chapter.

Kerouac enjoyed thinking up new stories, allowing each one to expand and fill up the vacant pages in his mind. He seldom resisted the urge to advertise his latest ideas in his correspondence. Each idea generated a spate of words. But he only took firm grip on the story he really wanted to tell – 'Neal, Neal, Neal, and Neal' – when he put all his other projects to the side, together with his various 'dialects', abandoned the theoretical structure borrowed from *Pilgrim's Progress*, based on the progressive stages of the soul, and began at the beginning: 'I first met Neal not long after my father died . . .'

In May, Kerouac wrote to Cassady to say that a 'special compartment' was reserved for him in his heart: 'I love you as ever.' Another special place was occupied by Joan.

At the end of a further three-week period, however, the second compartment was closed, and the marriage to 'great 20 yr old girl' Joan was over. In early June, she announced that she was pregnant. Kerouac said that he did not wish her to have the baby. Given the choice between husband and child, Joan chose the latter. She told Kerouac: 'I don't need two babies.' She returned to live with her mother in upstate New York. 'Jack hated me', she wrote later, 'and I felt completely indifferent.'

The stark, mean choice was indeed presented to Joan, but the subtext to the disagreement was surely this: with the writing of the road book over, there was no immediate need in Kerouac's life for a stable domestic set-up, especially one involving a child. With the sit-down job successfully completed, he wanted to be up on his feet and out on the road again. The stirrings of hatred for Joan (later fully expressed) are not included in his last letter written to Cassady from 20th Street, in which there is room only for self-pity:

Pops,

Now I sit here, with a sore phlebitis foot, my book finished, handed in, waiting for word from Giroux . . . my wife's not here, she's at her mother's, presumably, tomorrow I move out and we part, I don't know what to do, where to go . . .

When he moved out of the apartment, it was only as far as Lucien Carr's loft on the same street. So when Joan returned from her mother's place, Kerouac was her neighbour. One evening, not long after the break-up, he was granted the justification he was seeking for abandoning a pregnant woman. After work at the Brass Rail on Park Avenue, Joan was seen home by a Puerto Rican busboy named Angelo. She invited him in for coffee, and was in the act of showing him a copy of *The Town and the City*, and reading aloud from the opening page, when suddenly

we heard knuckles rapping at the door. Angelo ran, intuitively, to the window. It was stuck, and while I shouted to him that there was no need to worry, Jack yelled from outside, 'What's going on in there?'

Jack used his key to unlock the door, and he hurled it open. The minute the door budged, Angelo dashed out under Jack's arm. Jack jumped back, then, 'What was all that about?' he asked furiously.

I rescued the coffee and told Jack where we'd been, how I had asked Angelo in, and why he was afraid. It was obvious from the order of the room that nothing amiss had transpired. There wasn't so much as a wrinkle in the bedspread. But Jack's eyes had lit up by this point.

'How do I know you haven't been running around with that spic for the past two months?'

'How about, because I only met him two weeks ago.'

'Or some other spic! How do I know what you do with your time when I'm out?'

I wanted to lean into his face and unleash the most unearthly scream I could muster, but instead I ground my teeth together and seethed. 'Did you come to get your stuff?' I asked in a white fury. 'Then get it! And take your paranoia and type it onto a toilet paper roll and flush it down the toilet!'

When first presented with the scroll *On the Road*, Kerouac's editor, Robert Giroux, did not have anything as witty as that to say. He recalled how Kerouac brought to his office, on Madison Avenue, 'a big roll of paper under his left arm':

> he took one end of the roll and he flung it right across my office, right across the desk and stuff, and I thought, this is a strange manuscript, never seen a manuscript like this before, and he looked at me, waiting for me to say something, and I said, 'Jack, you know you have to cut this up. It has to be edited.' His face flushed and he said, 'There'll be no editing on this manuscript.'

This incident has become part of the legend of the scroll, and Giroux has recalled it in several different places; but it is contradicted by two letters, a fortnight apart (10 and 24 June), both to Cassady, which tell, in the first place, of Giroux reading and considering the manuscript, and, in the second, of turning it down. Giroux just didn't like it. Nor did Carr. Nor Ginsberg. 'I know you would like it', Kerouac wrote plaintively to Cassady, his 'sweet prince'.

Soon, Kerouac would begin work on another version of Cassady, longer than the first, and spatially redistributed; this one (eventually published as *Visions of Cody*) was intended as the 'vertical, metaphysical' study of Cassady's princely nature, whereas the road book, naturally, was 'horizontal'.

The hero of the road book, Neal Cassady–Vern Pomeray–Dean Moriarty, is not a one-dimensional idol; his character is complex, shaped by a conflict of opposites. He embodies both an innate generosity and a self-preserving animal greed, the latter inbred by his Old West ancestry and flophouse childhood. Comic and tragic, kind and callous, his romantic appeal resides in his spontaneous response to the world, his habit of acting without first negotiating social custom. He is himself a force of nature, both good and evil, and even those who are attracted to him are bound to be wary. In the finished *On the Road*, Sal Paradise is unable to disagree when Marylou (LuAnne) says: 'You see what a bastard he is . . .' Sal himself calls Dean 'a dirty rat' for abandoning him in San Francisco. Behind the sweet prince, 'charred ruins smoked'.

None the less, *On the Road* is a love story, and Dean Moriarty is its object. When the narrator arrives in Denver in spring 1947, at the beginning of the novel, the romantic motif plays between Dean and Carlo Marx, with Sal feeling like the spare wheel. The three-week version (in which Carlo Marx is simply Allen Ginsberg) shows how, from the start, Kerouac intended the Neal character to incorporate both light and dark:

> Allen was queer in those days, experimenting with himself to the hilt, and Neal saw this and a former boyhood hustler himself in the Denver night, and wanting dearly to learn how to write poetry like Allen, the first thing he was attacking Allen with a great amorous soul such as only a conman can have.

In this reading of his actions, Neal is only bestowing favours on Allen, or Carlo, because he wants to gain something by the transaction. This creates a space for the true romance of the book, which is between Dean and Sal. Theirs is a platonic love, though bedecked by romantic accoutrements, many of them subliminal, some even unconscious – including, surely, the symbolic wedding.

It takes place in San Francisco. Dean's reigning wife, Camille (Carolyn), has just thrown him out. He and Sal stand near the entrance to the house 'on top of a hill on a beautiful sunny day in San Francisco', and look at one another:

> There were triumph and insolence in his eyes, a devilish look, and he never took his eyes off mine for a long time. I looked back and blushed.

They possess nothing but their baggage and each other; they are poor but happy; they feel the world is theirs for the taking, and decide that as a first step in the taking of it they should go to Italy. Being thrust together with Dean like this inspires a new type of enduring bond in Sal: 'I'd never committed myself before with regard to his burdensome existence', he writes. It is at this point that Dean lets his eyes dwell on Sal's, and Sal blushes. His own eyes water 'with embarrassment and tears'. The half-playful, half-anxious questions lovers sometimes use to probe one another's feelings flash between them: 'What's the matter?', 'What was that look?' Sal understands that Dean recognizes his commitment, that he sees it as 'the pivotal point of our friendship'.

While they have been standing outside what Dean must now

regard as his former residence, talking, looking into each other's eyes, pledging their fates as one, the sounds of celebration have been drifting out of a nearby window. And just as Sal asks, 'What was that look?', a wedding party marches into the street from the house next door, and the members of the wedding line up to have their pictures taken. It is against this background that Dean proposes shyly: 'Shall we go?', to which the blushing Sal replies: 'Yes.'

Italy must wait. For now, they honeymoon no further than a bar on Market Street to toast their union – 'we would stick together and be buddies till we died'.

'Allen was queer in those days', Kerouac could write in the scroll *On the Road*, looking back at the Denver adventure. In present time (1951), he was trying to be not queer but normal – on doctor's orders. Enough of cock-Matterhorns, ass-canyons, of masturbating buddies under the elevated highway, of dismal pick-up bars where you went to find the faggot's delight in a sailor's uniform. What he desired, Ginsberg told Kerouac on the day he was discharged from the PI, 27 February 1950, was the love of a woman, the security of a career, the safe haven of normality. 'A turning-point has been reached in that I am no longer going to have homosexual affairs . . .' Homosexuality was 'camp, unnecessary, morbid . . . as bad as impotence'. So committed was he that he felt the need to put it in writing: it was, he told Kerouac, his 'final statement' on the matter.

There was a place of refuge in between queerness and normality, where it was unnecessary to make the choice between two opposites, and that was the land of visions. As he had prepared to enter the hospital, Ginsberg had struggled to hold on to the truth of his mystical experience. The vision – flashbacks of which were granted to him from time to time – had revealed a separate reality, an attainable Utopia of spiritual and emotional candour, a world of desire and tenderness, in which aliens such as he, now queer, now normal, seriously mother-phobic, deeply mother-loving, would be welcomed in all their nakedness, shedding confusion, guilt, wide-awake nightmares of going completely mad. The Vision (frequently capitalized in his correspondence) was sane. Socially induced guilt made you insane. 'I can only say', he wrote to Holmes on the eve of his hospitalization, 'that other people almost without exception have never had an inkling of what a world there is possible . . .' When his Blake experience seemed to him to be 'actual', he continued, he knew he was in touch with 'a light . . . What everybody who had known about it before the nineteenth century called God.' But when he found himself hovering on the threshold, he felt that he was 'the madman in an illusory world, trying to make my abstract metaphysical notions and systems stick'.

These affirmations and reservations were written in response to a request from note-taker Holmes for 'any and all information on your poetry and your visions'. It was not only the mystical side of Ginsberg's experience that Holmes wished to hear about, but the social aspect, too: 'I am interested in knowing also anything you may wish to tell . . . about Neal, Huncke, Lucien in relation to you . . .' Anything you say, he told Ginsberg, 'will evaporate here'.

Ginsberg replied with an eleven-page letter, omitting details of his friendships with Cassady and the others, but describing as completely as he could the divine revelation from 'the other side of the trick wall'. The letter exhibits a mighty faith in systems, a belief in the 'unity of being', and an assumption that everyone is seeking 'the road to perfection', requiring only guidance on to the 'necessary way' in order to find it. It is a letter written by someone who has had it pointed out to him that he is unhealthy, but who longs to believe that 'health is a possible thing'. It also gives a hint of the dogmatism to come, with its talk of the necessary way, and its expression of the feeling that 'it may be that I am one of a few people that has had contact with the real world'. It is the kind of talk that has always come from people who have a mission to change the world.

Over the course of his treatment, however, Ginsberg was persuaded by the doctors that the aim of resocialization should take precedence over everything else. He saw himself as a man who has lost his sense of balance, and must learn to walk all over again. His analyst, Dr Fagin, had told him that, in the PI, he would be subject to 'the works', and indeed the therapy he received had the effect of altering his way of thinking. A few weeks into the treatment, and he conceded the capitalized Vision to the scepticism of quotation marks: 'My "visions" were just moments of feeling', he wrote to Holmes, 'and I was confused because I did not know what was real: what I felt, or what I previously and subsequently thought . . .'

When Ginsberg stepped on to the city sidewalks in February 1950, it was with the determination to bend, to cramp, to squeeze himself to fit society's box, to stay on the blind side of the trick wall. The price of abnormality had been revealed (by the doctors) as being too high to pay, and he set himself the task of being straight. He told his friends about his 'normalcy program': normal in the head, normal in the heart, normal in the cock.

Burroughs wrote from his hideaway in Mexico City to say that word of his new form had reached even there. 'Lucien tells me you are become a virtual satyr – a mythological Greek creature characterized by insatiable lust, I mean, not Jean-Paul Sartre, the existentialist.'

Sardonic though it was, the compliment was accepted. Ginsberg's first girlfriend was a sophisticated woman called Helen Parker, married and divorced, a mother, a former girlfriend of a literary man (John Dos Passos). Ginsberg crowed: 'I love Helen Parker and she loves me.' It was the first time he had had sex with a woman, and she larded him with assurances that he was a great lover – as, he told Kerouac, he had always thought he would be.

The affair petered out after a few months, but there were other women to adore for a month or two, footnotes in the essentially masculinist archive of Beat love: Mardine, Dusty Moreland, Alene Lee, Elise Cowen, and others. Dusty had an apartment on West 12th Street, where she entertained Ginsberg in the evenings. She would undress in front of him, they would step into the shower, then make love. Doctors' orders were being carried out. The old nightmare of decomposition, of sex with a sailor in a vacant lot by a waterfront bar, could be kissed goodbye. Here was a second revelation to add to his hand-held tour of Eternity with William Blake: heterosexual heaven.

But one night, while drinking in a Washington Square bar used mainly by lesbians, the Pony Stable, he felt his body move again to the old rhythm, as he fell into conversation with a dark, curly-haired boy with sharp features. Gregory Corso did resemble a sailor, in a way, but a sailor in a music-hall act. Looks apart, he possessed two appealing characteristics for Ginsberg: he was a juvenile delinquent, and he was a poet. Under his arm, Corso carried a sheaf of poems, from which he might select one to read aloud to a stranger – such as the man he had just met – or to a crowd in a cafeteria, or to his probation officer, adding to the verse as he went along. When he read, the elevated lyricism of the language, carefully, almost laboriously, enunciated in a thick New York accent, played a music both streetwise and celestial:

> Within a delicate grey ruin
> the vestal lady on Brattle
> is up at dawn as is her custom,
> with the raise of a shade . . .
>
> Full bodied and randomly young she clings,
> peers down; hovers over a wine-filled vat,
> and with outstretched arms like wings,
> revels in the forming image of a child below.

Corso was twenty years old and had spent his life in society's lost-and-found rooms. He had been born above a funeral parlour, to an Italian mother whom he never knew, and a father who had drifted in and out of his life, and finally into the Navy at the start of the war, leaving his son to the care of others. En route to his meeting with poetry, Corso had had half-a-dozen sets of foster parents. In the intervals, he had lived among 'the alley cats in the wild and wonderful New York streets'. His life was a comic operetta with weepie touches. On one occasion, he stole a suit from a shop window, as his friends distracted the tailor. He was arrested, a small boy in a man's suit, when 'the tailor spotted me wearing the crime'.

The judge offered to send Corso back to his most recent set of foster parents, but this idea was rejected by the parents themselves, and Corso was taken to a detention centre for juveniles called the Youth House, where he only got into deeper trouble. Eventually, he was removed to the Children's Observation Ward at Bellevue: a thirteen-year-old in the dungeon, among 'the most awful human misery imaginable', according to his own recitative:

At the Children's Observation Ward there were old men. Calm yet unhealthy old men. But I was young and playful and mischievous, so one day I balled a piece of white bread the size of a pea, and flipped it

116

into the air. It hit an old man on the head, and God O God the screams that ensued. It was like a time bomb set off, a chain reaction, everybody started to scream along with him . . . I was whisked off to the Mad Violent Ward of Bellevue.

Men in sheets sitting hunched in corners their skin peeling off; men in sheets squeaking like mice; men in sheets peeing on other men . . . I don't know how long I was there; that it was summer and that I was thirteen I am sure.

Corso stepped outside this world only to write poems. When he met Ginsberg in the Pony Stable, he was on parole, having been released from his most recent, and longest, stretch of three years (again for theft) only a few months earlier. And yet his imagination chirruped operetta:

> I met her in the evening
> in the moon in the sky!
> She kissed me in the evening
> and wed me in her sty!
> Oh, dear! Oh, me! Oh, my!
> I married the pig's daughter!
> I married the pig's daughter!

> *Why? Why? Why?*

Perhaps as a way of indicating to his new friend that, although he had been found in a bar frequented by lesbians, he was not to be taken as homosexual himself, Corso engaged Ginsberg in a bit of boy talk. From his attic on West 12th Street, he said, he was able to look down into the apartment of a woman who lived across the street. Sometimes, in the evenings, her lover would visit; she would undress in front of him, they would step into the shower, then they would make love . . .

According to the legend (or his own version of it), Ginsberg then said: 'I have magical powers. Would you like to meet her?'

When Burroughs wrote to Kerouac about Mexico being a fine free place where a man could pack a gun and not take nothing off of nobody, it was with the rider that, since everybody minded his own business, the gun was superfluous anyway. He kept his with him,

117

however, and a short time later his warm feelings towards the tolerant local police force were confirmed in action:

> One night I got into a beef with a citizen in a bar and pulled my gun on him. A cop grabbed my arm. I was flabbergasted by this insolence and asked him what he was putting in his two cents for, and threw the gun in his stomach from which position it was transferred by the bartender who pulled my arm with the gun back across the bar. Then the cop takes me by the arm very respectful and says: '*Vámonos, Señor*', and walked me to a bus stop.

The incident, described here in a letter to Ginsberg, made the transition into the novel tentatively entitled 'Junk'. In the refined version, the policeman is 'the recurrent cop of my dreams . . . who would rush in when I was about to take a shot or go to bed with a boy'; the scene in the bar is characterized by an atmosphere which is 'unreal and flat and pointless, as though I had forced my way into someone else's dream'; and the life in Mexico City in general, like the life in New Orleans before, is a series of short progressions from drugs to violence:

> When my wife saw that I was getting the habit again, she did something she had never done before. I was cooking up a shot two days after I'd connected with Old Ike. My wife grabbed the spoon and threw the junk on the floor. I slapped her twice across the face and she threw herself on the bed, sobbing, then turned around and said to me: 'Don't you want to do anything at all? You know how bored you get when you have a habit. It's like all the lights went out. Oh well, do what you want. I guess you have some stashed away.'
>
> I did have some stashed.

One afternoon in a Mexico City street in 1951, Burroughs was host to a troubling visitation which, by the end of the day, would have come to seem clairvoyant.

Hearing the whistle of a travelling knife-sharpener outside his window, he took down a scout-knife (much like the one Carr had used to kill Kammerer) and handed it over to be whetted on the stone. The air was oppressive, and he had been anxious and downcast since the morning. Without warning, tears began to stream down his face as he turned back towards the house where Joan was waiting. ' "What on earth is wrong?" I wondered.'

★

Hal Chase: That William Tell stuff was a sham, a put-up thing to release Bill, to let him commit the ultimate crime.

Alan Temko: I knew that [Burroughs] was capable of killing someone. They were all very unattractive in that way. The level of violence was very high . . . It was very Dostoevsky.

Burroughs: I am forced to the appalling conclusion that I would never have become a writer but for Joan's death, and to the realization of the extent to which this event has motivated and formulated my writing.

★

Joan was not her old self. She told Kerouac that she hadn't read a book 'in about four years (since Benzedrine)'. Apart from the drug privation she had endured in Mexico, apart from her drinking from eight a.m. onwards, apart from the body sores and the limp, she was also suffering, so she told Hal Chase, from an incurable disease. To Ginsberg, she wrote: 'I'm out of the running.' She was twenty-seven. The relationship between husband and wife mystified onlookers. Huncke, who had stayed with them during Burroughs's first farming venture in Texas, was struck by Burroughs's indifference to Joan:

> She was sort of interesting to him, that's all. He didn't like to be annoyed with her too much. She demanded that he give her a little attention each night. She'd spend maybe an hour with him in his room . . . She'd leave and go on into her room.

On the evening of Burroughs's tearful foreboding before the knife-sharpener, he and Joan went together to the Bounty Bar on Calle Monterey. Billy junior, aged four, was with them. The situation was not unlike that of the first meeting with Huncke and his underworld friends, in that Burroughs had a gun for sale, a .38 Star automatic. He carried it in a bag into the apartment above the bar, where a private drinking session was in progress. Everyone was on Osso Negro gin. A young man with whom Burroughs had become obsessed, Lewis Marker, was present, accompanied by a friend, but whoever had expressed an interest in buying the gun had not turned up. During a gap in the conversation, Burroughs took the .38 out of the bag and said to Joan, as if it was an old party trick (though he claimed never to have suggested it before): 'I guess it's about time for our William Tell act.'

Joan placed an object on her head and turned sideways-on to her husband, who was sitting six feet away. He fired, shooting her through the temple. Marker, the reluctant lover, said: 'Bill, I think you've killed her.'

(*Fadeout to* New Year, 1965: Burroughs in his home town of St Louis is being interviewed for the *Paris Review*. He speaks at length about one of his favourite topics, the falsehoods perpetrated by the print media. Then he says: '. . . that terrible accident with Joan Vollmer, my wife. I had a revolver that I was planning to sell to a friend. I was checking it over and it went off – killed her. A rumour started that I was trying to shoot a glass of champagne from her head William Tell style. Absurd and false.')

Was it a champagne glass? Elsewhere, Burroughs described the putative target as a 'highball glass'. Carl Solomon, who may have got his information from Ginsberg, also called it a 'champagne glass', although unreliability is suggested by his dating the scene to 1950.

Edward de Grazia, a lawyer who was later to defend the work of Burroughs in court against the charge of obscenity, recounted the incident in his book about censorship, *Girls Lean Back Everywhere*: 'He aimed too low at a whiskey glass.' In a footnote, de Grazia qualified this assertion with proper lawyerly caution: 'variously also reported to have been a champagne glass . . . an apricot, an orange'. The publisher Barney Rosset once pointed out Burroughs to Alain Robbe-Grillet, with the recommendation that he was 'a very important writer'. 'Ah, yes?' said Robbe-Grillet. 'What has he done?' Rosset replied: 'He put an apple on his wife's head and killed her.' One of the witnesses, Marker's friend Eddie Woods, recalled that Joan had been drinking gin, and that when Burroughs came out with his William Tell quip, 'she balanced her glass on her head'. A *New York Post* reporter filled it up and made it 'a glass of gin'.

A historian of the Beat Generation, Steven Watson, called it a water glass, a more temperate view backed up by a recent collective biography of Beat women. The source of the detail could be a Burroughs biographer, Barry Miles, who described it with more precision as 'a six-ounce water glass'. A Kerouac biographer, Steve Turner, turned it into 'a wine glass'. Kerouac's publisher, Robert Giroux, who heard the news in New York soon after he had rejected the scroll *On the Road*, called it 'an old tin can'.

Billy junior was present throughout. Aged four at the time, he did not register what was on his mother's head as his father took aim, but his testimony has a poetry lacking in any of the others: 'she placed an apple or an apricot or a grape or myself on her head and challenged my father to shoot'.

Another crime, another headline: 'Heir's Pistol Kills His Wife' reported the *New York Daily News* of 8 September 1951; 'He Denies Playing Wm. Tell'.

Mexico City, Sept 7 – William Seward Burroughs, 37, first admitted, then denied today that he was playing William Tell when he killed his pretty young wife during a drinking party last night.

Police said that Burroughs, grandson of the adding machine inventor, first told them that, wanting to show off his marksmanship, he placed a glass of gin on her head and fired, but he was so drunk that he missed and shot her in the forehead.

After talking with a lawyer, police said, Burroughs, who is a wealthy cotton planter from Pharr, Texas, changed his story and insisted that his wife was shot accidentally when he dropped his newly purchased .38 caliber pistol . . . 'It was purely accidental,' he said. 'I did not put any glass on her head. If she did, it was as a joke. I certainly did not intend to shoot at it.'

He said there had been no arguments or discussion before the 'accident'.

'The party was quiet,' he said. 'We had a few drinks. Everything is very hazy.'

Burroughs and his wife had been here about two years. He said he was studying native dialects at the University of Mexico.

Once again, the family came to the rescue. His brother Mortimer arrived carrying the $2,300 bail money; he also arranged for Joan's burial, and took Billy away to be brought up by his grandparents. Julie went to live with the Vollmer family. The story of dropping the gun was altered to one of checking to see if it was loaded – pulling back the slide, and accidentally firing. Woods and Marker agreed to back him up, and the eventual charge was *imprudencia criminal* – criminal negligence – carrying a maximum sentence of five years. Having been detained for less than two weeks, Burroughs was released to await his trial.

The gruesome tale continues: the ballistics experts appointed by the court were paid off with a $300 bribe; while waiting for the case to come to trial, Burroughs's lawyer, Bernabé Jurado, shot a youth who had accidentally damaged his Cadillac – the youth died in hospital and the lawyer fled to Brazil; Burroughs followed him out of the country in December 1952, forfeiting his bail bond; he later learned that he had been given a two-year suspended sentence, in absentia; the love affair with Marker continued, unhappily, for a few months more; Billy lived with his grandparents, now resident in Florida, until he followed in his father's footsteps and became a writer and a drug addict; he died at the age of thirty-three, having undergone a liver transplant.

Down through the years, first in correspondence and then in published writings, Burroughs insisted that he took aim at the glass and not at Joan; at the same time, he did not discount the possibility of unconscious motivation. Ballistics experts could be bribed and magazine interviewers misled, but he never tried to pay off his conscience. Three and a half years after the shooting he wrote to Ginsberg that he had considered writing 'some account of Joan's death', but had been unable to face it:

> I suspect my reluctance is not all because it would be in bad taste to write about it. I think I am *afraid*. Not exactly to discover unconscious intent. It's more complex, more basic and more horrible, as if the brain *drew* the bullet towards it . . . I was concentrating on aiming for the *very top of the glass* . . . Why, instead of being so careful, not give up the idea? Why indeed? In my present state of mind I am afraid to go too deep into this matter.

Eventually, he would view his condition, in pre-Enlightenment terms, as a 'possession', literally, by a bad spirit. Many years later, in the introduction to a novel based on his relationship with Marker, he would write that the death of Joan had brought him into contact with 'the Ugly Spirit, and maneuvered me into a struggle in which I have no choice but to write my way out'.

A year before Kerouac sat down to write the scroll *On the Road*, Holmes had sent him a letter about their common interests:

> It's time we thought about our material. Call them hipsters, the 'beat generation', 'postwar kids' or our own displaced persons whatever you will.

It is not a letter Kerouac would have responded to warmly; it suggests too practical and shallow an approach to experience. Let's think about the best way to market ourselves, it seems to say. Nevertheless, a few months later, Kerouac wrote to Frank Morley of Eyre and Spottiswoode, the English publisher of *The Town and the City*, to say that he was planning a 'survey' of the generation 'known as the "Hip" ', which would depict a group of young men and women caught in a postwar, restless uncertainty.

Then, just three weeks before Kerouac started to write, Holmes turned up and presented him with a manuscript of his own, and asked him to read it. Holmes's notetaking had already resulted in a novel about 'our material . . . the "beat generation" '. It was called *Go*.

Kerouac was not pleased. The title was familiar, for one thing: 'Go, Go, Go' was a short story Kerouac had written about himself and Cassady in a jazz club; 'Go!' was the encouragement enthusiasts such as Kerouac and Cassady might shout at musicians while they were soloing. Reading Holmes's novel, Kerouac came across a jazz joint called The Go Hole, and 'the thud-thud-thud of stomping feet, and occasional "go!" [to] signify approval . . .' He also found a character based on Neal Cassady ('Hart Kennedy'), and one shaped out of the elements of Holmes himself ('Paul Hobbes'). The Holmes character responds to Kennedy's eighty-mile-an-hour dash through Manhattan in a car, his swerves and lights-jumping, with the same encouragement, 'Go! Go! Go!'

There was a brooding and sensitive would-be novelist with a

mother-fixation ('Gene Pasternak'); an excitable poet, 'David Stofsky', who has a vision of Blake in a tenement; Huncke, Cannastra and others were also depicted. Ginsberg, when he learned of *Go*, was annoyed at the treatment of his visionary experience, and at the overwrought poems attributed to Stofsky in the novel, which were, in fact, written by Holmes ('Flower of soul, flower of glare, / Stricken Rose who is so numb: / Is this shrunken impulse, like a star, / A prideful light where I succumb?'). When Holmes had asked Ginsberg to describe his divine revelations, it was with the assurance that they would then 'evaporate'; but here they were, an inkblot on a page in *Go*.

Although he grumbled to Ginsberg and others, Kerouac suppressed his displeasure when writing to Holmes. But the flat prose of *Go* contained an artistic lesson for him: that all the tea in the world, all the jazz, all the mad driving and wild parties, were not enough by themselves to make a book resonate. Holmes's novel may have been the first to dramatize the movements of the Beat Generation (a term which occurs in it several times), but its music had no beat; it was square, not hip, frantic, not cool. Holmes was nowhere. He had even wanted to call his book *Beat Generation*, but Kerouac warned him off that.

The arrival on Kerouac's desk of Holmes's manuscript is a more plausible explanation for the power of energy which fuelled his own beat book than Joan's questioning ('What was it like, Jack?'). By the spring of 1952, though, *On the Road* had been rejected by several publishers, while *Go* was being proofed, measured for a jacket, topped and tailed, and made ready for the bookstores. It had been bought by Scribner, publishers of Hemingway, Fitzgerald and Wolfe (and rejectors of *On the Road*). Scribner, in turn, had sold the paperback rights to Bantam for $20,000, a huge sum. As Holmes counted gold, Kerouac was scratching around in the lower reaches of the book trade looking for a deal, any deal. He got one – $250 advance, but the publishers never produced his book, even though, in a change of heart from his former artistic obstinacy, he offered to tailor it to fit any readership they believed would wear it.

With his sense of self-worth cast down, Kerouac's good will towards his friend cracked. Holmes was an outsider, he told

Ginsberg, a 'pryer-intoer' of the group which properly consisted of Ginsberg, Cassady, Burroughs, Huncke, himself, and 'mebbe Lucien someday'. No place for the author of *Go*. And there was something else to annoy him. He had had the idea of giving *On the Road* the subtitle, 'A modern novel', the distinction being carried over from modern jazz. And here was pryer-intoer Holmes's *Go*, bearing the legend on its front cover, 'A modern novel of the search for experience and for love'. The smell of Holmes's work, Kerouac announced when the novel was published in the fall of 1952, 'is the smell of death'.

Burroughs had also written a book, a beat book, though its tight-lipped, practical prose was nothing like that of either *Go* or *On the Road*. No one would have had the notion of subtitling Burroughs's book (still called 'Junk') 'A modern novel of the search for love'. Love was absent from it, though there were a few emotionally neutral references to 'my wife', including the account of slapping her in a fight over drugs; some homosexual encounters are described in sober terms. He had begun writing in March 1950, and by spring of the following year had a manuscript ready to show to a publisher.

But which publisher would be willing to consider a novel like this, full of drugs, guns, dubious sex, contempt for the law and everything that held society togther? As a commercial prospect, Burroughs's novel did not even have the advantage of cheap sensationalism. It had hardly any plot. It did not ask to be read as the story of a 'beat generation', or as a diagnosis of 'postwar' pathology. It had nothing of Kerouac's flighty vagabond romanticism, or Holmes's marketable brand of hip.

While Burroughs was waiting for his case to come up in Mexico City, his friends tried acting as agents for his novel. Kerouac sent it to James Laughlin, owner of the independent avant-garde house, New Directions, who had published Henry Miller, William Carlos Williams, and Ezra Pound. But Laughlin kept it for a year without replying, and eventually Kerouac was forced to write and ask for it back. Lucien Carr took over, without success, then Ginsberg, who finally found someone willing to publish the book. On 5 April 1952, Burroughs wrote from Mexico City:

I could kiss you on both cheeks. We should get used to calling each other sweetheart. I understand it is the standard form of address between agent and author.

The publisher was Ace Books, a specialist in the new cheap paperbacks. The company was owned by A. A. Wyn, uncle of Carl Solomon, Ginsberg's 'Kirillov'. He had heard about Burroughs from Ginsberg in the Psychiatric Institute, and, when his uncle gave him a job on his release, had brought him the novel. Ace Books paid $800 for 'Junk' by 'William Dennison', which became *Junkie* by William Lee (and eventually *Junky* by William S. Burroughs). The purpose of the pseudonym was ostensibly to shield the scandalous book from the notice of his parents, but as Lee was his mother's maiden name, and as he had rejected earlier thoughts of Al, Richard or James Lee, in favour of William, the pretence was thin.

There were other bumps to be smoothed out. *Junkie* had been completed before Joan's death, but when the publishers heard about the fate of the character referred to glancingly as 'my wife', they wanted the novel expanded and an account of the shooting worked in. The cover of the typical cheap paperback garishly blended sex and violence, and the Bounty Bar incident was just the kind of thing to inspire an Ace illustrator. But the normally unflappable Burroughs felt squeamish about the suggestion of developing the wife character. 'I wish you would talk them out of that idea', he wrote to his agent, Ginsberg, on 14 April (a few days later, he exclaimed: 'How I miss Joan!'), and the suggestion was dropped. There were cuts to make: for example, the original version contained several pages about Wilhelm Reich, exploring ideas on cancer and drug addiction derived from Reich's book, *The Cancer Biopathy*; these were deemed unsuitable for a novel the publishers wished to push as a dimestore pot-boiler, and were removed.

Then, even before *Junkie* had been made ready for the printer, Wyn, having heard from Ginsberg that Burroughs was writing a second novel, began to show interest in that one, too. It was called *Queer* (Kerouac's suggestion) and was based on a trip he had made to Panama and Ecuador with Lewis Marker in the summer of 1951, in a preliminary search for mind-expanding vegetable drugs used by South American Indians. Like *Junkie*, *Queer* was about addiction, but in this case the addiction of hopeless love. Burroughs thought of the novel as 'a sequel or Part II to Junk'.

Wyn conceived the idea of tacking *Queer* on to the back of *Junkie*. Burroughs had hoped that the new book would be published as a sequel to the first, but, though somewhat puzzled by Wyn's request, he worked hard to accommodate his publisher's wishes and made ready sixty pages of *Queer* within a month.

But it was cast in the third person, whereas *Junkie* was in the first. Ginsberg pointed this out to Solomon, who saw no problem: just switch from third to first, 'he / him' to 'I / me' and so on. Easy. Burroughs bridled at being told what to do in his own writing, which he had only lately restarted, but he was eager to get the book out and so wrote to Ginsberg that if Ace wanted the narrative voice in *Queer* 'switcheroo'd', then 'OK'. But: 'Why the hell can't you shift persons in the middle of a book? So it hasn't been done, so let's do it.'

The desire to experiment, coupled with a willingness to compromise, and a lack of concern over the structural integrity of his work, is typical of Burroughs. He was equally unprotective of the formal integrity of *Junkie*. Once Wyn had decided not to conclude *Junkie* with the sixty pages of *Queer*, after all, out of a fear of legal action over the homosexual content, there remained the question of how to end the original book. Burroughs, stuck in Mexico and desperate to leave, was growing impatient. 'Please let me know what is going on up there', he wrote in June. Ginsberg told him that Wyn wanted a new ending for the book before it went ahead, and he offered to do the writing himself, using the manuscripts of *Junkie* and *Queer* in his possession, and papering over the gaps with Burroughs's letters to him.

Finally, Burroughs undertook the job himself, and even supplied the biographical preface that Wyn had asked for, despite an earlier refusal: 'I have no idea what they want. Do they have in mind the – "I have worked as a towel boy in a Kalamazoo whore house, lavatory attendant, male whore and part-time stool pigeon . . ." routine, like you see on the back flap?'

After a year of delays, *Junkie: Confessions of an unredeemed drug addict* went on sale in drugstores in May 1953. Yet it formed only half a book. In spite of Burroughs's continuing hope, Wyn never did publish *Queer*. He said that to do so would land them all in jail. He feared legal action over *Junkie* as well, and so, instead of making an Ace Double-Book with its cousin, *Queer*, *Junkie* went back-to-back with a reprint of a memoir first published in 1941, *Narcotic Agent*, by Maurice Helbrandt.

The cover of the *Junkie* half of this beast with two backs was a triumph of bad taste and misrepresentation. It showed a handsome man holding a struggling blonde by the neck, while wrestling a syringe and cooking-spoon from her grip. She is dressed in tight sweater and pencil skirt. The book itself is almost woman-free, and, in the only scene which comes close to fitting the picture, it is the woman who knocks the syringe from the hand of the man. The spine held both authors' names and titles, and the price for the two-in-one was thirty-five cents.

Burroughs was not unhappy. He judged Helbrandt's book to be 'not so bad as I expected', and told Ginsberg that he didn't care 'what prefaces, apologies or explanations they paste on the deal' – a reference to the 'Publisher's Note', which joined forces with the jacket to conspire against the novel itself:

> This is more than the story of a drug-addict . . . we see the veins shrink at the needle's thrust, the 'bang' as the stuff takes . . . We witness the sordidness of every crevice of their lives. For all are a 'beat, nowhere bunch of guys' . . . there has never been a criminal confession better calculated to discourage imitation by thrill-hungry teenagers.
>
> William Lee is an unrepentant, unredeemed drug-addict. His own words tell us that he is a fugitive from the law; that he has been diagnosed as a schizophrenic paranoid; that he is totally without moral values. But . . . we realized that here was a document which could forearm the public more effectively than anything yet printed about the drug menace . . .

Wyn inserted parenthetical notes at selected places in the text, 'for the protection of the reader', where the author was judged to have 'departed from accepted medical fact . . . in an effort to justify his actions'. When Lee said that 'if a junkie could keep himself in a constant state of kicking, he would live to a phenomenal age', the publisher butted in to register caution: 'This is contradicted by recognized medical authority.' Or, following a similar remark, 'This statement is hearsay.'

Like Kerouac's novel, like Holmes's, *Junkie* was more or less a straight job of reporting on the unusual life of the author. (Huncke, the only indigenous inhabitant of the underworld in their circle, features in all three books – in *On the Road* as Elmo Hassel, in *Go* as Albert Ancke, and in *Junkie* as Herman, whose large brown eyes send 'waves of hostility and suspicion' flowing in Lee's direction when they are first introduced over a box of morphine syrettes and a gun; like Huncke, the thinly fictionalized Herman thinks the thinly fictionalized Lee is a policeman.) But *Junkie* is cool, whereas *Go* is uncool, and *On the Road* is slightly frantic (you can't picture Lee whooping 'Go!' or 'Whooee!' in the back seat of a car). In a style which shepherds all its notes at the lower register, suggesting restraint rather than technical limitation, Burroughs charts the drug addict's movements in New Orleans, Mexico City and New York:

> As the geologist looking for oil is guided by certain outcroppings of rock, so certain signs indicate the near presence of junk. Junk is adjacent to ambiguous or transitional districts . . . Stores selling artificial limbs, wig-makers, dental mechanics, loft manufacturers of perfumes, pomades, novelties, essential oils. A point where dubious enterprise touches Skid Row.

★

Among other Ace books published that year, in lurid colours, were *Twist the Knife Slowly*, *Dead Ahead*, and *Mrs Homicide*. They were popular: within a year, *Junkie/Narcotic Agent* had sold more than 110,000 copies, without the benefit of a single review.

The Ace list came close to including *On the Road* by John Kerouac. It was Wyn who had given Kerouac the $250 advance, together with an agreement to publish a book called *On the Road*, even though the form it would take was to be decided. He received news from Carl Solomon of Wyn's acceptance of the book in January 1952.

As usual with Kerouac when someone showed interest in his work, a mirage passed in front of his eyes; he reacted, overreacted, with giddy excitement. He urged Solomon and his uncle to publish not only his own book about Cassady, but Cassady's book as well – 'NEAL IS WRITING A GREAT NOVEL', he roared, though there was little evidence of it – and Ginsberg's too. He tried to get them to take a new novel he had embarked on, describing it one minute as '*Faust*, Part III', the next as a story of 'downtown redbrick neon in Lowell'. (It was published much later as *Dr Sax*.) Next he offered Solomon a novel on which he and Burroughs had collaborated, based on the Carr–Kammerer affair, *And the Hippoes Were Boiled in Their Tanks*, by 'Seward Lewis' (the two authors' middle names). As for *On the Road*, he suggested, getting into stride, why not publish an extract, say about 160 pages long, specially for the dime/drugstore market, then do the whole thing in hardback for the critics and serious readers? He had a spicy, sexy stretch in mind for the 25-cent edition, which he envisaged coming straight from the scroll version.

In the spring of 1952, Kerouac visited Neal and Carolyn Cassady in San Francisco, then moved south to see Burroughs in Mexico City. There, a new version of *On the Road* was typed on Burroughs's typewriter, and *Dr Sax* was written in pencil in tiny notebooks. He mailed Solomon the revised *On the Road* – 530 pages long – on 17 May. In his absence from New York, it was received into the Ace Books office, tried, judged, and condemned.

Taking his duties as an agent seriously, Ginsberg delivered the verdict in a letter which opened: 'Carl read it, I read it once . . . Wyn I'm positive won't take it.' Ginsberg made clear that, in Wyn's position, he wouldn't take it either:

> I don't see how it will ever be published, it's so personal, it's so full of sex language, so full of our own local mythological references, I don't know if it would make sense to any publisher . . .

Ginsberg praised aspects of the writing, but, as a whole, he said, 'It's crazy (not merely inspired crazy) but unrelated crazy.'

The next thing that happened was that Carl Solomon went insane again, and books were the particular target of his rage. He took a knife to all the books in his apartment. He stopped the traffic on Eighth Avenue by throwing books at passing cars. Eventually, he was whipped off to Pilgrim State Hospital (where he joined Ginsberg's mother and Little Jack Melody). Ginsberg told Burroughs that he could not get anything done at Wyn until Solomon 'calms down'.

Solomon calmed down long enough to write Kerouac a letter. He had always had a habit of jesting with Kerouac, which did not go down as well as he thought it did. In early correspondence over *On the Road*, he had accused Kerouac of 'work-shirking', of squandering his talent, of using too many drugs, of falling for a 'hip-bohemian-criminal-poetic conformism'. Now that *On the Road* had been ditched by Ace, Solomon let his mad self off the leash. He informed Kerouac that his pose was the pose of a 'nasty, stupid worthless, idiot-brat son of a royal house'. Neal Pomeray, as the hero of the novel was now called, was a symbol of 'the loss of respect for authority' (Solomon, in his madness, had forgotten Artaud), and of the 'loss of contact with this earth'. In daring to complain about the small advance he had received, Kerouac was acting like the 'Brilliant Young Punk', like an 'undertipped waiter', whereas, in fact, he was the 'turd in the toilet bowl'. What sort of novel could Ace expect from him, therefore, but a 'turd of the month'? They were not interested in publishing a book by him, and certainly not *On the Road*, which was a 'thoroughly incoherent mess'.

Poor Kerouac. He had left Mexico City conscious of Burroughs's grumbling. ('To be blunt, I have never had a more inconsiderate and selfish guest under my roof', Burroughs complained to Ginsberg.) Now he could think of nothing else to do but what he always did in times of trouble, limp off to be with his mother. He took a job in a textile mill for the summer, and wrote a bitter but dignified letter to Wyn and Solomon, invoking Hemingway, Joyce and Dreiser, all of whom had produced works which had been considered unpublishable by myopic publishers. When he himself encountered difficulty in a book, he said, especially if it was innovative in form, he laboured to understand its method, instead of rudely dismissing it as 'incoherent'. *On the Road* was among the first of a new type of 'modern prose book', as distinct from just a novel. 'I wrote it with joy in my heart . . .'

Burroughs departed Mexico as a fugitive in December 1952, arriving at his parents' new home at Cobblestone Gardens, Palm Beach, Florida, in time for Christmas. He saw Billy, took a cure based on the new wonder drug, Cortisone ('works like crazy'), and wrote a short story called 'The Junky's Christmas': 'It was Christmas Day and Danny the Car Wiper hit the street junk sick and broke after seventy-two hours in the precinct jail.' The family doctor told him his health was 'perfect'.

But escaping from Mexico did not correspond to returning to the US. 'I don't like it here', he told Ginsberg. 'I feel that my home is South of the Rio Grande.' After Christmas, he sailed down to Panama, the first leg of the search for a new kick, the drug called yagé used by Amazonian Indians. It was supposed to endow its users with telepathic powers. 'I do want usable knowledge of telepathy', Burroughs wrote. The man who all his life felt menaced by supernatural forces, both earthly – the corporate forces of the print media – and unearthly – the Ugly Spirit – wanted a supernatural power of his own with which to fight back.

On his previous trip to South America, with Marker, he had failed to find yagé. Among the few shards of *Queer* to survive in *Junkie* was the latter novel's last line: 'Yagé may be the final fix.'

While *Junkie* was running through the presses, the slumbering Beat Generation was kissed by the media (with which it would, one day, be trapped in an unhappy marriage) and awakened. An editor on the *New York Times* asked Holmes to write an article about the new mood, the Hip, the Knowing, the restless generation. Holmes got the brief: translate the Zeitgeist for the squares; introduce the cast of *Go* to their parents.

Holmes sat down and wrote 'This Is the Beat Generation'. It appeared in the *New York Times* on 16 November 1952:

> A man is beat whenever he goes for broke and wagers the sum of his resources on a single number; and the young generation has done that continually from early youth.
>
> Its members have an instinctive individuality, needing no bohemianism or imposed eccentricity to express it. Brought up during the collective bad circumstances of a dreary depression, weaned during the collective uprooting of a global war, they distrust collectivity. But they have never been able to keep the world out of their dreams. The fancies of their childhood inhabited the half-light of Munich, the Nazi-Soviet pact and the eventual blackout . . . The peace they inherited was only as secure as the next headline. It was a cold peace. Their own lust for freedom, and the ability to live at a pace that kills (to which the war had

adjusted them), led to black markets, bebop, narcotics, sexual promiscuity, hucksterism and Jean-Paul Sartre. The beatness set in later . . .

Burroughs, preparing to ship out to the jungles of South America and the final fix, wrote to Ginsberg to say that he had read Holmes's article: 'OK, in an obvious way.'

Behind the beat

The scroll

The scroll on which Kerouac typed *On the Road*, in less than three weeks, has undergone a series of metamorphoses over time. The most common description of it, no doubt because it is a convenient mental image of a seemingly endless sheet of paper, is of a 'teletype roll', the sort used to receive telegraph messages. This was the description offered by Kerouac's first biographer, Ann Charters – 'a 120 foot roll of teletype paper' – and also by a future biographer, Gerald Nicosia, in a preparatory essay he wrote on Kerouac. By the time Nicosia came to write his biography in 1983, however, he had changed the teletype roll to 'twenty-foot strips of Japanese drawing paper', taped together to form 'a roll that could be fed continuously through his typewriter'. In a subsequent article by Nicosia, twelve years after the publication of his biography, it had changed again, to a 'scroll of Japanese art paper', evoking something seamless and more oriental than separate sheets taped together.

Allen Ginsberg continued to insist that it was teletype paper, and even suggested a source: Kerouac procured this 'single piece of paper' from the 'United Press office in New York'. Joyce Johnson, Kerouac's girlfriend six years after the scroll *On the Road* was written, agreed that it was teletype paper, asserted that the scroll was 'huge', and said that Kerouac had got it from Lucien Carr, who was working at United Press. A later biographer, Tom Clark, begged to differ: it was 'oilskin art paper'. John Clellon Holmes remembered it as 'shelf-paper', stuck together 'like a Chinese roll', while a journalist from the *New York Post* who interviewed Kerouac in 1959 had it down – possibly from the mouth of Kerouac himself – as a 'roll of cannister paper'.

One month after finishing the scroll version of *On the Road*, Kerouac told Cassady in a letter that he had written the entire novel on a 'strip of paper 120 foot long'. But what sort of paper? Was it cannister paper, shelf-paper, teletype paper, Japanese drawing paper or oilskin art paper? No, it was 'tracing paper', said Kerouac. It did not come from Lucien's office at UP, but had 'belonged to Cannastra', the late boyfriend of Joan Haverty. In a later letter to Holmes, Kerouac modified this, making it 'that block long sheet of Cannastra's drawing paper . . .'

How long is a block? Ann Charters's teletype roll came out at 120 feet, as did Nicosia's Japanese scroll; Ginsberg's teletype roll ran to 'hundreds and hundreds of feet', while the Beat historian Steven Watson ('taped together rolls of tracing paper') estimated it at 120 yards.

According to Watson, the scroll contained 186,000 words. Nicosia knocked a digit off of that, and called it 86,000 words, whereas Kerouac himself, obsessive when it came to computing his output, reckoned 125,000 words, an average of 6,000 per day and 15,000 on the final day. He rolled it out on the floor like a carpet before his sweet prince.

6

Beat, in black and white

This is the Beat Generation, *circa* 1953.

Burroughs has wriggled out of prison, and a murder charge, sprung, yet again, by family money. Corso, who has no family money and practically no family, has spent his adolescence bouncing in and out of boys' homes but is now converted to Poetry. Cassady, who has had a similar in-jail-and-out-of-jail life, and has a similar love of literature, is disturbed by his lack of creative ability; by way of consolation, he has two wives and three children (in addition to the son by his bigamous wife, Diana, there is a second daughter by Carolyn). Ginsberg's taste of institutions, first in the company of his mother then as an inmate himself – briefly in prison, followed by the insane asylum – has put him off the nonconformist way of life of his closest friends. Carr, similarly mindful of the consequences of being 'deviant', of making the soul monstrous, is married and steadily working his way up the ladder at United Press; he has requested of the 'mad ones', of whom he was the first, that his name not be mentioned in any of their writings. Kerouac, who spent a month in jail during Carr's case, has again been pursued by the law, and has been briefly locked up for non-payment of maintenance to his wife Joan and their disputed child (it's a girl: Jan Michelle). Huncke is still doing time on Rikers Island as a result of the 1949 stolen-goods case.

Almost all have been subjected to psychiatric detention, or 'observation', and been held in mental wards of one kind or another. The exceptions are Cassady and Huncke, natural jailbirds, and, of course, Holmes, a natural good citizen. All have tried their hand at writing poetry, fiction or memoir.

And now some of it, with that deviant behaviour digested to form subject matter, is finding its way into print. 'Such great news about publishing etc', a friend from England wrote to Ginsberg while he was in almost daily consultation with Solomon and Wyn about getting into print. 'Great new generation of writing cats – Jack, Neal, Burroughs, yourself – John Holmes makes it too . . .' Kerouac had published one novel, and had an acceptance for another; Burroughs was waiting for *Junkie* to appear, and intended to follow it with *Queer*; Cassady, as Kerouac said (wrongly), was WRITING A GREAT NOVEL, and Corso and Ginsberg had collections of poems ready for the publisher, if only they could find one.

Ginsberg's title was 'Empty Mirror', a comment, maybe, on his haunting by vacancy as he attempted to remould his old homosexual, 'mad' (in both senses) self: 'I have dwelled on Hell on earth to write this rhyme, / I live in stillness now'. He approached William Carlos Williams – like him, a native of New Jersey – and asked the eminent poet if he would write a preface to his unpublished book. Williams obliged, presenting Ginsberg with a *tour de force* of flattering generality that mentioned Dante half a dozen times and the author of *Empty Mirror* once. The only lines of poetry quoted in the two-page preface to the collection – which would not be published for several years – were taken from the *Inferno*. Nevertheless, Williams came close to a true characterization of Ginsberg's work when he wrote that the poems in *Empty Mirror* 'sway to a beat that is far removed from the beat of dancing feet but rather finds it in the shuffling of human beings in all the stages of their day, the trip to the bathroom, to the stairs of the subway . . . the mystical measure of their passions'.

This is the libertine circle, 'Rimbauds and Verlaines of New York'.

Continuing on his mission to be sane, Ginsberg found one job on a newspaper, another writing advertising copy, yet another in market research. It might have helped to make him normal, but it did nothing to make him happy. In a poem written at the time, 'My Alba', he reflected that he had 'wasted / five years in Manhattan / life decaying / talent a blank'. In the evenings, he was seen with girls, but at night he dreamt about boys: 'O dear sweet rosy / unattainable desire'.

One person who was attracted to the loquacious, intelligent, but not libidinous (or at any rate not heterosexually libidinous) poet was Alene Lee, a black woman from Staten Island. In 1953, Ginsberg was living at 206 East Seventh Street, between Avenues B and C, on the Lower East Side, while working at a firm which did consumer surveys about cosmetics. Alene Lee lived nearby, on the corner of East 11th Street and Avenue A, in a building which contained a wide, busy courtyard, known as Paradise Alley – 'a big 20-family tenement of bay windows', as Kerouac described it, 'the wash hung out in the afternoon the great symphony of Italian mothers, children, fathers . . . yelling from stepladders, smells, cats mewing, Mexicans, the music of all the radios . . .' Traditionally an Italian neighbourhood, Paradise Alley had lately become the haunt of members of the hipper fringe of the Village scene, to which Alene Lee belonged.

As 'cool' was transformed into a tourist attraction, as Hollywood actors were heard to say 'You dig?' on screen, as the San Remo and the Kettle of Fish began to draw standing-room-only crowds at weekends, Hip stepped back, obscuring itself in the underground shadows, before turning up elsewhere, among a different crowd, in different bars – the latest residences being the Minetta Tavern, in tiny Minetta Lane, and the nearby Fugazzi's Bar and Grill on Sixth Avenue. The inhabitants – Stanley Gould, Anton Rosenberg, Alene Lee and others – nuanced their diction and their dress at the sharp edge, listened to the harder jazz, were familiar with the harder drugs, knew which books were in and why, and why and when the last in-things went out. Kerouac called this crowd 'the subterraneans'. Rosenberg, a painter and off-hours bop pianist, was 'the angel of the subterraneans', hipper than thou, and he was with Alene Lee when Kerouac first set eyes on her. Kerouac, who was far too forthright and vulnerable-sincere ever to be considered truly hip, coveted both the desirable aura that hung over the languid, heroin-using subterranean and the desirable black girl by his side.

Alene Lee could see that her group of ultra-hip friends 'didn't want to know him. They couldn't understand why he was coming at them.' But she herself, round-faced and headscarfed, was appealingly friendly, and she took up with the softer-edged, poetry-writing beat crowd. She was also in therapy and Ginsberg, whom she met first, found that less than appealing. His life was filled to the brim with therapy. He was living according to the A-B-C of therapy-dictated normality. As related by Kerouac, who was about to take over and begin an affair with Alene, Ginsberg put forward another reason for not responding to her: 'It's too much for me', Kerouac had him say in the account he wrote of the affair, 'and finally being a Negro I don't want to get all involved.'

We can ignore the solecism (Alene was the Negro, not Ginsberg), but the prejudice is startling: I don't want to get involved with her because she's black.

The sentiment would not have seemed so exceptional in 1953; but even if Ginsberg did not say the words attributed to him by Kerouac, they do get to the heart of Kerouac's own feelings: Alene's 'being a Negro' was both what attracted him to her, and what repelled him. The short, chaotic novel he wrote about their relationship, *The Subterraneans*, is structured round her exotic status, the sexual tug it exerts, and his romantic belief that the Negro was 'the essential American'. In successive scenes in the novel, however, the narrator's desire is stripped with unsparing candour, to disclose a mortal fear of the very same exotic quality – 'blackness' – that had aroused him.

You be Rimbaud, I'll be Verlaine . . . This time it was Alene Lee as the brown mistress Jeanne Duval to Kerouac's delirious Baudelaire. But that was a mere game of dressing up, yet another attempt to 'pass' and live for a day on the other side of the trick wall that bounds and regulates civilized society. The heavier burden of the story of *The Subterraneans* is how Alene – Mardou Fox in the novel – will, with her rich colour and its associated mythical passport into a life of the senses, destroy the narrator Leo's 'white man's life'.

The improvisatory technique which Kerouac had evolved while revising *On the Road* for Ace Books – 'sketching', he called it – was shaped by his liking for jazz, his belief that jazz was the essential American art form, and his feeling that no one else before him had seen the potential scope of a jazz prose. Kerouac's model for this new and self-consciously American melody line was adopted from the tenor man, 'blowing a phrase on his saxophone till he runs out of breath, and when he does, his sentence, his statement's been made'.

Kerouac's understanding of music is poetic rather than formal or even historical. In spite of his admiration for Charlie Parker, Dizzy Gillespie, Billie Holiday, Oscar Peterson and others, there is a striking absence, in his letters and books, of the sociology of black music, of the history that brought it into being. Nor is there much appreciation of the complexity of black taste and black life; of, for example, religious people's disapproval of blues and jazz, or of the snobberies and aspirations of the black middle class in general. He knew nothing of the colour prejudice that existed in black communities, which equated a light complexion with beauty and virtue and a black skin with their opposites. Kerouac's black was monochrome and monotonous: when he saw black, he heard bop.

Aware of this, Mardou Fox in *The Subterraneans* objects to being cast in a stereotyped role. When the narrator, Leo Percepied – Jack Kerouac – mentions modern jazz, Mardou's riposte surprises him: 'I don't like bop, I really don't, it's like junk to me, too many junkies are bop men and I hear the junk in it.' This rejection cannot unfasten Leo's grip on his stereotypes, and he persists: 'You never like what you come from. You're the child of bop.'

The Subterraneans progresses by way of long, highly coloured paragraphs which are loosely related to the impromptu streams of notes produced by a jazz musician. It is an attempt at a bop novel, in which the author wraps himself in a motley of themes and writes his way out. *The Subterraneans* was composed in three days. It is white man's art adapted from black, mixing exuberant and melancholy rhythms with what Kerouac himself believed to be an unsurpassable technique. 'I have completely reached my peak maturity now', he told Holmes the year before, crowning his usual comparisons of himself to the greats of world literature. The irony of *The Subterraneans* is that the black-based style is utilized in fearful defence of 'the white man's life'.

Kerouac did not read any contemporary black literature, and the same is probably true of Burroughs, Ginsberg, and Corso, despite it being the time when the Negro writer had at last become visible. Richard Wright was the first to be seen, with *Native Son*, which had reached the top of the bestseller list in 1940; five years later, his autobiography, *Black Boy*, the harrowing story of a Mississippi upbringing in the 1920s, emulated the novel's success. Ralph Ellison's *Invisible Man* – a novel which employs the conceit of improvisatory jazz techniques to express the skills required by the Negro for day-to-day survival – won the National Book Award for Fiction in 1952. The bright young Baldwin's first novel, *Go Tell It on the Mountain*, was published in the spring of 1953, six months before Kerouac composed *The Subterraneans*, and Baldwin's essays, written in a delicately modulated prose with Biblical inflections and bluesy ornaments, had been appearing in prominent journals for the past five years.

But 'the "Hip" (the Knowing)' read none of it, or if they did they never talked or corresponded about it; nor did Kerouac ever look or listen to an older generation of Afro-American poets, including Sterling Brown and Langston Hughes, who incorporated the rhythms of jazz and blues into their work, and, correspondingly, the rhythms of lives lived in time to the *beat* of the music.

The 'essential American' is spotted in a variety of guises in early Beat Generation traffic, sometimes as an object of fear or revulsion, sometimes of condescension, sometimes of romantic affiliation, but rarely just as himself or herself, as an American. There is Burroughs's redneck snarl as he receives the news from north of the Mexican border, 'Nigra laws eh?'; there are 'mad nigger joints' (Cassady to Kerouac), and 'good tea, yep, I met a nigger and brought some home' (Cassady to Ginsberg), and all the 'laughing', 'sensuous', 'patient', spiritual-moaning, blues-humming blacks of *On the Road*. Carl Solomon wrote to Ginsberg that he had found existence 'to display the affectations of a bloodthirsty Negro homosexual'; Ginsberg incorporated the aphorism into a poem, interpreting it to mean that 'the core of being is in human terms a frightening prospect'. One night in Denver, a 'big buck nigger' leered at Cassady's sister-in-law, causing a bunch of his relatives to pile into a car and head for the Negro section of town, intent on finding 'a dark goat to castrate' (not the one who leered, just any one).

Like Cassady (who wrote indignantly of the episode, without saying if the lynch-mob ever achieved its objective), Kerouac was introduced to racism at home. His mother was apt to spray insults at any of his friends whose race or nationality did not meet her approval – and no race besides the 'white' race did. The Jew Ginsberg was forbidden to enter the house. One of Kerouac's girlfriends was called a 'spic savage'. His father, Leo (the name Kerouac gave himself in *The Subterraneans*), was no different. During the war, he had tried to talk his son out of enlisting in the Navy, claiming that it was 'a war for Commie Marxist Jews'. One day, while walking down a street on the Lower East Side, arm in arm with Kerouac's mother, Leo came up against 'a whole bunch of rabbis . . . and they wouldn't part for this Christian man and his wife'. Kerouac recalled that 'my father went POOM! and he knocked a rabbi right in the gutter'. In 1952, Kerouac could refer to Carl Solomon as 'punk Jew Solomon'.

As with the scroll version of *On the Road*, the original *Subterraneans* contained the real names of its characters, and real locations, in addition to descriptions of actual events and conversations. Ideally, Kerouac would have preferred not to make 'fiction', in the conventionally understood sense, out of his stories at all. His practice now was to allow the imagination to play freely over remembered – though not invented – incidents as he wrote. The first version of *The Subterraneans* was set in New York, where the actual events described in it took place. Later, for legal reasons, he was constrained to shift the action to San Francisco. Paradise Alley became Heavenly Lane on Telegraph Hill, overlooking the Bay, though the atmosphere of 'Dostoevsky's Petersburg slums', and the 'narrow musty stairs' leading up to Mardou's 'hovel', were drawn from East 11th Street, New York.

Like Adam, the Ginsberg character, who is put off by Mardou's race and by her being in therapy ('always talking about it and really too much for my liking'), Leo has doubts at first about the wisdom of getting involved with her. What sort of doubts?

> Doubts . . . of, well, Mardou's Negro naturally not only my mother and my sister whom I may have to live with some day and her husband a Southerner would be mortified to hell and would have nothing to do with us . . .

The candour, and the honest obedience to instinct – that blood is thicker than water – are in their way admirable; less so is the absence of any criticism, or even questioning, of the racist fortifications enclosing his mother, sister and brother-in-law's lives; equally, the absence of consideration of any other option available besides excluding Mardou – whom Leo tells us repeatedly he loves – from his dream of the future:

> That Faulknerian pillar homestead in the Old Grandad moonlight I'd so long envisioned for myself . . . what would they say if my mansion lady wife was a black Cherokee, it would cut my life in half . . .

Leo admits to seeing Mardou as 'really a thief of some sort and therefore out to steal my white man's heart, a Negress sneaking the world sneaking the holy white men for sacrificial rituals later . . .'

As the story draws to a close, Mardou and Leo separate; for her, there have been too many drunken conclusions to the evenings, too much 'barging in on people and going this place and the other', too many abandonments at unexpected moments (Leo might climb into a taxicab and disappear with someone else after a night in a bar, leaving her on the corner); for him, the relationship contains too great a threat to his 'white man's heart'. When he discovers that Mardou has spent a night with the ragamuffin poet Yuri Gligoric (Corso), the romance is over.

But the romanticism is unchallenged and unchanged. Lovesick and repentant over the loss of Mardou, Leo wanders at night into a railway freightyard. As he reflects on his often foolish attitudes and behaviour, he begins to weep, and through his tears, he beholds a woman's face, accompanied by an auditory hallucination of her voice. She says: 'Poor Little Leo, poor little Leo, you suffer, men suffer so . . . I would very much like to take care of you all my days my angel.'

Leo hears the words in French. It is not his Baudelairean mistress who reaches out to him in his vision, however, but Gabrielle Lévesque Kerouac; not the black face of his lover that he sees, but 'the visage of my mother'.

Kerouac gave Mardou Fox 'an unknown Cherokee halfbreed father'; she had 'eyes of Indian watchfulness', a 'slightly Mongoloid' nose, a facial structure 'like the face on a beautiful porphyry mask . . . Aztecean'; in a bad humour, he was apt to lump her together with

'Mexican gal or Negress . . . "hustlers", they're all the same'. Or else, suddenly invoking deeper African roots, he would see Mardou/ Alene as 'the first, the essential woman . . . Eden's in Africa'. In life, Kerouac transported Alene Lee to Asia, telling his friends that she was Indian; when she was introduced to Lucien Carr, Lucien enquired: 'And what part of India are you from?'

Burroughs had also gone in search of the primitive, but there was no evasive romanticism involved in his voyage (and no 'on the road': where Burroughs was going there weren't any roads). His adventure in the jungles of South America was closer in spirit to a scientific expedition, the object being to experiment with yagé, and confirm or deny rumours of its telepathic powers. The basis of his enquiry was hardly strong. 'In South America at the headwaters of the Amazon', he wrote in *Queer*,

> grows a plant called Yagé that is supposed to increase telepathic sensitivity. Medicine men use it in their work. A Colombian scientist, whose name escapes me, isolated from Yagé a drug he called Telepathine.

How did he come to know all this? 'I read [it] in a magazine article.'

Burroughs embarked on a six-month trip, comically underprepared. Throughout, he kept up a correspondence with Ginsberg, which he hoped would form the final, revelatory chapter in his trilogy: from the hell of narcotics addiction, to the lesser, yet comparable torment of love-addiction, to freedom on a layer of consciousness beyond the reach of control, induced by yagé. (As with *Queer*, the yagé episode would not be published for many years, but even at this stage Burroughs intended that his letters from South America should form an epistolary novel.)

In Bogotá, Burroughs had the good fortune to encounter a team of professional botanists, American, English and Colombian, who were on an expedition sponsored by the Cocoa Commission; their brief was to encourage the Indians to plant rubber trees, and to try to discover the causes of the cocoa disease, broom. The expedition was led by Richard Evans Schultes, a world authority on hallucinogenic plants. Although he was puzzled by Burroughs's interest in the drug, Schultes none the less advised him about the best regions in which to find yagé, and what to do to counter its inevitable ill-effects. He also passed on his own experience of having taken it: 'I got colours', Schultes told Burroughs, 'but no visions.'

In some Amazonian tribes, the drug formed part of the creation myth. The Macuna Indians, for example, believed that they had sailed down the Milky Way in a canoe driven by an anaconda snake, with a triple cargo of tapioca, coca shrubs, and yagé. Preparation of yagé differed from place to place. Certain tribes chopped the vine into sections, which were then pounded with a rock by the *brujo*, or medicine man, and boiled in water with the leaves of another plant. When the mixture was reduced to a thick, oily substance, it was ready to drink. Elsewhere, the bark was considered the essential ingredient, scraped off the vine and soaked in cold water for a day, before being mashed and supped.

After a solo trial run on the Colombia–Ecuador border, in which he had no success in finding yagé, Burroughs teamed up with the Schultes expedition, and eventually got his hands round a cupful of the secret potion. The effects were not what he had hoped for. The local medicine man in Macoa was around seventy, he told Ginsberg,

with a baby smooth face, a sly gentleness about him like an old-time junkie. The liquid was oily and phosphorescent. I drank it straight down. Bitter foretaste of nausea . . .

After a few minutes, dizziness swept over him and the hut began spinning.

It was like going under ether, or when you are very drunk and lie down and the bed spins. Blue flashes passed in front of my eyes. The hut took on an archaic far Pacific look with Easter Island heads carved in the support posts. The assistant was outside lurking there with the obvious intent to kill me . . . I must have vomited six times . . . My arms and legs began to twitch uncontrollably. I reached for my nembutals with numb wooden fingers. It must have taken me ten minutes to open the bottle and pour out five capsules. Mouth was dry and I chewed the nembutals down somehow. The twitching spasms subsided slowly and I felt a little better . . . Next morning I was all right except for a feeling of lassitude and slight backlog nausea. I paid off the Brujo and walked back to town.

When he had recovered from his initiation, Burroughs continued to experiment. After sampling preparations of yagé in several different regions, always at the hands of the local *brujo*, he had a pleasanter trip, experiencing a feeling of serenity and 'possession by a blue spirit'. But it did not endow him with telepathic powers.

There were other dangers in tropical travel: worms, dysentery, a TB scare; and also the thieving habit of the boys Burroughs paid for sex:

> May 12: They'll steal all your fucking valuables (I lost my watch and $15 . . .)

> May 23: Rolled for the [$270] check . . . by a kid I picked up . . .

> May 24: *Ho hum dept.* Rolled again. My glasses and a pocket knife . . . This is a nation of kleptomaniacs.

The most valuable lesson to emerge from this botanical-cum-anthropological expedition was that the proper medium for Burroughs's talent was the letter, and that Ginsberg was the proper recipient. In among the yagé letters were a couple of 'routines'. The routine was a surreal skit, frequently a nightmarish sexual, scatological comedy involving both real and invented characters. He sent Ginsberg 'Roosevelt After Inauguration', which featured Jerk Off Annie, transvestite Lizzie, and Subway Slim, typical Burroughs characters of the future in embryo.

Returning to New York in the summer, Burroughs pitched his tent at Ginsberg's place on East 7th Street. He had brought a bunch of yagé vines with him from the jungle, and took pleasure in chopping them up with a machete in the living-room, in front of startled visitors.

Behind the beat

Broyard

What of the Hipikat now? There were a few blacks among the beat and subterranean crowds, but the Village overall extended a mean welcome, and the book-loving young black was apt to feel like a fugitive downtown and a misfit up on Lenox Avenue. Baldwin, once a Village denizen, had decamped to Paris at the end of the 1940s. He was driven out, he told the editor of *Partisan Review*, William Phillips, by a 'violent, anarchic, hostility breeding' pattern of racism which, once 'turned inward', had the power to kill.

Baldwin remained in Paris while the Beat Generation was conceived, born and raised. A few years into its infancy, the older black poet and editor, Arna Bontemps, having seen a collection of photographs of fashionable young writers in a magazine, wrote to Langston Hughes to ask 'whether or not you know Anatole Broyard. His picture . . . makes him look Negroid. If so, he is the only spade among the Beat Generation.'

Bontemps was not the only one to ask the question about Broyard, who had obituarized the hipster back in 1948, just as Holmes and Kerouac were baptizing the Beat. Five years later, his literary reputation was surprisingly advanced, given that it was based on a handful of essays and semi-autobiographical stories. They were stylish and intelligent pieces. In addition to 'Death of the Hipster', Broyard had written 'Keep Cool, Man: The Negro rejection of jazz', and 'Portrait of the Inauthentic Negro', an analysis of the effect of a pitiless environment – 'violent, anarchic, hostility breeding' – on the black personality, modelled on Sartre's essay, *Anti-Semite and Jew*.

The theme of Broyard's piece, which appeared in the magazine *Commentary*, was that the persona the Negro shows to the world is not to be trusted – not even by the Negro himself, whose protective poses have blended so harmoniously with his own skin that they have become his 'real' self; he is a walking survival kit.

Readers of Broyard's articles, and of the biographical note which described him as an 'anatomist of the Negro personality in a white world', would have assumed that he was black. But Broyard had stored his black identity in his parents' home in Brooklyn, and now presented himself to the world as white. The strategies employed in perfecting this deception were subtle, involving, eventually, literary production. In his early articles, Broyard made no attempt to mask the fact that he himself was black, but in a story written at about this time, he changed colour. 'Sunday Dinner in Brooklyn' replays the familiar contemporary theme of the ambitious son estranged from lowly parents who have sacrificed everything in order to enable him to fulfil his ambition of putting them and their values behind him. Readers who had taken Broyard's blackness for granted would have had the assumption confounded by his latest piece:

> When [my father] wasn't talking about boxing, his remarks were designed to show me that he was a liberal, a man who understands. Yesterday he gave up his seat in the subway to a Negress . . .

'Sunday Dinner in Brooklyn' is fiction, but the autobiographical skeleton behind it is clearly discernible, as if Broyard were laying a trail at the end of which, he hoped, the reader would come upon a white author. The father in the story is a carpenter, as was Broyard's father Paul; the son, given the proper name 'Paul' in the story, is more familiarly known as 'Buddy', which was Broyard's nickname in life; the parents, like Broyard's, live humbly in Brooklyn, and they project their hopes for a better future on to their son, who has migrated to the Village. All of it was true of Broyard. When he slipped his token into the slot at the subway station in Brooklyn, he was black; by the time he came up the steps in Manhattan, he was white.

In 1952, Broyard was made the subject of someone else's fiction: *Who Walk in Darkness*, by Chandler Brossard, is occasionally credited with being one of the first novels to make 'the "Hip" (the

148

Knowing)' its subject matter. The question of the protagonist's race – a question which Arna Bontemps was to repeat six years later – occurs in the opening sentence of the novel as Brossard wrote it. The author also managed to work in a thread from one of Broyard's own subjects, namely the gulf between the mask and the face it shields:

> People said Henry Porter was a Negro. But nobody knew for sure. I think the rumour was started by someone who had grown up with Porter in San Francisco. I suspect it was supposed to explain the difference between the way he behaved and the way the rest of us behaved. Porter did not show that he knew people were talking about him this way. I must give him credit for maintaining a front of indifference that was really remarkable.

Among the people 'talking about' Porter are Brossard's narrator, Blake, and his friend Harry Lees. Together with a few girls – one of whom, Grace, is attached to Porter but coveted by Blake – they go to a jazz club, where Porter shines on the dance floor (Broyard was famed for his dancing) and is seen to be on first-name terms with the black musicians. He makes attempts to deflect attention from his 'secret' by playing up his own race-related cynicism, scoffing at 'spade intellectuals' who 'think they've got it made' when they date a white girl. At the end of a novel, there is a showdown between Porter and Harry Lees, who asks Porter if what people have been saying is true. A scene ensues, and Porter departs, abandoning his girl, Grace, who falls into the protective embrace of Blake, one of Kerouac's 'holy white men'.

Who Walk in Darkness is a mucky piece of work. Whereas *The Subterraneans* is naïve and, in places, childlike in its clumsy honesty, the premiss of Brossard's novel is overtly and coldly racist. The idea that people were talking about Porter's furtive backness survives only in the French edition of *Who Walk in Darkness* (published as *Ciel de nuit* in 1954); for the American one, under threat of legal action by Broyard himself, the publishers altered 'a Negro' to 'an illegitimate', which leaves the reader puzzled at Blake's nudging remark about 'the difference between the way he behaved and the way the rest of us behaved'. In the original, also, Porter, like Broyard, was from Brooklyn; the amended version has him growing up in San Francisco. This, too, survived only in the French. ('Le bruit courait que Henry Porter avait du sang nègre ... Cette rumeur avait été lancée par une de ses camarades d'enfance de Brooklyn.')

Broyard lived out a 'white' life. He became a book critic on the *New York Times*, and kept many among his wide circle of literary acquaintance in ignorance of the fact that he was born into an Afro-American family. His skill on the dance floor crossed back over into his prose style, which is liquidly elegant, at its best, and, in its own way, hip. His denial of a part of himself must have inhibited the free dancing of his natural talents – which is ironic, as he was apt to base literary judgments on his estimate of the distribution of that gift in others. Here he is looking back at the *Partisan Review* editors who first encouraged his reflections on the subject (with perhaps, a sideways swipe at Brossard, who worked at the *New Yorker*):

> I had always felt that life was a rhythmical process. When I was happy, my rhythms, my tuning, were good – everything danced – and when I was unhappy, I didn't have any rhythm at all. It was my secret conviction that Delmore [Schwartz] and the other writer-intellectuals had very little sense of rhythm. It wasn't just that Delmore, for example, was clumsy – it went further than that. As Kenneth Burke said, the symbolic act is the *dancing* of an attitude – and I thought there was something about the way the New York intellectuals danced their attitudes. There was not much syncopation in their writing.

PART II

. . . further and further out

7

Sutra on the subway

'What joy! The nakedness!'
– Allen Ginsberg

The change in Allen Ginsberg's domestic life, which led to a change in his poetry, which disturbed American poetry as a consequence, and which caused a tremor of change in American society as a whole, can be traced back to a conversation with a doctor in San Francisco one day at the beginning of 1955.

Ginsberg had been attending sessions with an analyst called Philip Hicks, at Langley Hospital, a West Coast equivalent of the Columbia PI. He confided to Dr Hicks his fears that, after a faltering but, largely (he felt), convincing term as a heterosexual, office worker, good citizen, a sane type capable of stressing his father's genes rather than his mother's, he was standing on the brink of the pit of love once again. And in the pit was a young man. He told his doctor what he later told his journal: 'My mind is crazed by homosexuality.'

Dr Hicks pondered the matter. Then he asked: 'What would you like to do?'

Ginsberg admitted that what he wanted to do was live with Peter Orlovsky, the young man in question, to give up his job in advertising, and to write poems.

'Why don't you do that?' asked Dr Hicks.

yes, yes,
that's what

153

I wanted,
   I always wanted,
I always wanted
   to return
to the body
   where I was born

★

Before coming West in June 1954 – out of a desire to see Cassady – Ginsberg discovered Chinese art in the East. During a period of unemployment, he had spent his days browsing in the New York Public Library and had come upon

> book upon book of reproduction – coolie made volumes sewn together on fine linen paper by laundrymen in Shang-hai . . . China is a bleak great blank in our intimate knowledge.

Most of the Buddhist writings he read, Ginsberg continued in his letter to Cassady, were of no interest, 'vague etc because it has no context to us'; but the pictorial art gave him 'a very beautiful kick'. His enthusiasm led to a poem, written right there in the library, inspired by a painting of Sakyamuni ('a later form of Buddha, I think') coming down from his mountain hermitage. Here, for the first time, 'beat' is given a suggestion of what would be its favoured later gloss, 'beatitude':

He drags his bare feet
out of a cave . . .

    unhappy hands
clasped to his naked breast –
humility is beatness

Emerging from his mountainside cave, the beat Buddha appeared to be an icon of self-sufficiency, spiritually fortified against money worries, parent pressure, sex that crazed the mind, Lionel Trilling. Although Buddhist writing held little appeal, Ginsberg nevertheless told Cassady that he liked the Zen idea of philosophic insight triggered by an act of absurdity. He related a number of anecdotes to Cassady – including one in which a novice monk satisfactorily

154

answers a Zen master's question about what do with a disputed cat by placing his shoes on top of his head and walking out of the room. Zen reminded him of his old partner at the Columbia PI, 'Kirillov', and the Dadaist acts which had got him incarcerated. Here was a new Beat kinship: traceable from Carl Solomon, through Artaud, to Buddha.

As the years went by, while he struggled to get out of youth into maturity, whenever he looked to see where his fabulous freedom had brought him, Neal Cassady found he had just completed another aimless circuit in the track event that was his life. He knew of no way to use his energy, but nor had he any way to tame it, nor a place to confine it. It just inhabited him, like a monkey at loose in the house.

Kerouac and Ginsberg went on urging him to write, but Cassady knew that he could not, and this knowledge, and the knowledge that others didn't understand that his wild-man performances stemmed from artistic sterility, was the source of frustration and sadness. The crafts in which he was unsurpassable were little crafts: driving a car; doing the railroad brakeman's job on the Southern Pacific.

In the course of his work the previous year, Neal had had an accident. A fall from a moving train had almost severed his foot. As part of the medical examination, he was obliged to undergo some Rorschach inkblot tests, the contemporary favourite of psychologists. The results labelled him 'a sociopathic personality with schizophrenic and manic-depressive tendencies that could develop into psychosis'. The tests also threw up evidence that he was sexually sadistic.

Carolyn Cassady's optimistic nature kept her hoping that Neal's demons could be exorcized – by love, by domestic stability – and that family life could begin at last. The family (there were three children, not to mention the son Neal had with his bigamous wife, now abandoned, Diana Hansen) had moved fifty miles south of San Francisco, renting a house with plenty of room and a garden in the town of San Jose. He had restarted work on the railroad – the perfect job for Neal, providing routine motion between fixed points. The children were at various stages of infancy, all delightful; Carolyn and Neal were fixing up the house, and progressing towards comfort and calm. Her terminus was Domestic Bliss, and with her railroad man she was getting there.

But Neal was frequently restless (Carolyn later referred to the quiet times as having him 'in harness'). San Jose was nicknamed 'Nowheresville'. Neal had written to Ginsberg that he was 'a blank and getting more so'. In 1954, the legendary life-force, Neal Cassady, saw himself as Mr Blank living in Nowheresville.

So here came Allen Ginsberg – Allen the Stranger, as he had lately signed a letter to Carolyn – on his way West:

> If I had a Green Automobile
> I'd go find my old companion
> in his house on the Western ocean.
> Ha! Ha! Ha! Ha! Ha!

Would he succeed in filling the blank? He certainly intended to try. And he expected to be put up at the Cassadys'. What would he do when he arrived? 'I'd honk my horn at his manly gate' . . .

> We'll go riding
> over the Rockies
> we'll go riding
> all night long until dawn

Neal welcomed Ginsberg, but Carolyn barely tolerated him. His inverse sexuality, and the knowledge of its past claim on her husband, made her queasy at the best of times, but now it was like the introduction of electricity into a dark house. The Cassadys had a mutually acknowledged bedroom truce. He found it frustrating, she called it peace. He was priapic, she admitted she was frigid. Cassady masturbated 'every day at least three times', he told Kerouac. Before his marriage to Carolyn, he used to have 'all-day orgies where lying there by myself I think of a woman . . . & come 11 and more times in 6–7 hours'. Sex with more than one woman in a day was commonplace. Carolyn called it 'a sexual problem'. When he had sex with her, she felt that 'it had to be violent . . . like rape'.

She had rejoiced the previous year, when Neal joined her in seeking relief from his burden in religion. Together, they became followers of the 'psychic theurgist', Edgar Cayce, a believer in reincarnation, and eagerly expounded his teachings to one another and to Ginsberg. No household problem was so large or so small that it could not be soothed by applying the balm of Caycespeak. 'Mind is the builder. Thoughts are things.' 'You reach Heaven leaning on the arm of someone you have helped.' 'The stronger you are, the tougher the tests.' The Cassadys even called their cocker spaniel Cayce.

Ginsberg and Cassady were not discussing Cayce when Carolyn unintentionally interrupted them in Allen's room one afternoon. All the while Ginsberg was with them, she must have been seeing, somewhere in her mind, the picture of him and LuAnne and Neal together in bed in Denver, back in 1947. Now, as she tapped gently on the door and entered, without pausing for a reply, she saw her husband on his back on the bed, trousers down, and Ginsberg enjoying a meal of oral sex. Carolyn said she felt her stomach turn over. She let out a scream, but had the presence of mind to note that Ginsberg 'lifted his head towards me quizzically'.

'No one meets a circumstance he hasn't the power to overcome', Cayce taught, but this one was too much for Carolyn. Ginsberg left San Jose immediately, his Western adventure in ruins, like all his other adventures. He felt like a 'lovesick queer', a 'pervert'. That kind of love, he wrote in his journal, 'is a *sickness*, must be cured'. He beseeched himself to find 'Strength! to kill the whole affair' with Neal. But then, in the next line of the same entry (17 August) he wailed: 'to be free for what vapidity, what lack luster?' His poems of the early 1950s are stuffed with lines like 'How sick I am!' and 'Oh, God how horrible', and 'I have no hope and I am tired'. Kind Carolyn would have been touched by his repentance, but his sordid spiritual condition seemed to be visible to others. A friend of Holmes's, meeting him for the first time, told Holmes: 'I don't think I want him around my kids.'

When Ginsberg first set eyes on Peter Orlovsky, Orlovsky was naked, just as Cassady had been naked when first admired by Kerouac. The difference was that Ginsberg beheld his love-object in a painting. Then the painting came alive.

In Foster's Cafeteria in North Beach, San Francisco, Ginsberg had met a painter called Robert LaVigne, and, on being invited back to his apartment on Gough Street, was struck immediately by the portrait of a naked youth with tousled yellow hair, staring out of the canvas. He asked who it was. LaVigne called into the next room, and the real thing walked out (clothed) and was introduced. Before long, Ginsberg was sleeping with him, even though Orlovsky was primarily heterosexual – a strange feature of a relationship that was to involve a de facto 'marriage vow' and was to last for thirty years.

But then the Orlovskys were strange folk. The son of Russian immigrants, like Ginsberg himself, Peter had been raised in a converted chicken shack in Northport, Long Island, along with four other children. He was semi-literate, and described himself at the time of meeting Ginsberg as 'a dope, a creep, a hermit, a moron'. Although he liked girls, he felt helpless and invisible before them. Two of his brothers, Nicholas and Julius, were mentally ill, and another, Lafcadio, loved by those who met him for his pet-animal gentleness, teetered on the brink. His mother was deaf and partly paralysed. His father was often violent. Both parents were alcoholics.

Ginsberg took it all on, seeing redemption reflected in Orlovsky's idiot-savant innocence. After their meeting, Ginsberg began to shed the sanity that had been imposed on him by the doctors at Columbia PI, the professors at Columbia College, the worried family at home. He had never really succeeded in adapting to it. 'Oh, by the way', he had once told Holmes, 'gravely', 'I'm sane.' The session at Langley Porter Hospital, during which the analyst asked: 'What would you like to do?' was the overture to a striptease. Ginsberg peeled off his heterosexuality, then slipped out of his office-job collar and tie, finally divesting his verse of traditional forms. He continued the process of writing 'secretly', with no thought of publication and for no one else's eye or ear – just settling down, as he put it, 'in the muck of your own mind', to see if anything there was usable for art. 'Who will speak for his own wild naked mind will speak for the mass', Ginsberg announced in his journal in September 1955. 'We want to read the individual, not his public thoughts.' (The declaration led straight to yet another tilt at his old surrogate father: 'And Trilling doesn't think the individual is important ... He's rejected himself.') As a credo, it was deep in the American grain: Emerson's crystallization of the self as transcendental reference point, updated to 'Do your own thing.'

★

With a letter from William Carlos Williams in his pocket, Ginsberg sought out Kenneth Rexroth, one of the older San Francisco writers, and a natural father-figure to many of the young poets living in the Bay area. Almost fifty when Ginsberg came knocking, Rexroth had lived in Chicago before moving to San Francisco in the late 1920s. He chose the small West Coast city on purpose, as somewhere remote from the business centres of both commerce and literature. San Francisco, Rexroth said, was 'the only city in the US which was not settled overland by the westward-spreading puritan tradition, or by the Walter Scott fake-cavalier tradition of the South. It had been settled mostly ... by gamblers, prostitutes, rascals, and fortune seekers.' This suited a poet who was an anarchist in politics, and a champion of the radical and perverse in art.

From his bag, Rexroth unpacked, along with Gertrude Stein, the pamphlets of the Industrial Workers of the World movement (the Wobblies); along with James Joyce, Jack London; along with Pound's make-it-new translations from the Chinese, Thoreau's Orientally inflected musings on Walden Pond. By the time the war ended, Rexroth was at the centre of an intellectual group whose members were, in different degrees, disobedient in politics, experimental in verse, and mystical in religion. Among his allies were writers as diverse as Kenneth Patchen, Robert Duncan, Madeline Gleason, and Philip Lamantia; together they nurtured a postwar avant-garde on the Pacific rim, moving contrariwise to the New Criticism of Brooks and Warren, rejecting the unsyncopated New York quarterlies for their devotion to Eliot and obedience to his canonical strictures.

Rexroth wanted an 'I to thee' type of poetry. In the course of achieving it, he took to the stage with musicians and read aloud to jazz accompaniment. As well as being aesthetically testing in itself, this fulfilled two functions: it broke the mould of 'publication', and it kept up the bardic tradition in American poetry. Rexroth was equally at home in lyrical and polemical modes; he took elements from Oriental literature and religions, from modern radical politics, European modernism, and from other media when it suited him to do so, including journalism and music. His lament for Dylan Thomas, 'Thou Shalt Not Kill', is a typical blast from the dissenting horn:

You killed him,
Benign Lady on the postage stamp.
He was found dead at a *New Republic* luncheon.
He was found dead on the cutting room floor.
He was found dead at a *Time* policy conference.
Henry Luce killed him with a telegram to the Pope.
Mademoiselle strangled him with a padded brassiere.
Old Possum sprinkled him with a tea ball.

The young West Coast poets who regarded Rexroth as a mentor in the early 1950s, when Ginsberg arrived, shared no political programme, or literary programme, other than charting a direction in 'open form'; not Eliot's Frenchified *vers libre*, but an American line generated by American speech. Away from the formal, and back to the vernacular. Rexroth held Thursday night soirées at his home, where there would have been discussion of structuring the poetic cadence on the foundation of the breath, and suchlike refinements of the bardic manner. Robert Duncan, whose early mentors included Pound, Stein and Dylan Thomas, was engaged on a sequence entitled 'The Structure of Rime', of which the opening lines of the opening poem were

I ask the unyielding Sentence that shows Itself forth in the language as I make it,

Speak!

Rexroth could only be a good influence on Ginsberg. Hardly yet published, Ginsberg was in the habit of declaiming his poetry aloud, as a means of making it 'public'. (Carolyn Cassady was surprised when, one night in Neal's absence, he took off his clothes, lay down on the floor, and began to recite his poems.) Now the influence of Whitman and Williams converged with the poetic practice of the newly met San Francisco writers to increase his awareness of the elastic potential of his own line. In his journals, he continued his systematic study of prosody, imagery, and the effective use of ellipses and other devices, but the main project from now on was to allow imagination and desire free reign in the course of composing the poem; the structure ought to facilitate the poet's expression – if not actually to stem from it – never to inhibit it. ('In the feet that

160

measure the dance of my pages I hear cosmic intoxications of the man I will be' – Duncan.)

Since 1950, Ginsberg had been in correspondence with Williams, the anti-Eliot proponent of the American voice in poetry, and had already secured from him an introduction to his unpublished book. In 1955, he wrote again to Williams, enclosing a sheaf of new work intended to show what he had learned while working with the longer line. The term of reference was borrowed from Kerouac: 'The key is Jazz choruses to some extent; . . . With a long line comes a return to . . . expressive human feeling, it's generally lacking in poetry now, which is inhuman.'

One of Ginsberg's earliest attempts to write in a more spontaneous way was 'Love Poem on a Theme by Whitman', written in San Jose, and transparently about the *mariage blanc* of his hosts:

I'll go into the bedroom silently and lie down between the
    bridegroom and the bride,
those bodies fallen from heaven stretched out waiting naked and
    restless . . .

and I rise up from the bed replenished with last intimate gestures
    and kisses of farewell –
all before the mind wakes, behind shades and closed doors in a
    darkened house

(Shades and closed doors would have no place in the house which Ginsberg wished to share with Orlovsky.)

When he wrote to his father about his new insights, he mentioned a class that he taught at Ruth Witt-Diamant's Poetry Center at San Francisco State College, which functioned as the main institutional forum of the San Francisco Renaissance. He tried to get the students 'personally involved' in what they were writing, he told Louis (who continued to hope for normality in his son's life, and for decorum in his verse), and came down heavy on anything that struck him as self-consciously literary: 'I try to get them to actual [*sic*] express secret life in whatever form it comes out. I practically take my clothes off in class myself to do it.'

The desire to make the personal public had existed since the days when Ginsberg had feared to make his homosexuality known to Kerouac and Carr. Therapy, at last, had led him to conquer shame, and poetry was now becoming therapy by other means. The change was precipitated by the clement San Francisco air, which was kinder to the 'aberrant, idiosyncratic' developments in the arts, which Rexroth saw as characteristic of the age.

Ginsberg soon made friends among the local poets, while Robert LaVigne introduced him to other painters. With his endearing mixture of shyness and a desire to put himself forward, his comprehensive openness to others who were more shy, his free-rolling, unending conversation about poetry and politics, his knowledge of and enthusiasm for literature of other ages and cultures, Ginsberg quickly painted himself into San Francisco's bohemian scene.

Among the painters he met was John Ryan, who was associated with a gallery on Fillmore Street called the Six. Ryan wrote a letter to Ginsberg about a jazz and poetry 'whing-ding' at the Cellar club, in which Rexroth – 'Rexwrawth', Ryan styled him – 'came on like Elvis Presley, doing the rhumba'. When Ginsberg wrote back, in the middle of 1955, he mentioned that another Six Gallery painter, Wally Hedricks, had asked him to organize a reading by some local poets at the gallery. Ginsberg thought about it, but decided against, as he told Ryan, 'not knowing of any poetry worth hearing'.

The pre-publication history of *On the Road* is a dismal catalogue of rejection, prevarication, changes of mind – then a moment's optimism, to be followed by more postponements. The pattern continued even after the book had been accepted for publication.

Following his quarrel with A. A. Wyn and all at Ace, amid the mess of scatology flung at him by Carl Solomon, Kerouac tried the book on other publishers. Harcourt Brace, which had done *The Town and the City* (dedicated by Kerouac to his editor there, Giroux), had already rejected it; Knopf rejected it; Dodd Mead rejected it; Farrar Straus rejected it. For a spell in 1952, the manuscript dropped from sight, and had to be recovered by Ginsberg from the offices of the MCA agency. 'I finally got up off my ass', he wrote to Kerouac, 'and went to MCA, where I found your ON THE ROAD chapter mss lost, forgotten and gathering dust on the bottom of a dusty closet . . .' Kerouac began to feel that it didn't matter what it was called ('The Heroes of the Hip

162

Generation' and 'Beat Generation' were his preferred alternatives to 'On the Road'), or who rejected the book next, and he began to toy with the negative relief of not publishing it at all.

His one serious hope was Viking. At the beginning of 1953, Malcolm Cowley, an editor there and a significant critic in his own right, had liked *On the Road* and seen its potential appeal to the younger generation. He did not think it could be published in its present form, however, and so he too rejected it. Unlike all of the other publishers, though, Cowley could envisage the book as it might be after the onslaught of heavy editing. He invited Kerouac to lunch, where he detailed his scheme of revision.

The main problem, according to Cowley, was *On the Road*'s sprawling, repetitive form. The book careered from one side of the continent to the other, then lurched back again. It did the same thing a second time, and then a third. Where's the development? asked Cowley. Where's the story?

Kerouac's attempts to explain that a novel such as *On the Road* – a novel without an A-B-C development, a bop novel whose essence is improvisation – needs no story beyond the story posted by the signs along the way, that the journey *was* the story, that anything could happen and that that was the daring of the exercise for the author and the excitement of it for the reader, did not convince Cowley. In a general essay on the craft of fiction, 'The Limits of the Novel', published in the *New Republic* a little later, Cowley set out his definition of narrative fiction; he undoubtedly said something similar to Kerouac during their meetings. A novel, Cowley wrote,

> is a long but unified story designed to be read at more than one sitting, that deals with a group of lifelike characters in a plausible situation and leads to a change in their relationships . . . On pain of early death for his book, [the novelist] must create a mood of expectancy.

On the Road did not satisfy those qualifications, though Cowley thought it might be made to do so with a lot of work.

Kerouac was unimpressed by Cowley's aesthetics. Behind his back, he called Cowley 'a semi-pedantic Vermont professor type with a hearing aid'. But he still wanted his book published; and by then he had two others: *Dr Sax*, the neon-burning story of his early childhood in Lowell, and *Maggie Cassidy*, about his love for a girl there.

In July 1953, Ginsberg, again working as Kerouac's agent, wrote to Cowley to say that Kerouac had done some new writing, including another version of *On the Road*. Would he be willing to read the manuscripts? Cowley responded with patience, but from the same standpoint:

> You are right in thinking that I am interested in Kerouac and his work. He seems to me the most interesting writer who is not being published today – and I think it is important that he should be published, or he will run the danger of losing that sense of the audience, which is part of a writer's equipment. But the only manuscript of his that I have read with a chance of immediate book publication is the first version of *On the Road*. As much of the second version as I saw contained some impressively good writing, but no story whatsoever.

Nevertheless, he agreed to read the new *On the Road*, which the faithful Ginsberg delivered to his office, and again he liked what he saw. Others at Viking also thought the book worth publishing, but they shared Cowley's reservations. One senior editor, Helen Taylor, agreed with his view that *On the Road* had the potential to be 'a classic for our times', but then she recommended 'publishing it quietly for the discerning few'. Her reading of the novel demonstrates why:

> I am not shocked by this portrayal of the hipster generation as a portrayal, but by the fact that the generation exists, and was constantly forced to think of the why of it. It is a life slice so raw and bleeding that it makes me terribly sad. It is the quintessence of everything that is bad and horrible about this otherwise wonderful age we live in. The trickles of evil run small and unnoticed throughout the pattern of life today, and here they come together in a flood, in a bunch of young people who are irretrievably gone in the literal sense of the word. There is no redemption for these psychopaths and hopeless neurotics, for they don't want any.

Another editor, Evelyn Levine, wrote that the book 'must be and will be eventually published'. Had he had the opportunity to read

Levine's internal memo, Kerouac would have welcomed it as being among the most sympathetic comments on his writing to date:

> I loved Kerouac's prose style, and the sense of poetic rhythm in the prose: as they're driving thru the country you can actually feel the US passing by, feel the actual speed of the car; throughout there is a Whitman-esque style of expression for the US . . . The style of the prose adds to the descriptive passages about jazz because it sounded exactly like bop music.

As for what disturbed her colleague, Helen Taylor – 'use of narcotics, drinking, immoral sexual relationships' – Ms Levine wrote: 'I don't think the author is exaggerating too much'. However, Levine was not a senior editor at Viking, and anyway she agreed that the manuscript of this 'jived-up Whitman' needed work. *On the Road* was returned to Kerouac.

Cowley still regarded him as one of the most exciting young writers on the scene, though, and said so in print. Writing in the *Saturday Review of Literature* in 1954 about a group of young people in society who 'talked about being "underground" and called themselves "the beat generation" ', Cowley told readers of the magazine that 'it was John Kerouac who invented the second phrase, and his unpublished long narrative, *On the Road*, is the best record of their lives'.

The compliment was paid as a result of Cowley having read the 'narrative' – he could not bring himself to call *On the Road* a novel – yet again in the summer of 1954. Yet again the pedantic Vermont professor endeavoured to steer the novel past the conservative Viking editorial board, and yet again he failed. In the meantime, Kerouac's list of refusals lengthened: E. P. Dutton had rejected *On the Road*, Little, Brown had rejected it, Ballantine and Vanguard were about to reject it. As the refusals piled up, so did the manuscripts.

He despaired, and passed on to a place beyond despair. Having received the latest bad-news bulletin from Cowley, Kerouac wrote to his new agent, Sterling Lord, to say that he was quitting New York to go and live with his mother and sister in North Carolina, and that he wished to sort out his affairs before leaving. This involved retrieving all his unpublished manuscripts from the agency's office. Kerouac enclosed the melancholy inventory: two typed copies of *Dr Sax*, two of *Maggie Cassidy*, two of *On the Road*; one copy each of *The Subterraneans*, *Visions of Neal*, and yet another new work, *Book of Dreams*; several articles. Ten houses or editors are mentioned on the list, as either reading or having read his various manuscripts, together with Kerouac's comments: 'Rejected ... Rejected ... No information ... Whereabouts unknown ... Unread ... Rejected ...' And, finally, a publisher's report on the 512-page *Visions of Neal*, which had begun life as a revision of *On the Road* but had grown into a separate book: 'Unpublishable'.

He intended to 'forget publishing'. As mercurial as ever, however, he changed his mind a week later, after receiving a token of success, the proofs of a chunk of *On the Road* which had been accepted by *New World Writing*: 'Jazz of the Beat Generation'. Although he went on down to North Carolina – where he immediately embarked on yet another book, an exploratory essay on his new obsession: 'Your Essential Mind: The story of Buddha' – he left his manuscripts with Sterling Lord, after all.

Then, in the middle of 1955, Cowley asked to see 'The Beat Generation' (as it was again called) once more. This time, as he sent to the Lord agency for the latest version of the book, he was confident of the backing of a new young editor, Keith Jennison. He cautioned Kerouac that even if the board could be persuaded to agree, in principle, to its publication – and he thought that it could be – there were still difficulties of obscenity and defamation to overcome. However, Cowley was more hopeful than ever before that if he, Kerouac and Jennison worked together, they could turn 'The Beat Generation' from a dog-eared manuscript into a published book.

Kerouac agreed with that. He did almost everything that Cowley (and later Jennison) suggested, including removing the passages which were thought to be libellous and getting clearances from those of his friends he hoped would not mind being depicted in the book. He allowed Cowley to make his own changes ('okay with me') and to compress the cross-country trips. And he agreed to change the title back to *On the Road*.

One thing which he would not agree to had nothing to do with Cowley or the future publication of *On the Road*. Ginsberg had written, asking him to read in front of an audience in San Francisco, but Kerouac refused. He was planning to go West to see his old friends the Cassadys, but he would not take part in any public reading. 'I'm too bashful', he told Cowley (who considered Ginsberg a bad influence on his author). Ginsberg, though, said Kerouac, 'gets up on stage and howls his poems'.

When first asked to organize a reading at a gallery in San Francisco, Ginsberg begged off; but within a month he had written to John Ryan to say that he would do it, after all. His enthusiasm was charged by the thought of reciting some new work to an audience composed of the San Francisco bohemian set. He had already made an impression as an experimenter in verse, and an enabler capable of fusing the creative energies of others. Ginsberg liked movements, circles, groups, boy-gangs, generations – artists hunted most successfully in packs.

He was in a productive period. The long line of 'Love Poem on a Theme by Whitman' suited his naturally voluble statement comfortably. In a single day in September, he wrote 'A Supermarket in California' –

What thoughts I have of you tonight, Walt Whitman, for I walked
 down the sidestreets under the trees with a headache self-
conscious looking at the full moon

– and another poem transported, like that one, along the line of the poet's breath, 'A Strange New Cottage in Berkeley':

All afternoon cutting bramble blackberries off a tottering brown
 fence under a low branch with its rotten old apricots
miscellaneous under the leaves . . .

Ginsberg had met some San Francisco poets of his own age whose work appealed to him. First, he was directed by Rexroth to Berkeley, to seek out Gary Snyder, whom Rexroth considered to be the best among the young writers in the Bay area. Synder was a small, singular man who combined in his wiry body the ascetic philosophy of the Far East and the industrious principles of the Far West. He belonged to a rare, but established, species in America: the backwoodsman who studies Zen by the campfire. Ginsberg described him as 'a head, peyotlist, laconist, but warmhearted, nice looking with a little beard, thin, blond, rides a bicycle in Berkeley in red corduroys and Levis'. Snyder's employment skills were of the logging, merchant-marine sort, but his tendency of mind – like other San Francisco poets, like Rexroth himself in one of his guises – reached over the Pacific to connect with Asian philosophy, myth and poetry. Snyder had studied Oriental languages at Berkeley University; as an undergraduate at Reed College, Oregon, he had written a thesis on the folklore of a Native American people, the Haida; he wove scraps of tribal lore into his patchwork poetry, overlapping squares of Japanese and Chinese literatures. Sometimes he was rudely realistic, though usually within the framework of an ecological good. Snyder's planet-friendly verse was composed mostly of short, simple words, creating a tight surface texture, reminiscent at once of Far Eastern lyric and of domestic craftwork, such as quilt-making or dry-stone-walling ('Lay down these words / Before your mind like rocks'). It had nothing in common with Ginsberg's – neither his old formalism nor his new, long-line confessionalism.

> Down valley a smoke haze
> Three days heat, after five days rain
> Pitch glows on the fir-cones
> Across rocks and meadows
> Swarms of new flies.
>
> I cannot remember the things I once read
> A few friends but they are in cities.

Snyder spent his summers in solitude, as a fire-lookout on Sourdough Mountain, Oregon, or as a choker for a lumber company. He took his Buddhism seriously, practising meditation with the Berkeley Young Buddhist Association, which published his Orientally inflected poems in its magazine. When Snyder wrote of 'The world like an endless / four-dimensional / Game of Go', no one for a second would mistake it for a shout of encouragement in an East Coast jazz dive.

As Ginsberg arrived in Berkeley to visit in order to talk about the projected reading, Snyder was outside his house mending a bicycle. It was a characteristic introduction to a poet who was also a handyman, who was usually mending, or trying to mend, something, whether it be a puncture on his back wheel or a forest denuded by greedy loggers. The cottage itself was monkish, with straw mats and a table made from orange crates. Ginsberg might have recalled the Buddha, Sakyamuni, whom he had discovered, in the NYPL, emerging from his mountain cave,

> in ragged soft robes
> > wearing a fine beard
> > > unhappy hands . . .

Snyder, whose hands were always at work, whose prayer was self-sufficiency, was planning to go to Japan, in order to see and study Buddhist hermits for himself. He told Ginsberg about another San Francisco poet, Philip Whalen, who was also in Buddhist 'mind'; and Ginsberg mentioned Jack Kerouac, who had recently begun to read the Sutras on the subways, to talk in his letters about Tathagata, dhyana, dharma, and to advise his old beat pals: 'Perturb not your vital essence.' Kerouac was on his way West, and would arrive in San Francisco in a few days' time, and so Ginsberg organized a rendezvous at which Snyder and his Buddhist friend Whalen could meet him.

Here began the San Francisco Beat scene, September 1955, eleven years on from the killing of Kammerer in New York, and the break-up of the first libertine circle.

Ginsberg, not mad now in Naomi's sense, nor 'mad' in Kerouac's, nor even 'sane' in Trilling's sense, was doing as the doctor ordered, that is, doing what he wanted to do. He was fired up by a new love, the new coast, new freedom from his routine (he had quit his job as a researcher in San Francisco's financial district), new poet friends, a new dimension in his verse and a new determination to be spontaneous on the stage it offered. The preference for open form over regular metre and the handcuffs of rhyme was accompanied, by poetic command, by a shift into the vernacular. The long verse-sentence capable of containing realms of association was not the legacy of Whitman alone. Ginsberg, whose mind housed poetry of all ages, and who had a capacious memory for verse, could see a link between Whitman and, for example, the blank verse of Milton (of whom Eliot remarked that he could go from Heaven to Hell in one 'line'); or between open form in poetry and the unfolding sentence of Melville, Thomas Wolfe, or – increasingly – Kerouac. The long line enabled an outpouring in poetry; outpouring suggested 'the full heart', and that was precisely the ground – the open road – of Ginsberg's new poetics.

His most audacious attempt to ride his aesthetic and create a poem in the performance happened one afternoon in August 1955. It drew its inspiration from the thoughts of Carl Solomon, *il miglior fabbro* in the craft of Artaudesque mad-sanity (restrained, once more, in a psychiatric ward). Ginsberg had recently had a dream about Joan Burroughs, the most shocking of the casualties among their circle, which had affected him deeply and which he had recorded in a poem: 'clear eyes and downcast smile, her / face restored'. While in the PI, he had taken notes as Solomon came out with surreal squibs – talk about 'poets in their pubic beards' and 'the harlequin speech of suicide' and the 'heterosexual dollar'. Now, with both Joan and Solomon in view, Ginsberg sat down at his typewriter in Montgomery Street. 'I decided I'd let loose', he said later, 'whatever I wanted to let loose and say what I really had on my mind, and not write a poem, finally – break my own forms, break with my own ideals, ideas, what I was supposed to be like as a poet, and just write what I had in mind.'

Ginsberg typed:

> I saw the best minds of my generation
> generation destroyed by madness
> starving, mystical, naked,
> who dragged themselves thru the angry streets at
> dawn looking for a negro fix

By the end of the session, there were seven pages, chanted on to the page in a rhythm patterned largely by the pronoun 'who' – 'who screamed on all fours in the subway and were dragged / off the roof waving genitals and manuscripts'; some of it obscene – 'who copulated all weekend exstatic and insatiate / with a bottle of beer'; some of it surreal – 'who bit detectives in the neck and climbed green smokestacks'; some of it impenetrable; all of it startling with the force of unexpected juxtapositions – 'who demanded sanity trials accusing the radio of hypnotism' – and something of the temper of Hebraic liturgy.

On looking again at the opening, Ginsberg found it too sentimental. He changed 'mystical' to 'hysterical', changed 'angry streets' and 'negro fix' to 'negro streets' and 'angry fix', and made several more pencilled alterations to each page. Later, he would run the triadic 'ladder' unit, borrowed from William Carlos Williams, into a single long line. He jotted a title at the top, 'Howl for Carl Solomon', kept a clean copy, and sent the original to Kerouac.

When Kerouac threatened to withdraw from the world of publishing at the beginning of 1955 – not that there were many people to threaten – he concealed his despair and humiliation in a tangle of motives: revolt against the commercialization of the publishing industry; careless reading of his 'hard-worked' manuscripts; the paltry sums of money on offer to a writer (Jack Kerouac) who was compared to Dostoevsky, Joyce, Thomas Wolfe (by Jack Kerouac); the pressure of having to bear the venality of publication in mind while writing. He worked better, he told Sterling Lord, in a 'Saturday, no school' frame of mind, in which the imagination had nothing else to do but go out and play.

And another thing: 'From now on all my writing is going to have a basis of Buddhist teaching free of all worldly and literary motive.' *On the Road*, a cross between a magnum opus and an albatross, he now regarded as ' "pre-enlightenment" work'. He signed off his letter with an apology for being such a 'beat client'.

But here he is in the act of giving the B-word a new gloss. Beat Buddhism's most important ancestor came not from the Far East but the East Coast – Concord, Massachusetts, where, in 1845, Henry David Thoreau constructed a rough hut on the shore of Walden Pond. He turned his back on the traditional Puritan values of hard work and profit, and turned instead to the rigours of contemplation. In the time it takes to clap one hand, Thoreau ceased to be a cog in the machine and became a particle in the Universe. *Walden* is the ur-text of Beat Buddhism: practical in its backwoodsmanship, sound in its ecological principle, and useful as a guide to the classic Hindu texts. 'The reader is nowhere raised into and sustained in a higher, purer, or *rarer* region of thought than in the *Bhagavad Gita*', wrote

Thoreau in his first book, *A Week on the Concord and Merrimack Rivers* (the same Merrimack River as would flow into the first sentence of Kerouac's first book a century later). When he writes in *Walden*: 'I went to the woods because I wished to live deliberately, to front only the essential facts of life, and see if I could not learn what it had to teach', it could be Gary Snyder speaking.

Though temperamentally and intellectually ill-equipped to meet the tests of self-discipline set by a life of contemplation, Kerouac pursued it anyway, as part of his frenetic chase after inner calm. After rereading *Walden*, he began to study Eastern texts, starting with *Life of Buddha* by Ashvagosa, and, with his usual enthusiasm, made copious notes and quickly styled himself an expert. In two months, he wrote 70,000 words of his story of Buddha, now called 'Buddha Tells Us', and he offered to make Ginsberg his pupil.

> Here's the trick:
> Drink a small cup of tea. Lock door first, then place pillow on bed, pillow against wall, fold feet, lean, erect posture, let all breath out of lungs . . . listening to intrinsic sound of silence which as you know is the sea-sound shh under noises which are accidental . . . the mind-sound of mind-stuff everywhere . . . This is the only Teaching.

Ginsberg, he said, should think of him 'as though I was Einstein teaching you relativity'. From having as its primary meaning 'beat up', down on your luck, etc, beat became *beatific*, the repository of beatitude. In Eastern philosophy – or just in 'shh' – Kerouac sought a way of soothing his egocentrically conditioned self, his Western self, what he called 'the Kerouac-Me'.

Another route to oblivion opened up at about the same time. This was the period during which his drinking began to get the better of him. In *The Subterraneans*, he had described waking up in the night from his 'Beermares'; he often admitted to being drunk in the middle of writing a letter; he confessed to Ginsberg, just before administering his lesson on 'the only Teaching', that 'right this minute, because of silly elation, wine and benny, I cannot sit down and practise true dhyana'. To one to whom thoughts brought trouble, who drank to quell them – which brought more trouble – there was comfort in pieces of homespun Buddhist wisdom such as this:

Thinking is just like not thinking –
So I don't have to think
    any
    more

'The light has been vouchsafed to me since I stopped thinking', he harped at Ginsberg, beseeching him to seek the light himself, and renounce attachment (Ginsberg was far too attached to his new love, Orlovsky, to consider practising asceticism at that moment). Kerouac sought the essence of Buddhism – what he called 'the true morphine' – in the phrase 'Repose beyond fate'; but his marginal gloss on this aphorism was fatalistic and commonplace:

> since life is nothing but a short vague dream encompassed round by flesh and tears, and the ways of men are the ways of death . . . the ways of beautiful women are the ways of old age, and since nothing we do seems to go right in the end . . . 'repose beyond fate' meant 'rest beyond what happens to you', 'give it up, sit, forget it, stop thinking' . . .

His elaborations on the subject were apt to bring out his less estimable qualities – he claimed that Buddha was 'an aryan' with 'long, blond hair', which he cut off when retreating from civilization – and to exhibit what the non-Buddhist reader might well interpret as a banal fear of life: 'Buddha found out that the cause of suffering was *birth*! If we hadn't been born, none of all this would have happened.'

Kerouac began to read the Sutras – traditionally taken to be transcriptions of the words of Buddha himself – at all times, travelling to and from the city, or sitting at his desk by candlelight. In correspondence, he quoted from the Diamond Sutra, the Heart Sutra, the Surangama Sutra, and ploughed on with his Buddhist book, again retitled, this time as 'Wake Up!' He also managed to adapt the Buddha's teachings to his own jazz aesthetic. 'If you are now desirous of more perfectly understanding Supreme Enlightenment and the more enlightening nature of pure Mind-Essence', wrote the Buddha in one of the Sutras, 'you must learn to answer questions spontaneously with no recourse to discriminating thinking.'

It is 'First thought, best thought' – the aesthetic principle guiding *The Subterraneans*, *Dr Sax* and the scroll *On the Road* – from the mouth of the Buddha himself, circa AD 99.

'Your HOWL FOR CARL SOLOMON is very powerful', Kerouac wrote to Ginsberg after he had read the corrected manuscript which Ginsberg had sent him, 'but I don't want it arbitrarily negated by secondary emendations made in time's reconsidering backstep' – *no recourse to discriminating thinking*, in the Buddha's words – 'I won't read hackled handicapped poetry manuscripts.' From bebop to Buddhism was a short distance.

He wrote Burroughs a letter full of renunciation – no more drunkenness, no more rich diet, no more chasing women, no more benny – and received in reply a splendid exhortation to seek himself through life and love, not the not-is and not-I of Buddhism:

> Remember, Jack, I studied and practised Buddhism (in my usual sloppy way to be sure). The conclusion I arrived at, and I make no claims to speak from a state of enlightenment, but merely to have attempted the journey . . . was that Buddhism is only for the West to *study* as *history*, that is it is a subject for *understanding*, and Yoga can profitably be practised to that end. But it is not, for the West, *An Answer*, not *A Solution*. We must learn by acting, experiencing, and living; that is, above all, by *Love* and by *Suffering* . . . You were given the power to love in order to use it, no matter what pain it may cause you. Buddhism frequently amounts to a form of psychic junk . . . What I mean is the Californian Buddhists are trying to sit on the sidelines and there are no sidelines. Whether you like it or not, you are committed to the human endeavour.

But Burroughs, bobbing back and forth to Mexico, Texas, Florida, Panama, was on the wrong track. The Beat wind was no longer a West wind. Kerouac's pioneering, Go-West days were drawing to a close.

The question he set himself in his new contemplativeness was: where had all his frontiersmanship and hoboing taken him? The action of *On the Road* may be joy, but the scaffolding holding it in place is despair: 'Where go? What do? What for?' In its own way, the book is an effort to describe a life of not-thinking – something the traditionalist Cowley had failed to see – but without a spiritual dimension. Kerouac had fought back against his black dog with kicks – 'Dean gave . . . a goofy grin that said to us, Ain't we gettin our kicks *anyway*?' – in the form of sex, Benzedrine, liquor, travel, and a big fix of words. But the dog – purposelessness – had got him.

A long-standing ambition, or anti-ambition, of Kerouac's had been to get away from it all, 'smoke some deermeat and pack it in my saddlebag, and go away over the bluff', to save something, 'get a little tract of land . . . for farming', or to become a rancher. Sometimes these fantasies were elaborated to include details of the number of employees he would need, the type of crop he would favour, whether or not there should be cattle-grazing, how high or low the rent on the property might be, and the 'Western girl' who would settle with him there and bear him 'six kids'. There was usually a place for his mother in the dream, and for Neal and Neal's wife. In the light of his recent interest, the dream was redesigned with Eastern trappings:

> I'd like to found a monastery in the plateau country outside Mexico City . . . I cant imagine what my rules would be, what rules would conform with pure essence Buddhism, say. That would be, I spose, NO RULES.

Buddhism not for the West? It was the road East now.

Burroughs went East, too, at about the same time. 'Bill is sitting across from me fixing up, and he is going to Tangiers for a few weeks', Ginsberg had written to Cassady at the turn of the year, 1953–4. Much as he esteemed Burroughs, Ginsberg was not sorry to see him go. After returning from South America with a suitcase crammed with yagé vine and making for Ginsberg's place on East Seventh Street, Burroughs had fallen in love with the host. Ginsberg had tolerated some of his advances at first, out of friendship and sympathy, but without reciprocal desire.

It was not surprising. Burroughs's amatory longings had an intensity so great that he had had to coin a verb – *to schlupp* – to describe them. In *Queer*, he wrote about his desire to schlupp with Marker:

> Lee could feel his body pull towards [him], an amoebic protoplasmic projection, straining with a blind worm hunger to enter the other's body, to breathe with his lungs, see with his eyes, learn the feel of his viscera and genitals.

He lets slip a typical chat-up line in baby talk: 'Wouldn't it be booful if we should juth run together into one gweat big blob.'

Eventually, Ginsberg revolted, not in baby talk: 'I don't want your filthy old cock', he burst out one day in the apartment. Burroughs fixed up and went to Tangiers.

Burroughs had no social conscience; only a kind of ruthless personal integrity. He was a shameless plunderer of exotic cultures, not for material goods, in which he had no interest, but for breadth of mind – drug-induced or anthropologically researched – and boy-love. He had pursued his dream of out-of-body peace down through the tropics; now he put his engine into reverse and travelled to the Orient.

The original plan had been to spend just a few weeks in Tangiers, but, after a dismal start, the city smiled its licentious smile, and a few weeks lengthened into a few months, which stretched out to become several years. When Burroughs wrote to Ginsberg half a year after his arrival that 'there is an end-of-the-world feeling in Tangiers', it was a sign that he was starting to enjoy himself.

One of the city's main attractions was that sex with the type of clean-limbed, adolescent male that Burroughs liked was available, and cheaply. The concept of social censure was vague; indigenous customs governing licence and restraint were byzantine and often could be conveniently papered over with the American dollar.

Drugs were similarly given the nod by the police. 'Weed absolutely legal, and you can smoke it anywhere', Burroughs told Cassady shortly after arriving (he was trying to locate Ginsberg, his only purpose in writing to Cassady, for whom he had little affection). North Africa was a further step beyond the reach of the spectres that bedevilled him – his spotless moneyed background, and the dim memory of his infant soul being gnawed at in the woods by his governess and her boyfriend, which mocked the lie of cleanliness.

Burroughs bedded down in a damp room in the Hotel Villa Mouniria, the kind of place sometimes rumoured to be a brothel. Tangiers overlooked both the Mediterranean and the Atlantic, and the city contained several worlds. Whereas the rest of Morocco was under French rule, Tangiers was a separate city-state; an International Zone had been established by the Allies after the Second

World War, to be governed by a commission drawn from eight nations. There were three official languages (French, Arabic, Spanish) and two official currencies. What appeared to be an excess of government resulted, in practice, in an antinomian freedom. Sexual misfits came from Europe looking for sport, and black marketeers from all over seeking profit. The banking industry consisted of money-changers on the street; it was a free port, without import duties, and smuggling was a normal line of work. 'Tangiers is looking up', Burroughs wrote to Ginsberg, six weeks after settling in to the Villa Mouniria. 'Junkies. Queers. Drunks.'

The best-known writer in Tangiers was another American, Paul Bowles, coolly unconventional but certainly not hip. He and his wife Jane were the first couple of the International Zone. Bowles sometimes travelled in a chauffeur-driven car, with several suitcases on board, containing the proper attire for every conceivable social situation. From Ceylon, where he owned a small island, Bowles wrote to Gore Vidal that 'the way one is taken care of [here] by the servants appeals to me . . . there is no such thing as service in Europe.' He would have disdained the idea of a Beat Generation, had he ever heard of one, which he hadn't.

Bowles's two novels, *The Sheltering Sky* and *Let It Come Down*, were among the things that had drawn Burroughs to Tangiers. The latter, in particular, which described life in the International Zone, had fuelled his continuing desire to live beyond the accepted boundaries of behaviour. But Bowles snubbed him. 'He invites the dreariest queens in Tangiers to tea', Burroughs complained, which, when he considered the size of the international community in Tangiers, amounted to 'a deliberate affront'. Bowles was visited by other writers whom Burroughs would have liked to meet, including Truman Capote, Tennessee Williams and Vidal, but since they were part of the Bowles circle, 'I, of course, don't get to meet them'.

Then the old pariah in Burroughs growled in self-defence. Why would he want to meet them anyway? They were squares, 'rigidly conventional and frightened'. He referred sardonically to Bowles, his wife and their crowd as 'the intelligentsia of Tangiers'. His own circle of friends, for the time being, was composed of Kiki, an Arab boy, Antonio the Mooch, a Portuguese Huncke-type character, and a genial failure from England whom Burroughs called Eric the

Unlucky. He was a former civil servant who, at fifty, had 'no job, no money, no prospects'. Tangiers was 'full of people like that'. Both the Mooch and Eric the Unlucky were archived, and in time would be hauled out again and cast in Burroughs's book in the making.

What he lacked was a readership for his new, action-based form which he was calling his 'routines'. One reader would be enough. If he was lonely in the International Zone, it was the loneliness of the writer with no audience. And, he told Kerouac, 'Buddha doesn't help me a bit.'

★

Ginsberg: Wally Hedricks asked me if I wanted to do a reading at the Six Gallery, and I didn't several months ago, not knowing of any poetry worth hearing.

Michael McClure: Someone asked me to arrange it. But I got busy and I couldn't do it, so Allen said he *would* arrange it.

Ginsberg: Changed my fucking mind.

Kerouac: Allen Ginsberg has arranged for me to read before an audience but I won't do it because I'm too bashful. Poet ain't court jester, I say.

McClure: That was the last I heard about it until I got a postcard in the mail with our names on it.

Ginsberg: We sent out 100 postcards, put up signs in North Beach bars, and invited the well-known Frisco Anarchist resident poet Kenneth Rexroth to act as Master of Ceremonies.

INVITATION TO A READING
6 Poets at 6 Gallery
Philip Lamantia reading mss of late John Hoffman – Mike McClure, Allen Ginsberg, Gary Snyder & Philip Whalen – all sharp new straightforward writing – remarkable collection of angels on one stage reading their poetry. No charge, small collection for wine and postcards. Charming event
Kenneth Rexroth M.C.
8 pm Friday Night October 7 1955
6 Gallery 3119 Fillmore St
San Fran

Michael Schumacher: A recent production of Robert Duncan's play, *Faust Foutu*, had given the Six Gallery an aura of notoriety that helped attract a larger audience.

Kerouac: Anyway, I followed the whole gang of howling poets to the reading that night . . . Everyone was there. It was a mad night.

Rexroth: Allen Ginsberg read a terrific poem — a real jeremiad of unbelievable volume — 'This is what you've done to my generation . . .'

Schumacher: Rexroth compared the climate of San Francisco to that of Barcelona at the time of the Spanish anarchists, where culture survived an oppressive national political environment.

Ginsberg: Their approach was purely amateur and goofy, but they represented a remarkable line-up in terms of experience and character — it was an assemblage of really good poets.

Kerouac: And I was the one who got things jumping by going around collecting dimes and quarters from the rather stiff audience standing around in the gallery and coming back with three huge gallon jugs of California Burgundy.

Ginsberg: The poets got drunk, the audience got drunk.

John Goodman: Hemmed in by a lot of insulting black blotches painted on butcher paper that kept getting torn off the walls, there was a fine big crowd, wine punch and a kind of Greek chorus by the name of Carrowac.

Ginsberg: First Philip Lamantia, a surrealist blood poet, former member of the San Francisco Anarchist group, who at the age of thirteen had in imitation of Rimbaud written surrealist poetry, come to New York, consulted Breton and other surrealists, took drugs, underwent visions, became Catholic, became silent, and reappeared at age of twenty-eight in native town to take part in the reading.

Goodman: This Carrowac person sat on the floor downstage right, slugging a gallon· of burgundy and repeating lines and singing snatches of scat in between the lines; he kept a kind of chanted revival-meeting rhythm going.

Rexroth: By the time the second poet on the programme started reading, Kerouac was already banging his big gallon jug of wine on the floor just to show his enthusiasm.

Kerouac: Between poets, [Rexroth], in his bow tie and shabby old coat, would get up and make a funny little speech in his snide funny voice and introduce the next reader.

McClure: I read a poem that sprang from an article in *Time* magazine . . . about the slaughter of whales.

Time (April 1954): Killer whales . . . Savage sea cannibals up to thirty feet long with teeth like bayonets . . . often tear at boats and nets . . . destroyed thousands of dollars worth of fishing tackle . . . Seventy-nine bored GIs responded with enthusiasm. Armed with rifles and machine guns one posse of Americans climbed into four small boats and in one morning wiped out a pack of 100 killers.

McClure:

The sleek wolves
Mowers and reapers of the sea kine.
THE GIANT TADPOLES
(Meat their algae)
Lept
Like sheep or children
Shot from the sea's bore.
Turned and twisted
(Goya!)
Flung blood and sperm.

Snyder: This friend of mine who has been working in the mountains in Washington . . . his name is Philip Whalen . . . he ought to get in on the reading, too.

Ginsberg: Philip Whalen, a strange fat young man – in appearance a Zen Buddhist Bodhisatva – read a series of very personal relaxed, learned mystical-anarchist poems . . . written in post-Poundian assemblages of blocks of hard images set in juxtapositions, like haikus.

Whalen: Ptarmigan hunt for bugs in the snow
  Bear peers through the wall at noon
  Deer crowd up to see the lamp
  A mouse nearly drowns in the honey
  I see my footprints mingle with deer-foot
  Bear-paw mule-shoe in the dusty path to the privy . . .

Ginsberg: The poets were reading with abandon and delight.

McClure: It was like a hot bop scene. Ginsberg was real drunk and he swayed back and forth. You could feel the momentum building up and some of the people began to shout, 'Go! Go!'

Goodman: Ginsberg's main number was a long descriptive roster of our group, pessimistic dionysian young bohemians and their peculiar and horrible feats, leading up to a thrilling jeremiad at the end, that seemed to pick up the ponderous main body of the poem and float it along stately overhead as if it were a kite.

Ginsberg: I saw the best minds of my generation destroyed by
    madness, starving hysterical naked,
      dragging themselves through the negro streets at dawn
        looking for an angry fix . . .

Kerouac: Everybody was yelling . . . and old [Rexroth] was wiping his tears in gladness.

Ginsberg: The reading was delivered by the poet rather surprised at his own power.

McClure: Ginsberg read on to the end of the poem, which left us standing in wonder, or cheering and wondering, but knowing at the deepest level that a barrier had been broken.

Goodman: There was a lot of sex, sailors and language of the cocksucking-motherfucker variety.

Ginsberg: who let themselves be fucked in the ass by saintly
    motorcyclists, and screamed with joy,
      who blew and were blown by those human
        seraphim, the sailors, caresses of Atlantic and
        Caribbean love . . .

Goodman: The people gasped and laughed and swayed, they were psychologically had.

Rexroth: When he finished the audience of 250 stood and clapped and cheered and wept.

McClure: A human voice and body had been hurled against the harsh wall of America and its supporting armies and navies and academies and institutions and ownership systems and power-support bases.

Ginsberg: When I read long poems I get carried away like a cantor. Ruth Witt-Diamant kept sending messages to tone that down, the scandal, etc, but nobody seemed to mind after it was over.

Goodman: It was an orgasmic occasion.

Ginsberg: But this was not all! The last poet to appear on the platform was perhaps more remarkable than any of the others. Gary Snyder, a bearded youth of twenty-six, also from the Northwest, formerly a lumberjack and seaman, who had lived with the American Indians and taken the religious drug Peyote with them.

Snyder: My first thought was it was going to be a hard thing to hold the audience after Ginsberg.

Kerouac: His voice deep and resonant and somehow brave, like the voice of oldtime American heroes and orators. Something earnest and strong and humanly hopeful I liked about him . . . He was the only one who didn't look like a poet.

Ginsberg: He read parts of a 100-page poem he had been composing for five years, *Myths and Texts*.

Snyder: In bearshit find it in August,
　　　Neat pile on the fragrant trail, in late
　　　August, perhaps by a larch tree
　　　Bear has been eating the berries.
　　　　　high meadow, late summer, snow gone
　　　Blackbear
　　　　　eating berries, married
　　　To a woman whose breasts bleed
　　　From nursing the half-human cubs.

Kerouac: Come 11.30 when all the poems were read and everybody was milling around wondering what had happened and what would come next in American poetry [Rexroth] was wiping his eyes with his handkerchief. And we all got together ... and drove in several cars to Chinatown for a big fabulous dinner.

Ralph Waldo Emerson to Walt Whitman, July 1855: I greet you at the beginning of a great career, which must yet have a long foreground somewhere for such a start.

Lawrence Ferlinghetti to Allen Ginsberg, October 1955: I greet you at the beginning of a great career. When do I get the manuscript?

Behind the beat

City Lights

Ferlinghetti had spent the turn-of-the-decade years ferrying back and forth between New York, where he was born, and France, which had adopted him. He studied at the Sorbonne, translating the work of French poets in his free time. In Paris, in 1949, Ferlinghetti had met Kenneth Rexroth, who told him about the literary scene in San Francisco, whose leading members were Patchen, Duncan and himself. 'It was obvious that he would fit in perfectly', Rexroth said of Ferlinghetti. 'He went, and he did.'

Before leaving Paris, Ferlinghetti had become acquainted with another young American, George Whitman, who had set himself up as a bookseller on the Left Bank, specializing in English-language books. Whitman's shop was called Le Mistral; it was modelled on Sylvia Beach's Shakespeare and Co, which was frequented by Hemingway and Pound in the 1920s, and published James Joyce's *Ulysses* in 1922. When Ferlinghetti moved back to America for good in 1951, he took with him the happy memory of Whitman's shop (soon to be renamed Shakespeare and Co, in honour of Sylvia Beach).

In San Francisco, Ferlinghetti became reacquainted with Rexroth. He also met a man called Peter Martin, the son of an Italian anarchist. Martin had started a film magazine called *City Lights*, and Ferlinghetti offered some of his translations of the poet and sometime screenwriter Jacques Prévert, and had them accepted. The magazine operated from a small, second-floor office on the slope of Columbus Avenue, near Broadway; within eighteen months of his arrival in the city, Ferlinghetti had joined forces with Martin to open a bookstore on the ground floor. The spirit of the place (like Whitman's in Paris) was personal, informal, friendly. Rexroth described the kind of poetry he wanted as 'I to thee', and City Lights was an 'I to thee' kind of bookstore. Martin and Ferlinghetti decided to make it paperback only; it remained open till midnight, seven days a week; they put up signs saying: 'Pick up a book, sit down, and read'; they specialized in small-press publications, and literary and political magazines.

The publishing business was started two years later – by which time Martin had left for New York – and again Rexroth was an influence. He was a one-man anti-establishment university, who fought loudly against the Eliotic idea of art as an escape from the personality of the artist, and he championed the oral presentation of poetry, the first person, as 'a surgical instrument against the invincible ignorance of spiritual sloth'. He was also a committed libertarian, an opponent of the State, and in particular of 'an economic system that made man wolf to man'. In all departments, Ferlinghetti took after him.

Number One in the City Lights Pocket Poets series was Ferlinghetti's own book, *Pictures of the Gone World*, with the title and author's name printed on a white label which was hand-pasted on to the black card cover. It had unnumbered pages and untitled poems, which were whimsically surreal in style and consciously guided by the spoken voice:

> Away above a harbourful
> > of caulkless houses
> among the charley noble chimneypots
> > of a rooftop rigged with clotheslines
> a woman pastes up sails
> > upon the wind

The next in the series, by Rexroth (*Thirty Spanish Poems of Love and Exile*) and Patchen (*Poems of Humor and Protest*), uncles to the Beats, were in an older tradition of anarchist politics. Number Four, though, was of the future, as its title, and even its dedication – itself a brief, exegetic Book of the Beats – proclaimed:

Jack Kerouac, a new Buddha of American prose, who spit forth intelligence into eleven books written in half the number of years (1951–1956) – *On the Road*, *Visions of Neal*, *Dr Sax*, *Springtime Mary*, *The Subterraneans*, *San Francisco Blues*, *Some of the Dharma*, *Book of Dreams*, *Wake Up*, *Mexico City Blues*, and *Visions of Gerard* – creating a spontaneous bop prosody and original classic literature. Several phrases and the title of *Howl* are taken from him.

William Seward Burroughs, author of *Naked Lunch*, an endless novel which will drive everybody mad.

Neal Cassady, author of *The First Third*, an autobiography (1949) which enlightened Buddha. All these books are published in Heaven.

Lucien Carr, recently promoted to Night Bureau Manager of the New York United Press.

The first printing of *Howl and other poems* was 1,000 copies ('I wonder if we will actually sell the thousand', Ginsberg wrote nervously to Ferlinghetti), and was on sale in the paperback bookshop in the fall of 1956.

LuAnne Henderson,
Neal Cassady's first wife

Ginsberg, Lucien Carr and
Burroughs in New York, 1953

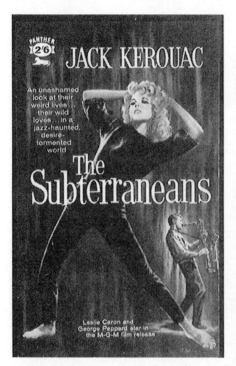

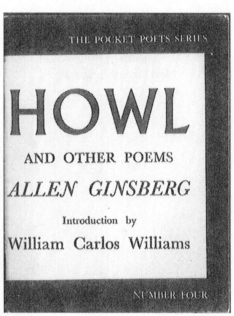

Clockwise: The film of *The Subterraneans* turned Kerouac's black heroine white, a switch reflected on the cover of the British paperback; the first edition of *Howl*, published by City Lights in 1956; the jacket for the original Paris edition of *Naked Lunch* was designed by the author himself; the cover of the Burroughs half of the Ace double-book, 1953

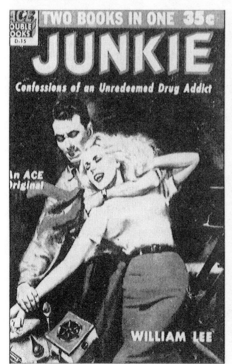

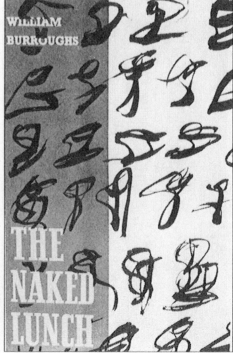

"But Jack I've told you before, if you continue going back to live with *mémère* you'll be wound tighter and tighter by her apron strings till you're an old man..." William Burroughs acting the André Gidian sophisticate lecturing at country bumpkin Thomas Wolfean American youth Jack Kerouac listening deadpan earnestly to "the most intelligent man in America." Fall 1953, my apartment 206 East 7th Street, Manhattan.
                                                                        Allen Ginsberg

Burroughs lecturing Kerouac in Ginsberg's East Seventh Street Apartment, 1953

The bar of the Beat Hotel in 1960. Madame Rachou is behind the bar

A break during the filming of *Pull My Daisy*: left to right, Larry Rivers, Kerouac, David Amram, Ginsberg; the white hat belongs to Corso

The original scroll typescript of *On the Road*

Kenneth Rexroth
and his wife, Martha

Anatole Broyard,
with friend, 1950s

John Clellon
Holmes and
Kerouac

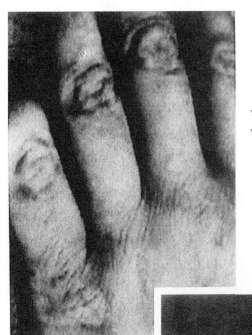

The first cut-up: Burroughs's left hand,
with mutilated finger

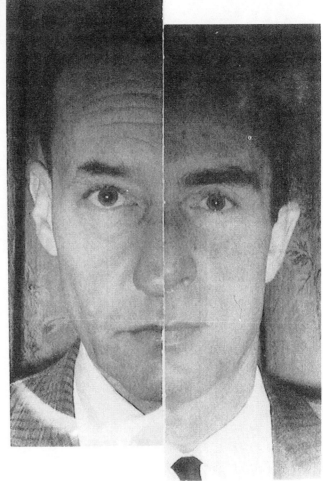

Ian Somerville's
diptych, featuring
Burroughs and Gysin

Burroughs leaving the Beat Hotel in the rue Git-le-Coeur, Paris, *circa* 1960

8

You're a Genius all the time

On 9 June, a few days after Ginsberg's thirtieth birthday, his brother Eugene sent a cable to San Francisco with the news that their mother was dead.

Naomi's mental state had scarcely improved after her lobotomy, not even to the extent of granting her an imbecilic peace. In a heartrending letter written on the day of her death, she told Allen:

> I still have the wire on my head. The doctors know about it. They are cutting the flesh and bone. They are giving me teethache . . . I am glad you are having your poetry published. I wish I were out of here and home at the time you were young: then I would be young. I'm in the prime of life now – . . . I'm looking for a good time.

Ginsberg had been seeking a solution to Naomi's dislike of confinement. The previous month, he had proposed to his brother that, since it was supposed she was relatively harmless, Naomi might be put out 'to pasture' with a family. He mentioned the Orlovskys – a bizarre suggestion, given what a mixed-up bunch they were themselves – but then discounted the idea. 'They say when you visit the Eskimos you need a double coat of fur', Naomi wrote in her last letter. 'Are you fit for that flying job?'

In accordance with Jewish custom, the body was buried within three days. On the West Coast and without the ready money to buy an air ticket, Allen did not attend. Eugene wrote from New York to say that a sexton offered a brief prayer in Hebrew, but 'could not give kaddish because a quorum of ten males was not present', as demanded by Talmudic law. Eugene (who had changed his surname to Brooks) penned a tribute to his mother, which was printed in the *New York Times*:

> Her spirit offended by insolence of slums,
> Besieged by truth, her eyes continually sad,
> No wonder, encircled by the great wreckage of beauty
> She mutinied, raging at evil, became quite mad.

Abruptly confronted by the fact of her death in a desolate room, Ginsberg grieved for his mother; but, in a not uncommon paradox, her going advanced his refurbishment. He understood that Naomi's madness and the consequent wreckage of his childhood, together with his early separation from maternal tenderness, lay behind his bisexuality; he had, he said, a 'longing for feminine bliss and yet a fear of it'. His erotic bias leaned towards the male, and the death of his mother affirmed it, clearing a space for his queer nature to live in.

The composition of 'Howl', the reading at the Six Gallery, the local fame the poem had acquired, the shocking discovery that lines such as 'who copulated ecstatic with a bottle of beer – and ended fainting on the wall with a vision of ultimate cunt and come' did not bring in the troops with fire hoses; all emboldened him.

Ferlinghetti needed to be bold as well. He was aware of the danger of prosecution, and while plans for the publication of *Howl and other poems* were progressing, he took the precaution of consulting the American Civil Liberties Union (ACLU). They pledged to defend the book if the police viewed it as obscene and brought charges against the author or the publisher. Ginsberg proudly relayed the news to his father.

When he had received a copy of the poem in the pre-publication, mimeographed form which Allen circulated among friends, Ginsberg *père*, unrepentant champion of rhyme and metre, defender of decorum, generously put his hands together for a spattering of applause: 'It has violence; it has life, it has vitality . . . it will give you a name.' But while Louis might have been relieved and proud that his son had followed him into poetry, it was evident to him that Allen took after his mother, too. Louis Ginsberg could not stop himself saying that 'Howl' embodied a 'one-sided, neurotic view of life', and continued to insist that 'there is no need for dirty, ugly words . . . They will land you in trouble.'

Others issued similar warnings, and Ginsberg looked for ways to comply with their wishes, without compromising himself. One night at the San Francisco State College Poetry Center, two weeks after the uproarious success at the Six, Ruth Witt-Diamant, the Center's director, had pleaded with him not to risk a potentially damaging scandal for the College by enunciating any of the dirty, ugly words in 'Howl' when reading it aloud. Ginsberg responded by saying 'censored' throughout his recital each time a taboo word occurred. The poem's most notorious line now had three variants. As written, it went: 'who let themselves be fucked in the ass by saintly motorcyclists and screamed with joy . . .' As set in type by the printers working for City Lights, it ran: 'who let themselves be . . . in the . . . by saintly motorcyclists' etc. And as read by Ginsberg at the Poetry Center, it was: 'who let themselves be censored in the censored by saintly motorcyclists' etc.

The law blushed with little provocation, but taboo and timidity stood as feeble adversaries in Ginsberg's path as he flexed his politico-poetic muscles and prepared to outstare the many-headed Establishment – academic, poetic, psychiatric, legal. In the material world, he had the ACLU behind him, a solid ally while under pressure; but in the firmament, where Good and Evil tussled over the length of a line, the breath controlling it and the words permitted to be used in it, Ginsberg, to whom Blake himself had spoken, had Right on his side. He was no longer compromised by his 'normality' – a fancy concocted by his father, the doctors and Lionel Trilling, in which he himself had briefly believed. 'There seems to have been enuf mercy around to get me to heaven anyway, no?' he wrote in a letter to Trilling, pointing back over his shoulder to the time when Trilling had tried to persuade him that the way forward lay through the portals of the Columbia Psychiatric Institute. With the letter, he sent a typed copy of 'Howl'. Never again would Ginsberg announce, as he had done to Holmes a few years earlier, 'Oh by the way, I'm sane.' He was 'lucky to be nutty' now.

It was more than a new set of insights – it was a world view, a coherent outlook on life which, as the years went by, would insist on its own completeness. For the time being, it would serve to protect him if his little black-and-white, four-by-five-inch book got him into trouble. 'I almost hope it does', he told his father.

Lucien Carr was still seeking anonymity in his own narrowly defined version of freedom. He made a friendly objection to being included in the dedication to *Howl*, and Ginsberg promised his name would be deleted if there happened to be a second edition.

Carr commented favourably on the poems. In addition to the title poem, the volume contained 'Sunflower Sutra', 'America', 'In the Baggage Room at Greyhound', 'A Supermarket in California', and other invertebrate, long-line poems. At the back, almost as an appendix, were some shorter, formal verses written earlier.

In 'Supermarket', Ginsberg spoke directly to his ideal geographer:

> Where are we going, Walt Whitman? The doors close in an
> hour. Which way does your beard point tonight? . . .
> Ah, dear father, graybeard, lonely old courage-teacher . . .

It is a beard not dissimilar to Rip Van Winkle's, but in Ginsberg's poem the time-travel happens in backward motion. Whitman's beard points to a territory of pure feeling; it is a pastoral vision of uncorrupted fertility, a ground on which the 'lucky / to be nutty' soul might stand with no fear of being incarcerated by the industrial, bellicose, moneymaking forces of the State, without fear of being destroyed by madness.

In a longer poem, 'America', Ginsberg enlarged the theme:

> America, I've given you all and now I'm nothing.
> America two dollars and twentyseven cents January 17, 1956.
> I can't stand my own mind.
> America when will we end the human war?

It ended with a pledge from the new Allen Ginsberg: 'America I'm putting my queer shoulder to the wheel.'

In response to the poems he had sent Lionel Trilling, he received a reply which suggested Trilling was growing impatient with the failure of his attempts to reform his old pupil:

> I'm afraid I have to tell you that I don't like the poems at all. I hesitate
> before saying that they seem to me quite dull . . . They are not like

Whitman. They are all prose, all rhetoric, without any music . . . As for the doctrinal element of the poems, apart from the fact that I of course reject it, it seems to be that I heard it a very long time ago and that you give it to me in all its orthodoxy, with nothing new added.

Copies of the mimeographed 'Howl' were also sent to T. S. Eliot and Ezra Pound. Eliot did not write back. Perhaps he recalled the letter that poet and dedicatee had written jointly from the PI in 1949 – 'we know a good literary dictator when we see one' – signed on behalf of the 'Yisraeli Soccer Team'.

Pound, locked up in St Elizabeth's mental hospital as punishment for his alliance with wartime Fascism, forwarded his copy to William Carlos Williams, with the message: 'You got more room in yr / house than I hv / in my cubicle.' But he couldn't let the verse pass without a Poundian stricture, not far removed from Trilling's:

> If he's yours why dont yu teach him the value of time to
> those who want to
> read something that will tell 'em wot they dont know.

Williams himself had consented, once again, to write a preface for the collection (there had not yet been an opportunity to use the introduction he wrote for Ginsberg's earlier sheaf of poems, *Empty Mirror*). The elderly Williams praised the young poet's work, even though his praise was issued sometimes in contradictions – 'It is a howl of defeat. Not defeat at all . . .' – and he seemed to think that Ginsberg was someone he had known just after the First World War (Williams may have meant to write 'Second World War', though the statement was left uncorrected). However, he delivered a resounding salute to the title poem, and a caution to its readers, in the final line of his short preface: 'Hold back the edges of your gowns, Ladies, we are going through hell.'

Back in the bughouse, Carl Solomon responded favourably, at first, to the poem which would make his name famous: 'an excellent piece of writing', he wrote back to Ginsberg, who had sent him a copy of the book; 'and just to my taste'.

But he soon began sending letters of complaint and self-pity ('no one regards me as an important thinker'), culminating in the kind of abusive criticism with which he had pelted *On the Road* while

191

working at A. A. Wyn's four years earlier. Letters were darted off to Ginsberg at random: 'Dear Allen, I disapprove of "Howl" and everything that was contained therein.' Solomon also sent a mind-unravelling letter to City Lights, which nevertheless, in that mad-sane way of his, contained a grain of reason: 'If I ain't Carl Solomon, why is my name in the book . . . If I ain't Carl Solomon, who is? . . . I sent the book to a place, explaining who I am, Carl Solomon, so when they write to you to have this confirmed, you may tell them.' Finally, after more in the same vein, he pointed out that: ' "All rights reserved" is on a page of the book. Does this mean I can't use my name any more?'

In the same envelope, Solomon included a parody of 'America', which mocked Ginsberg's poetics on roughly the same grounds as Trilling had dismissed them:

> America the nickel ain't no good.
> Why do you make pennies?
> America, Russia ain't no good
>   Hydrogen bomb it . . .
> America is the income tax a threat or demand . . .
> America look what you done to my pal Hitler.

In a brief synopsis, Solomon charted the progress of his life up to the moment when he became, in his own view, no more than a cipher in the title of a poem of which he disapproved. He called it 'The Education of Carl Goy':

Chapter One	701 Prospect Avenue
Chapter Two	Years Aboard the Mast
Chapter Three	Madness
Chapter Four	Encounter with Allen Ginsberg . . .
Chapter Five	Downfall –
	the hero of HOWL

Solomon continued to protest against 'Howl', occasionally back-tracking and praising it, eventually letting go a broadside which was published in one of his own collections of miscellaneous writings. 'Howl', he wrote, was

> compounded partly of truth, but for the most part raving self-justification, crypto-bohemian boasting à la Rimbaud, and esoteric

aphorisms plagiarized from Kierkegaard and others . . . Thus [Ginsberg] enshrined falsehood as truth and raving as common sense for future generations to ponder over and be misled.

★

The first hint of legal trouble for *Howl and other poems* came in March 1957, when part of the second printing was held up at Customs as it was making its way from the English printers Villiers to California and the City Lights bookshop. Five hundred and twenty copies of the book were seized. The *San Francisco Chronicle* reported the action: 'Collector of Customs Chester MacPhee continued his campaign yesterday to keep what he considers obscene literature away from the children of the Bay Area.' Collector MacPhee told the *Chronicle* that 'the words and the sense of the writing is obscene', before adding, in a distinct echo of what John Clellon Holmes's friend had said in a private conversation about Ginsberg after meeting him years before, 'You wouldn't want your children to come across it.'

In partnership with the ACLU, City Lights braced itself to contest the action. In the meantime, Ferlinghetti arranged to have a new edition of the book printed within the US, which would therefore not be subject to Customs jurisdiction. It was a piece of cleverness that caught the eye of the San Francisco police department, and when the US Attorney at San Francisco decided not to institute proceedings against *Howl*, prompting Customs to release the books, the police immediately stepped in. They arrested a counter assistant at City Lights, Shig Murao, for peddling literature likely to corrupt juveniles, and also arrested Ferlinghetti for publishing it. The *Chronicle* reported the event with the headline 'The Cops Don't Allow No Renaissance Here'. Ferlinghetti, meanwhile, had written an article for the same newspaper, in which he recommended that a special medal be struck for the Collector of Customs, since his action had already made the Pocket Poets books famous. 'But', Ferlinghetti added later, 'the police were soon to take over this advertising account and do a much better job.' Before long, the little press would have 10,000 copies of *Howl* in print.

Ferlinghetti was briefly held in the city jail, on the upper floors of

193

the San Francisco Halls of Justice. 'And a charming sight it is', he wrote, 'a picturesque return to the early Middle Ages.' Ginsberg himself was not legally involved. Nor was he on hand to make the symbolic gesture of bailing his publisher out of jail, for he was off on the road and on the seas again, this time en route to Europe and then North Africa. The main purpose was to reach Tangiers, with its hint of the Orient, and visit Burroughs, whom he had not seen since the last days of 1953.

Gary Snyder's interest in the arts of China stretched back to his boyhood in Washington State. In the Seattle Art Museum, at the age of nine or ten, Snyder was impressed by Chinese landscape paintings in a way that he had never been struck by anything before. 'I saw first that they looked like real mountains of an order close to my heart . . . [and] they were mountains of the spirit and that these mountains pierced into another reality which both was and was not the same reality as "the mountains".'

He carried the vision into adult life, to be enlarged when he read the translations of Chinese poetry by Arthur Waley, and then those by Ezra Pound collected in *Cathay*. While still a student, in the early 1950s, before his meeting with Ginsberg, Snyder began to attempt translations from the Chinese himself:

> Empty mountains;
>   no one to be seen;
> Yet – hear –
>   human sounds and echoes.
> Returning sunlight
>   enters the dark woods . . .

Summer spells as a fire lookout in Washington State provided Snyder with the real 'Empty mountains . . . / Returning sunlight' landscape, in the image of which he wished to decorate his mind. By the time he met Ginsberg and Kerouac, he was already deep in Eastern studies and planning a visit to Japan (China being out of bounds), a self-made exile which would last, with occasional interruptions, for twelve years. Even Snyder's face had an Oriental appearance, as if by predestination, 'a mask of woeful bone' as Kerouac described it, with eyes 'twinkling like the eyes of old giggling sages of China'. In Japan, in a monastery near Kyoto, Snyder studied Zen and meditation (or 'sitting', as he preferred to call it) with a *rōshi*, or 'old teacher'. There he made a series of translations from the hermit Han-shan, who lived in the eighth century, during the T'ang era.

Han-shan was the first Dharma Bum. According to the contemporary account by the Governor of T'ang prefecture, Han-shan wore a hat 'made of birch bark, his clothes were ragged and worn out, and his shoes were wood'. Snyder was a Beat dynasty update. He wore 'a funny green alpine cap', in Kerouac's description of him, 'rough workingman's clothes he'd bought secondhand', and mountain-climbing boots.

Han-shan lived 'seventy li west of the T'ang hsing district of T'ien t'ai at a place called Cold Mountain', after which he took his name. When he came down from his cave to a temple where the monks provided him with leftover food, he was heard before he was seen, 'shouting happily, talking and laughing to himself'. On Cold Mountain, Han-shan wrote the poems which Snyder translated:

> In a tangle of cliffs I chose a place –
> Bird-paths, but no trails for men.
> What's beyond the yard?
> White clouds clinging to vague rocks.

Another of Han-shan's descendants, Philip Whalen (the 'strange fat young man' who had read at the Six), was also in the habit of doing lengthy duties as a fire warden on the high peaks of Washington State. Three summers in succession, Whalen manned a fire station in the Skagit Valley, Mt Baker National Forest, brooding on mind and spirit throughout the months of solitude and sitting. When he came down, the poems he wrote were like translations from a hidden book of Chinese:

> Flies & other insects come from miles around
> To listen
> I also address the rock, the heather,
> The alpine fir

Whalen's poem, 'Sourdough Mtn Lookout', above, is a Beat dynasty echo of Han-shan's, written 1,200 years earlier:

195

> I wanted a good place to settle:
> Cold Mountain would be safe
> Light wind in a hidden pine –
> Listen close – the sound gets better

This English version is Snyder's. For most of his translations of Han-shan, he elected a cool, still tone, similar to that employed by Pound and Waley; in some poems, he introduced 'cars' and 'money' and hip West Coast terms such as 'hung up' or 'try to put me down'; at times, Snyder's Han-shan affects a superior attitude, which does not sit well with Tao or perfect mind or 'the pearl of the Buddha-nature':

> My heart's not the same as yours.
> If your heart was like mine
> You'd get it and be right here.

Most of Han-shan is less exclusive, more carefree, more beat, than that. The Governor describes him as laughing and singing, 'his nature happy of itself', replying to every remark or question put to him with a 'HO!' or a 'Ha ha!', just as Sal Paradise replies to remarks and queries with a 'Whooee!' In *On the Road*, Sal envisages himself arriving in Denver for the first time, in search of Dean Moriarty: 'I would be strange and ragged like the Prophet who has walked across the land to bring the dark Word, and the only Word I had was "Wow!" '

At that time, Kerouac had not read the Cold Mountain poems, but he did so after meeting Snyder in 1955, and eventually dedicated his novel about the Beat–Buddhist connection, *The Dharma Bums*, to Han-shan. The book ends with Kerouac (as narrator Ray Smith) following the example of Japhy Ryder (Snyder) and Warren Coughlin (Whalen) and signing on for fire-lookout duty on a mountain-top in Washington State. For sixty-three days and nights, Kerouac lived alone in a tiny Forest Service cabin perched on low stilts on Desolation Peak (6,600 ft), surrounded by the pristine and very cold mountains of the North Cascades. It required two weeks' training. Then came a journey by track, trail and boat, and finally a three-and-a-half-hour climb by mule up through dense forest, and aross scree and snow (it was June), to reach the low, pagoda-like structure on the most exposed spot on Desolation Peak, the only position to provide the necessary 360-degree view for fire-lookout. The pay was $700 for the season – not much, but it could all be saved, as there was nowhere to spend it. During his training, Kerouac would have been advised of the danger of black bears, but counselled that no fire warden had ever been killed in the line of duty. Deer flies were a more likely enemy.

On his first morning, he woke to the sight of the twin-peaked Hozomeen and the blue mountains unfolding behind, as far as the eye could see: 'hundreds of miles of pure, snow-covered rocks and virgin lakes and high timber'; below, 'instead of the world, I saw a sea of marshmallow clouds as flat as a roof . . .'

By then, Kerouac had read Snyder's version of Han-shan's poems in manuscript:

> The moss is slippery, though there's been no rain
> The pines sing, but there's no wind.
> Who can leap the world's ties
> And sit with me among the white clouds?

The 8,000 ft Hozomeen was a mirror. And, looking into this mirror, what did Kerouac see? 'The Void'. While hitch-hiking up to the Skagit Valley to take up his post, he was full of incorrigible romantic notions about the virtue, the relief, the ultimate release, even, of solitude: 'When I get to the top of Desolation Peak and everybody leaves on mules and I'm alone I will come face to face with God or Tathagata and find out once and for all what is the meaning of all this existence and suffering . . .' *Who can leap the world's ties?* For Kerouac now, this was the overwhelming question. Before his ascent, he had quipped to a friend, with a competitive allusion to Ginsberg's satori in Harlem, 'If I don't get a vision on Desolation Peak, my name ain't William Blake.' Instead of that, 'the Void'. Looking at vast Hozomeen, he came face to face with himself, 'no liquor, no drugs, no chance of faking it but face to face with ole Hateful Duluoz Me . . .'

As his term on high reached its end, though, he occasionally recaptured the spirit of karmic adventure. With a spark of Zen wit, he yoked together the two dynasties, the T'ang and the Beat:

Night, made hot cocoa and sang by the woodfire. I called Han-shan in the morning fog: silence, it said . . . 'Woo!' I yelled, and the bird of perfect balance on the fir point just moved his tail . . .

★

There are many fine passages, phrases, entire solos, in Kerouac's spontaneous bop prosody; and even more obscurities, blurry tones, fluffed notes, and flourishes born flat. But, to him, everything was of equal value – a lesson he had adopted from Buddhism, a lesson misunderstood. The first of the Four Noble Precepts of Buddhism, 'All life is suffering', particularly appealed to Kerouac. But, he wrote, it might just as well be 'All life is joy' – since 'What's the difference? . . . Why not? . . . Who says?'

The cat – as the Beat dynasty Buddhist scholar and doctor of divinity Alan Watts remarked of Kerouac's Buddhism – is out of the bag.

Until Kerouac arrived early in 1957, as the advance guard, Burroughs had been much on his own, and lonely, in Tangiers. Nobody wanted to know him. Nobody could *see* him. The street boys called him *el hombre invisible,* and even the clear-sighted Paul Bowles had difficulty in focusing on him:

> I first saw Bill Burroughs in 1954, passing along a back street of Tangiers in the rain. He was on H at the time, and he didn't look very fit . . . His life had no visible organization about it . . . He goes on his way enjoying even his own misfortune.

In his correspondence with Ginsberg, Burroughs had confessed that the 'nightmare feeling' of his childhood was 'more and more my habitual condition'. He began to keep a journal – 'Lee's Journal' – a record of self-effacement:

> Lee's face, his whole person, seemed at first glance completely anonymous. He looked like an FBI man, like anybody. But the absence of trappings, of anything remotely picturesque or baroque, distinguished and delineated Lee, so that seen twice you would not forget him.

He was still, as Bowles said, 'on H', reducing Burroughs himself to the same cipher, the mere initial, that Bowles had seen, or had strained to see, slinking through the narrow streets of the medina. Then he went off heroin. Then back on again. He invested heavily in the latest cure, swearing the efficacy of each one, swearing each time that he was off for good.

'I think junkies relapse because they are not *metabolically* cured by the usual methods of treatment', Burroughs told Ginsberg in September 1956. In May, he had undergone an apomorphine cure in London, at the hands of Dr John Dent. The treatment consisted in regulating the patient's metabolism with apomorphine, produced by boiling morphine with hydrochloric acid. First used as an emetic in the treatment of cattle – a detail certain to appeal to Burroughs – apomorphine was found by Dr Dent to be an effective cure for heroin addiction. Administered at Dent's London clinic, the course of treatment lasted two weeks. Back in Tangiers, and visible at last, Burroughs could confidently proclaim to Ginsberg: 'Man I don't *need* junk.' He stayed clean for about a year, before picking up another habit.

Heroin was one thing that remained constant. Another was his loathing of his family background. Writing was resistance against it. Burroughs had never submitted with any confidence to a psychoanalyst, and he must have looked on with satisfaction as Ginsberg – who had – healed his wounds not on the couch but at the desk. Burroughs, drug-sick, lovesick, sick with conscience, surrounded by an indefinable, lifelong nightmare feeling from which all his other nightmares derived, embarked on a similar process. He began to write something he called 'Word'. It wasn't 'Wow!' or 'Whooee!' or 'Ha-ha' or 'HO!'; Burroughs's word was a spurt of pure, uncut scatology in the face of Mortimer and Laura Lee Burroughs, of Palm Springs, Florida. 'I'm shitting out my educated Middlewest background for once and for all', he told Kerouac as they passed the slow days together in Tangiers. 'It's a matter of catharsis where I say the most horrible thing I can think of.' At times it came out like dictation. 'I can't keep up with it.'

The family had found out about *Junkie*, not taken in by the flimsy pseudonym in which Burroughs had cloaked it. So you were shocked by that, he seemed to say. Okay, try this:

Money all over him like shit you can smell it. And Rocky smell so sweet of junk . . .

The operator want to suck the emergent maleness of the passing queen . . . wise prick know when the bones will change and jump on that wagon break its ass with his weight of centuries . . .

'Like this,' he say on all fours, cup the boy's tits with hard palms, shove it in with a slow sideways wiggle, pull the boy's body on to him with long strokes sculpt stomach . . .

He sit me down and make the strip motion, and I undo belt silent and shaking and shove my pants down slow. Cock spring out hard, turn me around, sink slow fence post in hole . . . die in quick convulsions allergic shock − come five times

Ginsberg arrived in March, Orlovsky in tow (much to Burroughs's displeasure), and then Burroughs's friend Alan Ansen came from Italy. Together with Kerouac, they contemplated the butcher's shop of Burroughs's life and literary career, which were one. They scrutinized the shambles on the floor around his desk in the Hotel Mouniria, and tried to piece together the bits to find out what kind of beast it actually was, that 'endless novel that will drive everybody mad', which Ginsberg had advertised in the dedication to the now infamous *Howl*.

Kerouac, Ginsberg and Ansen worked in relay, typing and editing the material which had been produced over the past three years. 'Then the harder job', Ginsberg, ever the diligent archivist, told Lucien Carr, 'of going thru the letters from 1953–1956 extrapolating and integrating autobiography, routines and fragments of narrative'.

And then they left − Ansen first, then Ginsberg and Orlovsky to Venice, and finally Kerouac, back to New York to await the publication, at long last, of his own book. But they were leaving Burroughs with his 'horrible thing' typed up in clean pages. And with the satisfaction of having gained an audience, of four.

Writing to Cowley on 4 July, with the publication of his book only two months away, Kerouac resorted to Biblical quotation in a final effort to convince his editor of the authenticity − the Truth − of his aesthetic of spontaneity:

Take no thought beforehand what ye shall speak, neither do ye premeditate; but whatsoever shall be given to you in that hour, that speak ye; for it is not ye that speak, but the Holy Ghost.

Underneath, in case Cowley should have missed the point, he added his own scripture: 'spontaneous prose'. Cowley saw the point, but was unmoved. 'That's a fine quotation', he said of the bop prosody Kerouac had winkled out of the Gospel of St Mark. 'If the Holy Ghost is speaking through you, fine, let him speak.' Sometimes, however, he added, what sounds at first like the voice of the Holy Ghost 'turns out to be Simple Simon'.

The struggle between writer and editor continued as before, with New-World Kerouac attempting to make Old-World Cowley see the validity of spontaneous prose, and Cowley trying to tune Kerouac's gifts to what he believed would be maximum fitness: 'A good writer uses his subconscious mind and his conscious mind, one after the other, and uses them both as hard as they can be used.'

By now, though, Kerouac's aesthetic criteria were fixed. He must have hosted a riot of emotions when he received Cowley's letter – pleasure, pride, relief, disappointment, anger – for it was accompanied by a batch of advance copies of *On the Road*, and these criteria were not fully reflected in it. The novel which was to make him famous for a 'spontaneous' method was anything but spontaneous. To Cowley, this was cause for satisfaction – Kerouac 'revised well', when he could be persuaded to revise at all, he said later – but to Kerouac, who could call on one of the Apostles to be his witness, it was a form of sacrilege.

Three years earlier, in San Francisco, he had drawn up a list of twenty-seven 'essentials' of spontaneous prose. Some consist of simple, sound advice – 'Submissive to everything, open, listening'; some are comprehensible only by way of good will – 'Be crazy dumbsaint of the mind'; others are plain daft – 'Like Proust be an old teahead of time'. They show that Kerouac's mind worked like a camera – 'Dont think in words but to see picture better' – and that his pen raced to keep up as he found his picture 'swimming in language sea'. From Cowley's point of view, the problem lay in number 25 – 'Composing wild, undisciplined, pure, coming in from under, the crazier the better' – and, worse, number 26: 'You're a Genius all the time'.

To get Viking to publish the solid, black-jacketed book he now held in his hands, Kerouac had made numerous emendations, or had stood back while Cowley made them and submitted the results for his approval. He could now see that further cuts and changes had been made without consultation (he had not been shown a final set of galley proofs, as an author usually would have been). In a letter to his editor, he cooled his anger – the extra 'few cuts' were for the better, he said – but to Ginsberg and others he complained about 'crafty Cowley', and he continued to criticize him for ever after.

With the appearance of the troublesome book, the relationship between Kerouac and Cowley disintegrated. Kerouac still had his several other manuscripts, all of which he was eager to publish, but Cowley would not be rushed. Even if *On the Road* turned out to be a success, he would be in no hurry to exploit it. That voice of Simple Simon, whether it said 'Take no thought beforehand what ye shall speak' or 'Be crazy dumbsaint of the mind', still worried him. He complained, over and again, to Kerouac and his agent Sterling Lord, that the novels being submitted as possible follow-ups to *On the Road* (there were two more to be added to all the other books: *Visions of Gerard* and *Tristessa*) lacked one non-Kerouacean 'essential'. 'I told him', Cowley wrote to Lord in the week of *On the Road*'s publication, 'that any book he did for us would be fine, so long as it was a story.' And two weeks after the novel came out, he circulated a memo at Viking:

> I agree with [Helen Taylor] that DOCTOR SAX is impossible, at least as it stands – it's an exercise in self-abuse. Seems to me that I must have read it first in another version, much more public, much easier to read.
>
> Furthermore, Jack's Mexican story, TRISTESSA, is even more (if possible) impossible. It raises the question whether Jack has been completely ruined by Allen Ginsburg [*sic*] and his exercises in automatic or self-abusive writing.
>
> I don't think he *has* been ruined. I will continue my efforts to get something publishable out of him.

Ginsberg did not ruin Kerouac – the force of influence was the other way round – but Ginsberg came to believe that the original scroll *On the Road* was superior to the published version, which had been 'hacked and punctuated and broken – the rhythms and swing of it broken – by presumptuous literary critics in publishing houses'.

★

Also published in 1957 were Mary McCarthy's *Memoirs of a Catholic Girlhood*, James Jones's second novel, *Some Came Running*, *The Assistant* by Bernard Malamud, and *Pnin* by Vladimir Nabokov. None of these books – nor *The Town* by Faulkner or *The Wapshot Chronicle* by John Cheever – caught the rhythm and mood of the 1950s as *On the Road* did. And yet *On the Road* was a novel of the 1940s. Almost ten years had passed since Kerouac had confided to his pocket-sized journal that he was considering a story with that title, and added: 'More later'. Ten years to complete his 100,000-word gloss on the word 'Wow!'

While the tattered and endlessly worked-over manuscript hibernated in Kerouac's rucksack or slept in Malcolm Cowley's office drawer, the Western world's youth had been dreaming of the adventures it contained. Viking's frustrating procrastinations, it turned out, were the making of a happy anachronism. The 1950 *Life* magazine survey of 'teen idols' had included F. D. Roosevelt, Abraham Lincoln, General MacArthur and Florence Nightingale. In the seven years that had passed, America had made the H-bomb, heard the McCarthy hearings on UnAmerican activities, fought the Korean War, seen the launch by the USSR of Sputnik I (introducing the unpatriotic suffix -*nik* to the language), created Disneyland, published *Playboy* and *The Kinsey Report*, and given the country transcontinental television, which involved the concept of a 'TV community', an entire nation held together by a single screen image.

Kerouac's novel moved in a different direction; it married the hipster to the old-time hobo; it harked back, in Kerouac's own words, to 'the pioneering instinct in American life'; and yet it would seem to its young readers – *free* in an unprecedentedly modern sense – to be the future.

The legend is that Kerouac awoke to fame on Thursday, 5 September. Late on Wednesday night, with his girlfriend of the time, Joyce Johnson, he bought a copy of the *New York Times* containing an enthusiastic review of *On the Road*. Under a streetlamp on Broadway, they stood reading, mesmerized by Gilbert Millstein's praise:

> *On the Road* is the second novel by Jack Kerouac, and its publication is a historic occasion . . . *On the Road* is the most beautifully executed, the

clearest and most important utterance yet made by the generation Kerouac himself named years ago as 'beat', and whose principal avatar he is ... There is some writing on jazz that has never been equalled in American fiction, either for insight, style or technical virtuosity. *On the Road* is a major novel.

Johnson and Kerouac returned to her 68th Street apartment to sleep, and were awakened in the morning, romantic-movie style, by the arrival of the happy publisher (not Cowley, but Keith Jennison) bearing bottles of champagne. They drank it,

> as the phone kept ringing with news of excited reporters who wanted to interview Jack, and excited old friends, and invitations ... Three bottles of champagne were emptied with a rapidity that astonished Keith Jennison ... The first of many interviewers of the author of *On the Road* arrived to get the inside story on the Beat Generation and its avatar. What was it really like to be Beat? ... 'When did you first become aware of this generation? And how many people are involved in it, in your estimation? Is America going to go Beat? Are you telling us now to turn our backs on our families and our country and look for kicks? What kind of society will we have in two years?'
>
> 'Hey', Jack said. 'Have some champagne.'

Three days later, the more influential Sunday *New York Times Book Review* ran an unfavourable review of *On the Road*, 'In Pursuit of Kicks' by David Dempsey. He found it 'plotless' (Cowley and Kerouac's job of cutting and stitching had made no impression) and warned readers off 'a road that leads nowhere'. Most other reviewers were of a similar mind. The *Chicago Tribune* deplored the 'completely uncontrolled' story by a writer who 'slobbers words'; the headline in the *San Francisco Chronicle* – 'Sick Little Bums' – constituted a mini-review in itself; the *Atlantic* magazine described the book as monotonous and repetitious, while the review in the *Nation* – written by Herbert Gold, a novelist sometimes grouped with the Beats – said that the knowledge in *On the Road* was contained in one word: 'Whooee'. Of the character of Dean Moriarty, Gold wrote: 'He began as a psychopath and ended as a psychotic ... not much of a journey.'

Nevertheless, Kerouac, suddenly, burdensomely, famous, was showered with offers of work. *Esquire* wanted him to write for them, so did *Playboy*. Another girlie magazine, *Escapade*, offered him a monthly column, which he accepted. 'Buddha . . . preaches against entanglement with women', wrote Kerouac, his didactic thoughts on the Four Noble Precepts interleaved among the acres of pink flesh. Other magazines, including *Holiday* and *Life*, paid good money (up to $500 an article) for a quick look round the Beat Generation.

Famous Kerouac could not keep his footing. He did not enjoy the attentions of journalists, or of the groupies of both sexes. He wanted his other books published, and he wanted money to enable his mother to leave her job in the shoe factory, and to fulfil his dream of a house far from the travails of city life, or just of life. But in spite of the celebrity of its author, *On the Road* was not a great commercial success. It climbed no higher than number ten on the bestseller list, and dropped off the chart altogether after only a few weeks. A tentative offer from Warner Bros to buy the film rights for $100,000 or more flared into the gossip columns with the word that Brando might take the role of Dean . . . then it fizzled out, and movie interest in the book came to nothing. Within two weeks of publication, the verdict arrived from Viking – the rejection of *Dr Sax* and *Tristessa*, books which embodied the holy you're-a-genius-all-the-time aesthetic, unlike *On the Road*, which was old news to Kerouac anyway.

Others had been more brutally catapulted into the peculiar non-life of fame; what distinguished Kerouac was his inability to cope with the subversion of his natural shyness. He failed to turn up to a party which Gilbert Millstein, the *Times* book reviewer, had organized in his honour. All he wanted to do was get drunk and go home to Mémère. He would appear sozzled in front of journalists, which in their eyes made him good value, 'a story'. The story was that the King of the Beats was a clown with silly ideas about the sacredness of every word he wrote, a writer incapable of seeing that there are two sides to every sentence, a revised and an unrevised.

He did his book's unjustified reputation for incoherence no good at all by being the very model of incoherence in person. To those who were close enough, the reason was plain to see, or smell. 'Drunk all the time', he wrote to Cassady, '. . . no more wine, just whiskey.' On a television talk show hosted by Mike Wallace in early

1958, Kerouac blundered into a discussion about the Beats and mysticism. What do the mystics believe in? asked Wallace.

Kerouac: Oh, they believe in love . . . and . . . all is well . . . we're in heaven now, really.

Wallace: You don't sound happy.

Kerouac: Oh, I'm tremendously sad. I'm in great despair.

Wallace: Why?

Kerouac: Oh, it's a great burden to be alive.

★

In an essay written before either *On the Road* or *Howl* had been published, Kenneth Rexroth called Kerouac 'in his own small way the peer of Céline and Beckett . . .' He leavened his compliment by adding: 'the disengagement [from society] of the creator is one thing, but the utter nihilism of the emptied-out hipster is another . . . I believe that most of an entire generation will go to ruin . . . voluntarily, even enthusiastically.' The Beat transgressed both in his actions (taking drugs, stealing cars, picking pockets, committing sodomy, committing murder) and in his movements (Central and South America, North Africa). He was the writer as juvenile delinquent, without faith in the society that bred him or hope for the future. 'We are all guttersnipes', wrote the Artaud disciple Carl Solomon, unintentionally echoing Rexroth: 'Gide and Cocteau have made us what we are.'

The figure of the poet as delinquent or thief, relatively familiar in France (Jean Genet was the latest incarnation), was all but unknown in America. But here they came, one by one: Ginsberg's *Howl* was currently under investigation in the District Attorney's office, and the case was about to come to court. The appearance of *On the Road* had been delayed for years, partly because of publishers' unease over the sexual content (a scene in which Dean takes money from a man in exchange for sex in a motel room, while Sal reclines next door, provoked disgust in some reviewers). As for Burroughs, *Junkie* had crept out unseen either by the censors or the critics, hedged about with publishers' cautions and semi-apologies; but *Queer*, the book that A. A. Wyn had said would 'land us all in jail', still languished. Burroughs was presently engaged in trying to create something that

206

would 'put me in real danger, a danger I willingly take on myself . . . some excess of feeling or behaviour that will shatter the human pattern'. The effort behind 'Word' was to restate the first Word – the 'in the beginning' Word – in his own soul, thereby expelling all the evil words that still inhabited him.

Rexroth, at first an encouraging mentor, then a co-conspirator, now became just another worried grown-up. 'What is going to become of an attitude like this?' he asked. 'It is impossible to go on indefinitely saying: "I am proud to be a delinquent." '

But the Beats were fulfilling their early delinquent promise. Of no other group, in San Francisco or elsewhere, could it be said, in the same way, You are what you write. Rexroth had missed the point, as grown-ups usually do. Indulgent in criminality in their early youth, ranging from the mild to the monstrous, the Beats had come of age and made their books crimes as well.

Where was the real Cassady while Dean Moriarty was being reviled as a psychotic and one of a group of sick little bums? Kerouac's name was lighting up highways all over America; Ginsberg was transformed, a poet, a lover, a piping, naked seer; Burroughs was in dank Tangiers, but writing and off junk; even Holmes, on his second marriage and living outside New York, was finishing another novel. But Neal was still only 'mad' Neal. It was a mundane existence. He needed Sal Paradise to make his adventures metaphysical.

Among Cassady's latest kicks was an addiction to gambling. His new girlfriend, Natalie Jackson, with whom he was living in San Francisco, had recently forged Carolyn's signature, at Neal's insistence, to release the family savings. He promptly lost the lot at the racetrack. Carolyn discovered the fraud – a total of $10,000 disappeared in Neal's 'system' – when a caller from the bank rang her up at home: 'When you and your husband were in the other day to withdraw the money, I forgot one paper for you to sign . . .' You must be mistaken, Carolyn said. She had not set foot in the bank since the previous year.

A few months later, Natalie's name was added to the list of casualties, when she killed herself by leaping from the roof of a building on Franklin Street, San Francisco. 'The next day', the dutiful Carolyn recorded, 'Neal moved his things back home.'

The theme of psychosis in *On the Road* was developed in a review in *Time* magazine, in which the author claimed to have observed in Dean Moriarty's words and actions 'a prison psychosis that is a variety of the Ganser Syndrome', named after the nineteenth-century Dresden psychiatrist S. J. M. Ganser. With a copy of *On the Road* to hand, the *Time* journalist sounded out a contemporary psychiatrist, then reported his findings in the review. The symptoms of Ganser Syndrome, he wrote,

> sound like a playback from Kerouac's novel: 'The patient exaggerates his mood and feelings; he "lets himself go" and gets himself into highly emotional states. He is uncooperative, refuses to answer questions or obey orders . . . At other times he will thrash about wildly. His talk may be disjointed and difficult to follow.' The significant thing about sufferers from Ganser Syndrome is that they are not really mad – they only seem to be.

It was not uncharacteristic of *Time* to snipe against unconventional behaviour, but at the Cassady household, where conformity and nonconformity battled eternally like incompatible elements, it caused distress. Carolyn consoled Neal by reminding him of his fine work record: had anyone on the railroad ever said that he was 'uncooperative' or unwilling to obey orders? Never. To Neal, she quoted their spiritual guide, Edgar Cayce: 'Bless those who despitefully use you.' But to herself, she admitted that *Time*'s remarks 'got too close to home'.

Her dream was still to have Neal 'in harness', neatly uniformed and clean-shaven. She took a batch of photographs which show him this way – no Allen or Jack or madness, just the proud father with his trio of well-scrubbed kids lined up in front. There you are, she would say to doubters: the real Neal.

More than one reviewer of *On the Road* criticized the portrayal of blacks in the novel. In *Partisan Review*, Norman Podhoretz cited the phrase 'happy, true-hearted, ecstatic Negroes of America', and held it aloft for all to see. 'It will be news to the Negroes that they are so happy and ecstatic', Podhoretz jibed. He quoted the passage in which Sal Paradise wanders through the Denver coloured district, 'wishing I were a Negro', glimpsing the 'dusky knee of some mysterious sensual gal', smiling at the little children 'like sages in ancient rocking chairs', and then asked readers of *Partisan* if a more idyllic picture of Negro life had been painted since 'Southern ideologues tried to convince the world that things were just as fine as they could be for the slaves on the old plantation'.

Ned Polsky, a writer on the new weekly, the *Village Voice*, called this and other passages 'an inverted form of keeping the nigger in his place'. Herbert Gold gawped at the descriptions of blacks, and wondered what writers such as Ralph Ellison and James Baldwin would say about them. Baldwin gave his answer: 'I would hate to be in Kerouac's shoes if he should ever be mad enough to read this aloud from Harlem's Apollo Theater.'

Although a contemporary of Kerouac and Ginsberg, Baldwin had little time for the Beats – 'the Suzuki rhythm boys', he called them, invoking the Buddhist writer whom Kerouac and others cited increasingly in articles and talks. It was not until the second generation came along that black faces (the white Negro, Broyard, excepted) began to show up among the Beats. Among the first was LeRoi Jones, a college graduate and ex-serviceman from a middle-class home in Brooklyn, twelve years Kerouac's junior, twenty years younger than Burroughs. Jones would desert the Beat movement and raise the Black Power salute in the 1960s, adopting the *nom de guerre* Amiri Baraka. For now, though, he was an aspiring poet who had been alerted to the potential of a colloquial, hip poetics by 'Howl', as an earlier generation had read the future in 'The Waste Land'. Jones had a white girlfriend – whom he would soon marry and then jettison as part of his move from downtown to uptown – a job in a record shop – his 'slave job' he called it later, but not then – and a batch of free-form poems. He was also writing a history of jazz, the first exclusively AfroAmerican-centred study of the music's development.

Black Power was a distant drumbeat, but for Jones in Manhattan in 1957, the Beat Generation was the only rebellion around. When Podhoretz published his attack on Kerouac in *Partisan Review*, entitled 'The Know-Nothing Bohemians', it was Jones who leapt to the novelist's defence. After reading *Howl*, he wanted to meet the author; but enquiries among mutual friends revealed that Ginsberg was hoboing round Europe, and was currently holed up in a little hotel on the Left Bank in Paris. Someone gave him the address, and Jones decided to write.

Just to seem a little bit weird, he scribbled his note on toilet paper. 'Are you for real?' he asked at the end.

In the reply, also written on toilet paper, Allen Ginsberg asserted that, yes, he was 'real', but added that he was tired – so soon – of being 'Allen Ginsberg'.

Behind the beat

As good as Proust

The Rimbaud–Verlaine masquerade, in which the lover (played by Kammerer) is attacked by the object of his affections, was not given a revival; nor was the 'Van Gogh kick', starring the amputated finger, rerun; nor the final scene of William Tell, nor 'I'm Prince Myshkin . . . I'm Kirillov'; but the parallels between life and literature went on, if only on paper.

We heard Kerouac tell a Navy shrink: 'I'm only old Samuel Johnson', and explain to his hometown friend George Apostolos in 1943: 'My schizoid side is the Rakolnikov–Dedalus–George Webber–Duluoz side'. The most arresting feature of this quadripartite reference is that it includes not only the heroes of Dostoevsky, Joyce and Wolfe, but Kerouac's own name for himself in his then unwritten novels.

As the books came into existence, the comparisons with the Greats continued. In a letter to Cassady, written after *The Town and the City* had been published, Kerouac compared himself to Melville, Tolstoy and Faulkner within a few lines. Worried about the deteriorating effects of age even then (he was twenty-eight), he drew comfort from the fact that Dostoevsky's five great novels – *Crime and Punishment*, *The Idiot*, *A Raw Youth*, *The Possessed*, and *The Brothers Karamazov* – were all written after he had passed the age of forty-five.

Dostoevsky was a favourite, and consoling, point of reference: *On the Road* was rejected, Kerouac wrote in an article after the book had finally come out, 'though an editor, a very intelligent man, said,

"Jack, this is just like Dostoevsky, but what can I do?" ' Another was Goethe; it had been Kerouac's intention to write 'the third part of *Faust*, which I have done in *Dr Sax*' (when published, the novel would be subtitled '*Faust* Part Three').

On the Road was not only like Dostoevsky, it was 'like *Ulysses* and should be treated with the same gravity'. A Civil War novel he flirted with briefly in early 1952 was intended to 'parallel Tolstoy's 1812 hangups'. Switching tack, he pictured the same book as 'a big personal *Gone with the Wind* about . . . Melville-like Bartlebies [and] Whitman-like nurses . . .' In June 1952, Kerouac was, by his own estimation, 'probably the greatest living writer in America today'.

If Kerouac should ever have doubted that he belonged among the aristocracy of letters, Ginsberg was there to reassure him, comparing him to Melville – 'great prose Melville Jack' – to Thomas Wolfe, and to Milton. Ginsberg made comparisons not only with writers, but with jazz musicians, too: Kerouac was like 'Charlie Parker, like Lester Young'. This was pleasing to Kerouac, who fancied himself as 'America's new Jazz Critic Expert'.

Ginsberg also likened Corso to Keats. Or sometimes it was just that Corso was 'the greatest poet in America today'. Kerouac said that 'Gregory Corso and Allen Ginsberg are the two best poets in America', while Corso called Kerouac the greatest novelist and Ginsberg the greatest poet. To Ginsberg, the writing of Herbert Huncke was 'equal in delicacy of expression to Sherwood Anderson', while a page of Burroughs was 'as dense with imagery as anything by St John Perse or Rimbaud'. To Kerouac, Burroughs was 'the greatest satirical writer since Jonathan Swift'. Burroughs's first novel, *Junkie*, was 'a classic . . . better than Hemingway'.

Cassady was also better than Hemingway, according to Kerouac – more than that, he had 'as much talent as James Joyce'. When Cassady sent Kerouac the 'Joan Anderson letter' at the end of 1950, explaining his practical method for writing, and pointing the way forward for Kerouac (whom he knew to be the real writer), Kerouac reached for the usual names, then threw in a few more: Cassady's writing gathered together the best of the styles of Joyce, Dostoevsky, Céline, and Proust, mixing them all together 'in the muscular rush of your own narrative style & excitement. I say truly, no Dreiser, no Wolfe has come close to it; Melville was never truer.' In an interview given some years later, he threw out the same list, then added Twain. Briefly, in 1952, it was Holmes's turn: the prose in *Go* was 'the best in the states right now'.

To be compared to Proust was the ultimate compliment. He himself, Jack said, was a 'modern Proust', but Neal was something more, even, than that: 'think how wild it is for you to be Proust, which you are'. He was writing this letter while listening to the radio in the spring of 1955. He broke off to tell Cassady that Monte Irvin had just hit a home run, tossed in 'I'm not queer', in case there should be any doubt, then continued with the letter, only to discover that he had run out of comparisons. Neal Cassady was simply 'the greatest writer in America'.

9

Death to Van Gogh's Ear

Ginsberg seldom hesitated to place himself among those he considered truly great – not merely in the comparative stakes, but by actually knocking on the great one's door. In the summer of 1957, he and Orlovsky took the slow route up through Europe from Tangiers, instinctively nosing towards Paris, Mecca for the boy-gang from its earliest formations as the libertine circle and the New Visionaries, where Rimbaud would greet them – Rimbaud the exemplar and legitimator of bad-boy behaviour, Rimbaud the 'natural ignu in his boy pants', as Ginsberg portrayed him in a poem, who 'may be queer'; 'Rimbaud the child', as Corso preferred it.

On the way, Ginsberg and Orlovsky stopped off at the island of Ischia, near Naples, to knock on the door of W. H. Auden, who spent his summers there. They came unannounced. After asking around, they found Auden at a bar in the town, sitting with a group of friends. Crammed full of poems, visions, confessions, ecstasy, Ginsberg wanted to launch into one of his marathon monologues about literature, the Buddha, the lot. But he got off to a bad start, by quoting the opening lines of Whitman's 'Song of Myself':

> I celebrate myself, and sing myself,
> And what I assume you shall assume,
> For every atom belonging to me as good belongs to you . . .

Auden recoiled after the opening words. 'Oh, but my dear, that's so wrong, and so shameless, it's an utterly bad line.'

Ginsberg attempted to stress Whitman's universality. Auden

replied: 'When I hear that, I feel I must say, "Please don't include me."'

The next move was to give Auden a sample of his own poetry. But he inhabited the same galaxy as Whitman, his work was a satellite of Whitman's work – a world away from Auden's – with its tumbling-out of I, me, my, mine, and it met with no greater sympathy.

He read a poem from his recent collection:

> I began to feel my misery in pallet on floor, listening to music,
>   my misery, that's why I want to sing.
> The room closed down on me, I expected the presence of the
>   Creator, I saw my grey painted walls and ceiling, they
>   contained my room, they contained me . . .

Auden had no time for it. He told Ginsberg his poetry was 'full of the author feeling sorry for himself'.

Ginsberg tried a different approach. There had to be revolution in poetry, he said. The age demanded it.

Auden: 'Pshaw. Nonsense.'

Ginsberg mentioned Shelley.

Auden said he hated Shelley.

Ginsberg: 'You old fool. Discouraging the revolutionary young. That's not the right spirit for an older poet.'

Auden, who had no faith in the relationship between poetry and politics, looked as if he couldn't care less. Then Ginsberg called him a 'spiritual wet blanket', and, turning to the group of Auden's friends whose tea-time chatter he had interrupted, called them 'a bunch of shits'. To the surrounding tables and anyone who would listen, he announced that they were 'a table full of literary fairies'.

Since he had come into his own, he seldom doubted his own rightness, and others' wrongness when they doubted him; never doubted the potential for affecting worldwide spiritual change through the creative will of one person; never doubted that the one person could be Blake-appointed Allen Ginsberg.

The morning after the Auden fiasco, he dashed off a letter to Louis: 'All this . . . strengthens the conviction I have had that the republic of poetry needs a full scale revolution and upsetting of "values".'

★

'The plague is on!'
– Ginsberg, to his brother, from Paris (23 January 1958)

Bad-boy behaviour was now an established part of the artistic repertoire. Rimbaud, who awaited them in Paris, endorsed it. Arriving in the capital from the provinces three-quarters of a century earlier, Rimbaud was on a mission to scandalize not only *les bourgeois* – traditional, easy targets – but the city's poetocracy as well. At a recital by a well-known (now forgotten) poet, he greets every line with the exclamation 'Merde!' During a scuffle afterwards, he stabs the photographer Carjat (author of a famous portrait of the bad-boy poet) with a sword-stick. He stands at the window of his lodging in rue de Buci and strips off his clothes until he is as naked as Allen Ginsberg and the neighbours call the police. As a guest *chez* Verlaine, his literary patron, he disgusts the older poet's wife and in-laws by refusing to wash. He smokes marihuana and is noted for gnomic utterances such as 'Dogs are liberals' ('Les chiens, ce sont des libéraux').

And now here came the anti-bourgeois, anti-republic-of-poetry Beats, unwashed, smoking marihuana, exclaiming 'Merde' or 'bunch of shits' to everything that failed to please them or failed to notice them, making gnomic utterances such as 'Death to Van Gogh's Ear' (the current favourite, used to sign off letters).

Corso was the first to put the bad-boy aesthetic into performance in Paris. He had left New York for Europe at the same time as Ginsberg, Orlovsky and Kerouac, but had not become involved in the Burroughs project; while they were sifting through the results of Burroughs shitting out his educated Middlewest background 'once and for all' (he hoped), Corso shuttled back and forth between Paris and Amsterdam. While they were revolting Auden in Ischia, he was on the Left Bank, meeting Jean Genet. But Genet, the ultimate mentor for the delinquent *littérateur*, was not delinquent enough for Corso. 'Genet is so fucking bourgeois', he wrote to Ginsberg,

phoney, pugilistic-face poet. Pomerand, the man who gave me his place to stay, came back from his vacation and screamed at me when he saw that I did beautiful oil paintings on his walls and doors, he ran to his buddy Genet and cursed me to him. Genet shook his head and looked badly upon me as if I were some evil person.

He signed off: 'Death to Van Gogh's Ear'.

At a party to celebrate the opening of an exhibition, Corso met Picasso, whom he would have liked to speak to. But Picasso knew very little English, and Corso no French, and anyway Corso's companion messed everything up,

> by asking Picasso what he thought about BROWN – 'What, the color?' asks Picasso, in French – 'No' says my idiot friend. 'Brown that is biscuits that taste like sardines on the tongue of God!' Picasso ignored us after that.

He was cashing bum cheques on the Paris black market – 'hope I aint caught' – and stealing food from grocery stalls on the street. Ginsberg and Orlovsky, meanwhile, had moved on from Ischia to Assisi, where they sought shelter at a Franciscan monastery. To their surprise, the monks refused them, so they waited until darkness fell and camped down on the monastery's front lawn anyway, a night commemorated in the line, 'With Peter in Assisi, the clouds afright over the Umbrian plains in moonlite, cocksucking in the darkness on the grass in front of the cathedral doors'. The next morning, the monks went through their early routine to the accompaniment of an impromptu poetry reading.

Once they had got to Paris and teamed up with Corso, they met the painter Marcel Duchamp at a party. Allen kissed him. Then he put his hands between Duchamp's legs and asked for a blessing. Then he got down on the floor on his hands and knees and crawled through the other guests' legs, following Duchamp wherever he went.

The poet and painter Henri Michaux came to visit them at their hotel. He welcomed the conversation about the effects of mescaline, but was shocked when Ginsberg stood up and went to piss in the sink. Corso, noticing Michaux's reaction, asked: 'What's wrong with that?' Had they all forgotten Rimbaud, these bourgeois French writers?

More bad-boy behaviour: they stole books ('Genet is with us stealing books', Ginsberg wrote in a poem); Ginsberg and Orlovsky went to the office of the *Paris Review*, unannounced, and demanded to see some archival material relating to Ezra Pound; when the request was refused by the lone female secretary, they got down on the floor and started to make love; they used heroin; while Gregory slept only with girls, Peter slept with Allen and girls, and Allen slept with Peter and boys and girls ('Dogs are liberals').

Although his homosexuality was theoretically confirmed, Ginsberg was still occasionally of the other persuasion in practice. 'Been balling with a beautiful Indonesian girl named Joy', he wrote to his brother as 1958 came round. 'Have to fight off the women here.' He knocked on the door of another great bad boy of French literature, Céline, the author of *Voyage au bout de la nuit*, who had sided with the Nazis during the war. Ginsberg found him skulking in a suburb in an overgrown garden, surrounded by ferocious, noisy dogs. He had to keep them, Céline explained, 'because of the *Jews*'. Ginsberg gave him a copy of *Howl* and saluted him as the greatest living writer in France.

Corso had compiled a second collection of poems, *Gasoline*, which City Lights planned to publish in 1958. Ginsberg supplied an introduction: 'Open this book as you would a box of crazy toys . . .' And he gave a resounding endorsement to the poet whom he placed – as he placed all his friends – in the international parliament of all-time greats, mentioning, almost in a single breath, as Corso's compeers, Shelley, Lorca, Mayakovsky, and a new hero, Apollinaire.

The leading experimentalist in the France of the generation after Rimbaud, Apollinaire was more mischievous than delinquent. Before the First World War (Apollinaire died on Armistice Day), he had been put in prison, along with Picasso, for stealing sculptures from the Louvre, an experience he did not enjoy. Two years later, in 1913, he published a catalogue entitled 'Merde et Rose', doling out abuse or praise to a list of personages, the choice of which the Beats would have approved. Top of the list were critics – 'Mer . . . de . . . aux critiques', wrote Apollinaire, cleverly avoiding the printed obscenity (*Mer . . . de . . . aux . . .* Herbert Gold, Norman Podhoretz, even Auden) – followed by 'professeurs' (*Mer . . . de . . . aux* Trilling and Van Doren).

Apollinaire also invented a new form of writing – the 'conversation poem', he called it – which is similar in spirit to Kerouac's spontaneous poetics, and to Ginsberg's own improvisatory method of composition. Apollinaire's best-known conversation poem is 'Les Fenêtres', which reflected, said the poet (pre-echoing Kerouac by almost half a century), 'a totally new aesthetic'.

Sitting in a restaurant in the rue Danou with two friends, André Billy and René Dupuy, one day in 1912, Apollinaire suddenly remembered that he had promised to write a preface for the catalogue to an exhibition of paintings by Robert Delaunay. To meet the deadline, the essay should have been posted that very day. Apollinaire called to the waiter for pen and paper, and began to write:

> Du rouge et vert le jeune se meurt
> (From red to green the yellow dies away)

Dupuy was then asked to contribute a line. He dictated:

> Quand chantent les aras dans les forêts natales
> (When the aras sing in the native forests)

Apollinaire wrote this down, and added:

> Abatis de pihis
> (Pihi giblets)

Then followed Billy's contribution:

> Il y a un poème à faire sur l'oiseau qui n'a qu'une aile
> (There is a poem to be made about the bird of one wing).

A poem of thirty-seven lines was eventually composed, which was conveyed to the publisher by way of a 'message téléphonique', a pre-First World War form of telegram which guaranteed delivery within the hour. The suggestion to do this had arisen during the course of composition, and was commemorated in the line: 'Nous l'enverrons en message téléphonique.'

Whether they had already read 'Les Fenêtres', or whether this kind of literary mischief was simply in the air in Paris, Ginsberg, Corso and Orlovsky settled down and wrote their own conversation poem, 'Moon Prevention', each typing one line at a time:

> Will the moon be at least the beauty parlor for the warthog!
> Oh!

The world owes the Moon to the warthogs!
What great restaurants and what great cities?
I want to ride on the Metro! What will the name of the stops be?
Artaud, Apollinaire, Marlon Brando
    Sophie Eluard, Maybe we think so . . .

Even in a harmless game such as this, space was made for the irresistible communion with the immortals:

> Can we conjure up Kerouac on the moon?
>   Peter, Allen, Gregory, Neal?
> Rogozhin? Alyosha? Jean Arthur? Guillaume?
>   Dmitri? Walt? Edgar? Emily? Hart? Emily?

Apollinaire was probably the first poet to discard punctuation completely (he found it 'useless', he said), leaving 'the rhythm itself and the division into lines to provide the real punctuation'. And he disdained revision, just as his American descendants (and the Holy Ghost) did. 'Almost all my poems have been written as I wrote them in the first draft', said Apollinaire, while Ginsberg said: 'First thought, best thought', and Kerouac said: 'No emendations in time's reconsidering backstep.'

Ginsberg went in search of Apollinaire's grave in Père Lachaise cemetery, coming away with the inspiration for a long poem, which he set down in the little hotel in which he and the others were lodged, at 9 rue Gît-le-Coeur, unpunctuated and revised.

The hotel was of the unpunctuated, unrevised sort, too. Ranked thirteenth in the thirteen grades of hotel in Paris, it was already known among the raggle-taggle set before Corso found it, or had it recommended to him, in the summer of 1957.

At 9 rue Gît-le-Coeur, you were likely to be living next door to a pot-smoking artist who collected straw, or a photographer who was a penitent mute, or an American Negro writer who was penniless but sharp-suited and at the extremes of hip, or a Scottish guitarist who had married the maiden of border ballads to the dervish of Moroccan dances. There was a pleasure-trade in erotic books published by the English-language Olympia Press, among which could be found the works of Henry Miller and Jean Genet. (In a farcical play on French justice, Genet's *Oeuvres Complètes* were published in a splendid uniform edition by Gallimard, while the Olympia translations were banned from sale.) The Beats did not 'discover' the hotel in rue Gît-le-Coeur – among others the black novelist Chester Himes had stayed there, on and off, over the past few years, moving out for the last time as Corso moved in – but they did, in time, give it a name which it never lost, even after it had changed hands and been reconstructed: the Beat Hotel.

As it stood, the hotel had no proper title. It was simply called after its owner, Madame Rachou, a tiny, blue-rinse woman who had had a soft spot for artists ever since, as a girl, she had been a waitress at an inn at Giverny where Monet came to eat. The hotel had no carpets, hole-in-the-floor toilets, last week's *Figaro* for toilet paper, a smell of bad feet in the corridors. On the right, as you entered, was a little bar with a zinc counter, where wine and coffee were cheap. The hotel had forty-two rooms. Madame Rachou could keep an eye on who was in and what was happening in each one, by referring to her light-control panel, which displayed a bulb for each room. If someone was using more than the permitted amount of electricity, a light flashed on the switchboard, and a visit would be made to investigate the cause of the extra wattage. Her clients enjoyed her mixture of discipline and libertarianism, and her happy smile from behind the zinc counter managed to cheer up even William Burroughs when he came to stay in early 1958.

First, though, Ginsberg and Orlovsky joined Corso at the Hotel Rachou, just a stone's throw from the Seine, if you looked right out of the door, or the place St André-des-Arts, if you turned left. Ginsberg wrote to Lucien Carr, two weeks before Christmas 1957, that the hotel was getting rather crowded: 'one bed, me, Gregory & Lucky Pierre'. For the equivalent of a dollar a day, they got radiator heat most days, and hot water every day. 'Have usual choice collection of interesting screwballs dropping in for supper', Ginsberg continued, 'heroin or whatever's on menu.' Olympia Press books were one of the literary treats of modern Paris for a broadminded visitor from Britain or America, and Ginsberg told Carr that he had bought lots of 'unexpurgated Miller & Genet & Apollinaire'.

Paris, for Ginsberg, was happening not only in the present but also in the past. Baudelaire and Rimbaud he had expected to meet, and did, but Apollinaire was a surprise, appearing from behind his own gravestone 'in the black cloak of French poetry'; even the faces on the street looked as if they had 'stepped out of paintings by Lautrec and Van Gogh'. The cafés and boulevards which he was seeing for the first time were superimposed upon a Paris created in his imagination from readings of Hemingway and others. Poor Lucien, as Kerouac had written when he and Carr were arrested and imprisoned in 1944, on the eve of the Liberation, 'he who had wanted to be in Paris among the first'. They had been dreaming ever since.

Ginsberg settled into the Beat Hotel for the next eight months. Eventually, Corso was given a space of his own up in the attic, no. 41 out of the 42 rooms, a tiny, triangular garret hardly tall enough to stand up in or wide enough to stretch out while he slept. Allen and Peter stayed on the third floor, in a room with a window giving out on to the narrow street with the river at the end. In January, Burroughs blew in from Tangiers and was installed downstairs. Madame Rachou took a liking to the author of *Junkie* and the unpublished *Naked Lunch*, with his three-piece suit, shirt and tie, spectacles and hat, and he ended up staying longer than any of the others.

Orlovsky left the day after Burroughs's arrival. The ostensible reason for going was that he had heard from New York that one of his brothers had been taken ill; but he also found it necessary to get out of the way of *el hombre invisible*, whose snuffling, satirical presence made Peter uncomfortable. 'Me and Bill B don't get along', he wrote to a friend. 'To maney blocks and pre-conceived attitude he has about me. Thinks i'm a dope . . . don't even read my peotry.'

One of Ginsberg's first artistic acts after they had joined Corso at the hotel was to pose Peter for a photograph, staring at the camera, through a shock of hair, poet-savage-like. He called it 'Peter Orlovsky, Rimbaud portrait'.

★

Among many idiosyncratic things about Madame Rachou was this, which struck Burroughs for obvious reasons:

In a room adjacent to the bar and separated by a curtain, Madame gave occasional lunches, usually for the local inspectors of the police, with whom she always maintained good relations . . .

The bright side of this, for Burroughs, was that her clients were spared 'searches and harassment'.

But what's this? According to the memory of another guest, a friend and collaborator of Burroughs, Brion Gysin, who arrived slightly later, Madame Rachou

> had no use for the police, none at all . . . She was 'pugnacious' with them, determined not to let them set foot in the place, not even her little bistro . . .

Or how about this?

Burroughs: 'Madame Rachou was very mysterious and arbitrary about whom she would let into her hotel. "She has her orders", Brion Gysin always said.'

Gysin: 'William Burroughs used to say sententiously: "Madame Rachou has her orders." Whatever did he mean?'

As Burroughs insisted, 'the word' could not be trusted; and he was currently engaged in engineering a method to 'rub it out', and yet, by textual magic, still leave a book behind. If a publisher existed anywhere in the world for that kind of book, it was in Paris.

'Howl' was declared not obscene by Judge Clayton W. Horn of the San Francisco Municipal Court, on 3 October 1957. The verdict was greeted with relief, not only by the poet, Ginsberg, and the publisher, Ferlinghetti, but by other poets and publishers. 'We will await the outcome of this case before we go ahead with other books', Captain William Hanrahan of the police department's Juvenile Bureau had announced while the trial was in progress. The case lasted throughout the summer, with days in court occurring at weekly, sometimes fortnightly, intervals. Letters and written statements in support of the poem – it was the title poem alone among the contents of the book that was on trial – were accumulated by the defence; Rexroth, Duncan and Patchen were among those who stood up for it, though each in his own way, members of an older 'San Francisco Renaissance' and living in the encyclopedia of world literature, had reason to be impatient with the unruly Beat movement.

The chief defence counsel was J. W. 'Jake' Ehrlich. His opponent was an elderly district attorney, Ralph McIntosh, something of a veteran in smut cases, having tried to ban, among other obscenities, the film *The Outlaw*, starring Jane Russell. The case was covered by several journals. The fullest account was given in the *Reporter*, 12 December, written by David Perlman. He provided a vivid picture of the prosecutor McIntosh wrestling with the principal witness for the defence:

> The first major encounter of the trial came when Ehrlich carefully pitted McIntosh against Mark Schorer . . . one of America's leading critics . . .
>
> In his characteristically imperturbable drawl, Schorer testified on direct examination by Ehrlich: 'I think that "Howl", like any work of literature, attempts and intends to make a significant comment on or interpretation of human experience as the author knows it.'
>
> He said the theme and structure 'create the impression of a nightmare world in which the "best minds of our generation" are wandering like damned souls in hell' . . .
>
> Judge Horn having carefully read the evolving law on the subject, ruled that while Schorer and other experts could not testify whether they thought the poem obscene, they could state whether they thought the controversial language contained in the poem was 'relevant' to the intent and theme of the poem.
>
> 'Ginsberg uses the rhythm of ordinary speech and also the diction of ordinary speech', Schorer said. 'I would say the poem uses necessarily the language of vulgarity.'
>
> Then came the cross-examination. For an hour, McIntosh pecked at Schorer, stormed at him, and read him nearly every questionable line in the book. The prosecutor railed at the poem too, and it was sometimes difficult to tell which he objected to more, its dirt or its incomprehensibility.
>
> 'I presume you understand the whole thing, is that right?' McIntosh asked Schorer at one point, a dare in his voice.
>
> Schorer smiled. 'I hope so', he said. 'It's not always easy to know that one understands exactly what a contemporary poet is saying, but I think I do.'
>
> McIntosh flourished the book triumphantly. 'Do you understand', he

demanded, 'what "angelheaded hipsters burning for the ancient heavenly connection to the starry dynamo in the machinery of night" means?'

'Sir, you can't translate poetry into prose', Schorer answered. 'That's why it's poetry.'

The audience, among whom were North Beach writers, downtown booksellers and a few criminal-courts regulars, roared. The judge smiled tolerantly, but McIntosh would not give up.

'In other words', he asked, 'you don't have to understand the words?'

'You don't understand the individual words taken out of their context', Schorer explained patiently. 'You can no more translate it back into logical prose English than you can say what a surrealistic painting means in words because it's *not* prose.'

Having established the impossibility of translation, the prosecutor then read aloud one line of 'Howl' after another, each with its quota of Anglo-Saxon words or vivid sexual images, and demanded more translations.

Schorer patiently declined to give them, and McIntosh finally turned to Judge Horn to complain: 'Your Honor, frankly I have only got a batch of law degrees. I don't know anything about literature. But I would like to find out what this is all about. It's like this modern painting nowadays, where they have a monkey come in and do some finger painting.'

The judge declined to instruct the witness to enlighten McIntosh on the poem's meaning, so the prosecutor tried another tack. He read a few more vivid phrases into the record and then asked Schorer: 'Now couldn't that have been put another way? Do they have to put words like that in there?'

But Judge Horn disallowed the question, and offered a bit of literary criticism himself: 'I think it is obvious', he said, 'that the author could have used another term; whether that would have served the same purpose is another thing; that's up to the author.'

After several more witnesses had spoken of the merits of 'Howl' – Rexroth called it 'probably the most remarkable single poem published by a young man since the second world war' – McIntosh produced two witnesses of his own to testify in rebuttal. One was a woman named Gail Potter, who passed out little printed brochures announcing that she gives private lessons in speech and diction, and who offered a formidable array of qualifications as an expert.

'You feel like you are going through the gutter when you have to read that stuff', Miss Potter said of 'Howl'. Then she shuddered in distaste and added: 'I didn't linger on it too long, I assure you.'

Jake Ehrlich bowed Miss Potter off the stand without a question, and that was the prosecution's case.

In summing up, McIntosh spoke first: he asked the Judge to consider the effect on the city, the state, and the nation, if the type of language used in 'Howl' were to be allowed to become common currency. 'In other words, Your Honor', concluded McIntosh, 'how far are we going to license the use of filthy, vulgar, obscene, and disgusting language? How far can we go?'

Judge Horn took two weeks to arrive at his answer to those questions. Writing to Ginsberg in Paris earlier on during the case, Ferlinghetti had said that an article in *Life* magazine was helping to sell 300 extra copies of *Howl and other poems* per week. As he waited now for Judge Horn to make up his mind, Ferlinghetti wrote: 'Question of Fucked in the Ass not yet settled in court.' In just over a fortnight, though, it would be.

The 'unexpurgated Miller & Genet & Apollinaire' which Ginsberg wrote about to Carr would have been, respectively, *Tropic of Cancer* and *Tropic of Capricorn*, *The Thief's Journal* and *Our Lady of the Flowers*, and *The Debauched Hospadar* and *Exploits of a Young Don Juan*, the last two being translations of pornographic novels Apollinaire wrote at the beginning of the century. All the books were published under one of the many imprints – Atlantic, Ophelia, Ophir, Othello, Traveller's Companion – of the Olympia Press, run from a small, Left Bank office by an Anglo-Frenchman, Maurice Girodias.

Girodias was a pornographer by trade and a rascal by repute, but he was also an aesthete, a dandy, a gourmet and an oenophile, a lover of beautiful women, beautiful cars and good writing. In addition to publishing paperback books, his firm had embraced the literary magazine *Merlin*, which had recently gone out of business but in its short life had published work by Sartre, Ionesco, and Paul Eluard. Olympia, which stabled such frisky rides as *School for Sin*, *Until She*

Screams, The Whip Angels, was also home to the novels of Beckett (*Watt* and *Molloy* had already appeared; the one-volume Trilogy was in production), *The Ginger Man* by J. P. Donleavy, and a neat, two-volume edition of Nabokov's story of nymphet-love, *Lolita*.

All in all, Girodias, who was the son of Jack Kahane, the original publisher of Miller's *Tropic* books in the 1930s, liked nothing better than a banned book, or a book that was likely to be banned, or likely to become notorious by other means. So he would have been interested to meet Allen Ginsberg, when, one day around the turn of the year, 1957–8, he walked into the Olympia office just across the boulevard St Michel from the no-name hotel, and to hear the news about the censorship battle being fought across the ocean by his own publishers.

There was no suggestion of Girodias publishing anything by Ginsberg himself – poetry was not commercial enough for Olympia, unless it happened to be bawdy limericks – but Ginsberg had brought him *Naked Lunch*, transported all the way from Tangiers, in his rucksack, in the hope of finding a publisher in Paris for the unpublishable book. Girodias's ears pricked up as Ginsberg spoke. Might the book be unpublishable for the right reasons? Girodias normally requested a sex-scene every six pages at least, and a colourful pseudonym to go with the spicy title. *Naked Lunch*? Hmmm. It was a promising start. The main idea was to bait the hook to lure the American sailors, and tourists from England and elsewhere, who were Olympia's main customers.

Ginsberg left the manuscript with him, but when Girodias sat down to read, he couldn't make head nor tail of the thing. It was hard to know which way up to hold it. The subject matter was pornographic, in a grotesque manner – but it was a world away from the arousing capers of Olympia bestsellers such as *Helen and Desire*: 'At first the girl lay unresisting on the floor like a crushed flower . . . but as the exploring member moved more easily at her shy vehicle, her softened buttocks mushroomed slowly upwards', and so on. Compare that with what Girodias found in *Naked Lunch*:

Johnny extracts a candiru from Mary's cunt with his calipers . . . He drops it into a bottle of mescal where it turns into a maguey worm . . . He gives her a douche of jungle bone-softener, her vaginal teeth flow

out mixed with blood and cysts . . . Her cunt shines fresh and sweet as
spring grass.

That last sentence came closer to the kind of thing Girodias usually
looked for, but as for the rest, *Qu'est-ce que c'est que ça?* There was no
discernible logic in the narrative, if it could be called a narrative, and
what's more, the pages were tattered and torn, some of them pasted
together, and so clumsily that they stuck to the ones underneath. To
Girodias, the only audience for this book could be the rats of Paris,
who seemed to have made a start on editing it already, nibbling the
edges of the pages so as to leave Burroughs's prose looking in places
like poetry.

After a few days, Ginsberg called back at the office in rue St
Séverin, and a thankful Girodias relieved himself of *Naked Lunch*.

★

Editor: Who are you?
Burroughs: Sole male heir of Burroughs Machine Corps St Louis Mo
Harvard Phi Beta Kappa 37 with postgraduate work in anthropology
and psychology Columbia For the past 15 yrs have been acknowledged drug addict and homosexual Who are you???

Ginsberg announced to his brother Eugene on 23 January 1958, that
there were 'lots of things coming up'. He meant literary things. He
meant that he and his pals, though still happily expatriated, were the
advance guard. He gave notice of an upcoming article in *Esquire* on
the movement, poems in *Partisan Review* (they never happened), a
special number of a new publication, the *Evergreen Review*, devoted
to Beat writing ('with 15 pages of mine'), and something similar in
the *Chicago Review*, which was planning a San Francisco poetry
number. There would also be substantial concentrations of Beat San
Francisco writing in the annual *New Directions in Poetry and Prose* (no.
16), and in the *Black Mountain Review* (no. 7), edited by Ginsberg's
friend Robert Creeley. When Ginsberg proclaimed 'The plague is
on!', this is what he meant.

The *Chicago Review* – whose editor had asked Burroughs for a
biographical note ('Who are you?') – had no strong tradition of
avant-garde advocacy. It was published in academia (from the

University of Chicago), an institution Ginsberg increasingly despised. The Summer 1957 issue – just before the storm – had led with an article by the recently deceased poet Isaac Rosenfeld. Entitled 'The role of the writer and the little magazine', it came out of a talk given by Rosenfeld to the staff of the *Chicago Review* the previous year. In retrospect, it appears smudged by irony. Rosenfeld's theme was that 'the avant-garde, strictly speaking, does not exist any longer'. Little magazines were traditionally the organs of the avant-garde, their function determined by the lack of ready outlets for progressive political and artistic ideas. The *Chicago Review* might have been such a magazine, were it not that now, in 1957 when Rosenfeld was talking, paperback books, written from all manner of political viewpoints, expressing every conceivable progressive artistic idea, were available to all. The independence and integrity of the avant-garde was compromised, paradoxically, by the attainment of one of its own objectives, which was to spread the radical word. The avant-garde, Rosenfeld repeated more than once, 'I am sorry to say, is largely non-existent nowadays'.

What about the new breed of young radicals, who were prominent on the campuses and overrunning the adjoining coffee bars? Rosenfeld could find in himself no fellow feeling with them.

> In a place like Jimmy's [coffee bar] you have a sort of student atmosphere . . . and the dominant values are the ones taken over from jive – where the key words and the key metaphors are, well, the words are 'cool' and 'crazy', 'gone', 'gas' and so on. The dominant metaphors therefore are of insanity and death . . . Once you get used to the murk and the darkness, the paradox of the noise becomes clear to you – namely, you get a headache from the din, but nevertheless, you can't find anyone talking to anyone else.

While Rosenfeld's article was being read and discussed in and around the University of Chicago (possibly even in Jimmy's), a box containing what Ginsberg referred to as 'poison' was sailing across the Atlantic from Paris. The poison came in the form of a batch of chapters from *Naked Lunch*, and it eventually landed on the desk of Paul Carroll, the incoming poetry editor of the *Chicago Review*. Together with the new editor, Irving Rosenthal, Carroll intended to compile an issue which focused on the San Francisco scene.

Ferlinghetti was already known to the editors of the *Chicago Review*, and he suggested Ginsberg as someone to consult about who and what might be included in such an issue. Ginsberg offered his recommendations, in the hectoring tone which was now a vital part of his armoury. He gave an Apollinairean 'Rose' to his friends (and to himself):

> Whalen's and Snyder's poems are hard and will stand . . . Print all my poems you can . . . Corso says he's including some Zany short poems. Make a Zany issue, if you can't convince yourself it's literature . . . Print everybody madly! . . . Don't worry what people say if you turn out a screwy magazine full of idiotic poetry – so long as it's alive – do you want to die an old magazine editor in a furnished room who knew what was in every cup of Tea? Put some arsenic in the magazine.

And a last word before signing off: 'Some final poison for your pot – Burroughs!'

The San Francisco Renaissance issue of the *Chicago Review*, Spring 1958, contained work by Ferlinghetti, McClure, Whalen, Duncan and Ginsberg himself, among others. It came with a preface by Kerouac, now 'a name' – he was King of the Beats, to him a detestable description. 'The Origins of Joy in Poetry' showed him to be even more loose-tongued than his reputation made him out to be.

> The New American Poetry . . . is a kind of new-old Zen Lunacy poetry, writing whatever comes into your head as it comes . . . . Poetry & prose had for a long time fallen into the false hands of the false. These pure new poets confess forth for the sheer joy of confession. They are CHILDREN. They are also childlike graybeard Homers singing in the street. They SING, they SWING. It is diametrically opposed to the Eliot shot, who so dismally advises his dreamy negative rules like the objective correlative etc which is just a lot of constipation and ultimately emasculation of the pure masculine urge to freely sing . . . I could say lots more but aint got time or sense.

Burroughs stood apart from the others in having no association with the San Francisco group, besides his friendship with Ginsberg and Kerouac; and while the others offered poetry, his contribution was in prose. The chapter published in the *Chicago Review*, which eventually would form the opening of the book, was entitled simply, 'Excerpt: *Naked Lunch*':

> I can feel the heat closing in, feel them out there making their moves, setting up their devil doll stool pigeons, crooning over my spoon and dropper I throw away at Washington Square Station, vault a turnstile and two flights down the iron stairs, catch an uptown A train . . .

It was Burroughs in *Junkie*-mode, a Dashiell Hammett ringer, with some illicit substance rubbed in, saying goodbye and hello in one breath, as he began a new book and introduced a new style. The drug theme aside, however, there was little poison in it, and little to offend any reasonable member of the Chicago intelligentsia.

The following issue, Summer 1958, stuck to the Beat Generation in spirit, by proclaiming a 'Zen' theme. There were essays by Orientalists such as Alan W. Watts – 'Beat Zen, Square Zen, Zen', in which Watts criticized Kerouac's 'Buddhism' as another word for 'anything goes' – and work by Snyder, Whalen and Kerouac himself. For the Autumn issue, Rosenthal and Carroll avoided the Beat Generation as a dominant topic, but they did include 'Chapter 2 of *Naked Lunch*'. It contained an apposite passage:

> Chicago: invisible hierarchy of decorticated wops, smell of atrophied gangsters, earthbound ghost hits you at Dearborn and Halstead, Cicero, Lincoln Park, panhandler of dreams, past invading the present, rancid magic of slot machines and road houses.

This was more toxic, and the trustees, the advisory board of the magazine, and the 'invisible hierarchy' of the University at large, did not like it, or anything else about the extract. 'Fuck 'em all', Burroughs wrote when he heard about the complaints. 'Squares on both sides.'

In the same issue, they would also have read 'Two Letters from Allen Ginsberg', including one in which he introduced Carroll to Burroughs for the first time: 'That's William S. Burroughs – see dedication to my book if you have it.' Cross-referring to the scandalous (though legally not obscene) *Howl*, the invisible hierarchy would have sniffed the poison now directed at the *Chicago Review* in the part-dedication to the 'author of *Naked Lunch*, an endless novel which will drive everybody mad'.

'Wot about that fellow who is a model for Neal Cassidy in Jack's novel?' Paul Carroll asked Ginsberg in a letter. So eager was he for more Beat matter that, as well as spelling the name wrongly, he got character and model reversed.

Carroll was not alone, however, in confusing the man and the invention. As Cassady himself wrote to Carolyn, the association was getting on his nerves: "*On the Road* is in the library here and Doug . . . bewails that it's always checked out, so he still hasn't read it, as I wish no one would, frankly."

'Here' was prison, Vacaville, California, a temporary halt for Cassady on his way to San Quentin. A few months after the publication of *On the Road*, the hip hero at the centre of the novel, the incarnation of freedom and joy, was beginning a sentence of five years to life for possession of marihuana. The only prose he was writing was in the form of letters to his wife. In one, he described the circumstances of his arrest:

> I was at a party at the Fergusons' apartment. When I said I had to go to work, a couple of guys offered to drive me to the depot. When we got there, I offered them a couple of joints in return and went to my locker to get them. I gave them three. Then, on my way home, it hit me; something told me they were narcs . . .
>
> You see, a couple of months ago two other guys asked me to buy them some pot. They gave me forty dollars, and I said I'd try. I was sure they were agents, so I took the money to the racetrack. This, of course, told them I knew who they were. Somehow I think it's all connected.

Time passed, without further developments, and Cassady assumed he had seen them off. Then, on 5 April 1958, two detectives came to the house where he was living with Carolyn and the children in Los Gatos, and arrested him. There was a feeling of inevitability about it. Twelve years before, Cassady told Kerouac that, passing any prison, anywhere, he was always reminded of his 'jail problem'. ('. . . they walked in on me that morning at 8 o'clock . . . Hauser and O'Brien. They had been on the City Narcotic Squad for twenty years . . . "Well well", says O'Brien . . . "Long time no see, eh?" . . . "Put on your coat", says Hauser . . .' – *Naked Lunch*.) A few weeks after his conviction and imprisonment in the county jail, Cassady was transferred to San Quentin in the company of twenty-three other convicts, all in leg-irons. He told Carolyn that he had to share a cell with a 'thug who'd escaped 8 times', and that his 'sagging bunk' permitted, at best, only 'troubled sleep'. Prison proved to be a strong breeder of contrition, mixed with self-pity, and Neal informed Carolyn that, as her husband was in prison, 'the state will grant you an uncontested divorce for only one dollar'. What would Carolyn, 'Dear, Dear Carolyn . . . Diligent Dharma Decoding Directness Carolyn . . . Dearest Everything Carolyn', want with a husband like this, who had blown the family savings at the racetrack, had only returned home after his girlfriend had committed suicide, and had now been forced to abandon her again, with three children to feed and debts to pay off, including $800 worth of personal loans?

But Carolyn was not seeking a divorce. She took solace from the teachings of Cayce – 'What we sow, we reap' etc – and she might have been comforted by the idea that Neal, under lock and key, was 'in harness' at last, protected from Dean Moriarty, from the wayward imaginings of Sal Paradise, from the always abnormal Ginsberg; and that he was hers in a way he had never been before.

A visit was arranged for Kerouac to see Cassady in prison, but he didn't turn up.

The most effective censor was not the one who held out the threat of the law, but the one that manipulated the in-built allegiance to good citizenship, to taste and propriety; convention's press gang. The censor was in the living-room in the suburbs, surrounded by the latest in labour-saving gadgets, and Doris Day on TV. It was the tyranny of Mom and Pop. 'Allen get married', Naomi wrote from the mental hospital. And he tried. 'Exorcize Neal', wrote Louis. And, however briefly, he tried that, too.

But then, after trying, he refused. By the same gesture, he refused the nine-to-five job. And, by means of a system of articulation in which all segments of life and work are linked, refused the five-foot line of verse. And so it continued. From Paris, Ginsberg wrote to his father, as pithy a mission statement as he ever composed:

People keep seeing destruction or rebellion in Jack's writing, and *Howl*, but that is only a very minor element, actually; it only seems to be so to people who have accepted standard American values as permanent.

What we are saying is that these values are not really standard nor permanent, and we are in a sense I think ahead of the times . . . When you have a whole economy involved in some version of moneymaking – this just is no standard of values. That it seems to offer a temporary security may be enough to keep people slaving for it. But meanwhile it destroys real value . . . Only way out is individuals taking responsibility and saying what they actually feel – which is an enormous human achievement in any society.

Kerouac was different. He shouted 'Wow!' and ran away from home, scat-sang in the street, wished he were a Negro, squatted on a mountain for two months, renounced all worldly goods, renounced grammar, embraced 'Zen lunacy' . . . but, through it all, remained tethered to law and custom, and to its reigning symbol in his own life, his mother. His love-affair with a black woman, Alene Lee, posed questions which, imprisoned in his do-it-yourself white identity, he was not equipped to answer except by reference to the old literary fantasy of Parisian adventure, 'I am Baudelaire and love my brown mistress', and all that jazz.

Of the many paradoxes strewn behind Kerouac on his way to becoming King of the Beats, none was more absurd, or more grotesque, than this – that, in 1958, when he was thirty-six, his mother acted as his censor, his actual censor.

'I read Mrs Kerouac's letter', Burroughs wrote to Ginsberg less than a year after *On the Road* had been published. 'Evidently she intercepted your letter to Jack. The woman is mad.' After opening the letter, Mémère warned Ginsberg against trying to contact her son ever again, threatening to report him to the FBI for drug-taking and homosexuality. 'She is really evil in her small way', Burroughs went on. As for Jack himself, if he continued to allow his mother to open his mail and tell him whom to see and correspond with, 'he is a lost cause'.

Sightings of Kerouac reported an increasingly desperate, alcoholic figure. His habit of drinking with the specific aim of getting drunk had always been dominant, but had been kept under control by his desire – almost a natural appetite in itself – to create a body of work that would prove his worth. There was no need for such restraint now.

His girlfriend, Joyce Glassman, sat down to eat with Kerouac and his mother at their home in Richmond Hill. Mémère prepared a big meal, 'that everybody ate except Jack. He ended up with his head in his plate'. His first wife, Edie, having read about his success in the papers, called up and suggested a reunion. Kerouac had always had a soft spot for her. She came into town especially for the occasion, and Jack took her down to the Village for old times' sake. Before she had a chance to start enjoying herself, however, he was lying on the pavement outside a bar, drunk and crying.

In another Village bar, the Kettle of Fish on MacDougal Street, he made such a commotion inside that when he stepped out three thugs set upon him. He staggered up to Joyce's apartment, bleeding. By this time, their romance had diminished to a brother–sister relationship. Joyce understood that the only woman for Jack 'wasn't me or Edie Parker or Carolyn Cassady or any of the dark felaheen beauties of his longings, but Gabrielle L'Evesque Kerouac, aged sixty-two, with her bun of iron-grey hair'.

When he found a new girlfriend, Dodie Muller, and brought her home, the visit ended with Mémère calling Dodie a witch. Why? Because she had long, untied hair. Mémère had never liked Joyce Glassman either; she disapproved of the way Joyce did the dishes.

Kerouac's response was to write, in a poem:

> I keep falling in love
> with my mother . . .
>
> The doll-like way
> she stands
> Bowlegged in my dreams,
> Waiting to serve me.

And he beat his chest and added: 'I am only an Apache.'

Ginsberg departed Paris on 17 July 1959, sailing out of Le Havre aboard the *Liberté*, bound for New York. Eighteen months had passed since he left San Francisco. His fame at home, and the fame of the Beats, had grown without him. 'This is the Beat Generation', Holmes had announced in 1952; and now it was.

Stashed in Ginsberg's luggage on the *Liberté* was a folder full of poems – 'At Apollinaire's Grave', 'Death to Van Gogh's Ear', 'To Aunt Rose', 'Europe! Europe!', 'The Lion for Real' – poems in which the personal was intimately involved with the political. The world was headed for destruction, and only the ignu-poet – 'he hears Blake's disembodied Voice . . . No woe on him . . .' – was capable of saving it.

> Poet is priest
> Money has reckoned the soul of America
> Congress has broken thru to the precipice of Eternity
> the President built a War machine which will vomit and rear up
> Russia out of Kansas
> The American Century betrayed by a mad Senate which no longer
> sleeps with its wife
> Franco has murdered Lorca the fairy son of Whitman

This poem, which took its title from their current trademark slogan, 'Death to Van Gogh's Ear', marked a deliberate shift away from the pastoral, lyrical voice of most of the poems in *Howl*. The major 'protest' poem in that collection, the title work, was driven by a feeling of sociological exclusion, rather than a wide-scale political complaint.

Although he had cut himself adrift socially, and was floating further and further away from conventional life, Ginsberg was not, now or ever, a drop-out. Even his most exhibitionistic public pantomimes were prompted and shaped by what he saw as the immoral manoeuvrings of the government. You threaten to bomb the Russians and blow up the planet; I take off my clothes in public. Who is the sane one and who the insane? If it was in danger of coming across as a simplistic ideal, Ginsberg was willing to take the risk; far from being an unAmerican philosophy, it was firmly in the Emersonian tradition of self-reliance. With his stated intention to 'Widen the area of consciousness', and his plucky support for 'poetry that will save the world', Ginsberg stands here, in 1958, at the founding of the philosophy that will dominate the coming decade – 'Be yourself'.

The mystical was political, too. From Paris, earlier in the year, he had written another letter to his ever-patient father about the profound disaffection he felt from the 'flow of organized life around me'. He recalled his vision in Harlem, when, in a few moments of mental release, he felt 'completely free of my own guilts [and] the forces that molded & structured me'. He saw 'a living God'. It was a revelation of a 'creative freedom of the will', which 'every government is scared of . . . the enemy of both capitalism and communism'.

Among the sheaves of poetry carted home from Europe, intended for a new collection to be published by Ferlinghetti, were the beginnings of a long elegy to his mother. It would become 'Kaddish', the title poem of the projected book. Two years earlier, she had been denied proper Jewish rites at her funeral in New York, which Ginsberg had been unable to attend. In time, the irony had struck his conscience that, while his mother was lowered into her grave without kaddish, he was on the other side of the continent lamenting 'the best minds . . . destroyed by madness' among his peers. Now he began to pick at his childhood, passed in a household presided over by a mad mother; or, when she was absent, the spectre of her madness. The poem is a grand accumulation of love and pain in memory, mediated by the poet in a spirit of absolute fidelity to his recollections and the sensations which accompanied them. The finished poem, which runs to thirty pages in the original Pocket Poets edition, is his masterpiece.

It was begun in Paris, at the café Le Select in Montparnasse. The first of the five sections to be written was 'Litany', which became Part Four of the completed work. Ginsberg wrote to Kerouac telling him how he sat in the cafe, 'once haunted by Gide and Picasso . . . writing first lines of great formal elegy'. He reproduced part of what he had done so far:

> with your eyes of shock
> with your eyes of lobotomy
> with your eyes of divorce
> with your eyes of stroke
> with your eyes alone
> with your eyes
> with your eyes
> with your Death full of Flowers

More than eighteen months elapsed before he took up the work again, and the poem incorporates its own second wind of inspiration:

downtown Manhattan, clear winter noon, and I've been up all night,

talking, talking, reading the Kaddish aloud, listening to Ray Charles
blues shout blind on the phonograph
the rhythm the rhythm – and your memory in my head three years
after –

He shut himself into his room in the apartment he shared with
Orlovsky at 170 East Second Street, and remained there until ten
o'clock the following night, writing the bulk of the poem on an
engine fuelled by heroin and Methedrine, long lines with Jewish-
emigrant inflexions, having at times the character of a prose memoir:

> But you stared out the window on the Broadway Church corner, and
> spied a mystical assassin from Newark,
> So phoned the Doctor – 'OK go way for a rest' – and so I put on my
> coat and walked you downstreet – On the way a grammarschool boy
> shouted, unaccountably – 'Where you goin Lady to Death?' I
> shuddered . . .

By the end of his thirty-four-hour confinement, Ginsberg had a
poem composed of fragments of speech, shards of memory, the
reactions of relatives – everything seen from the twin perspective of
distance in time and imaginative close-up, all helping to put Naomi
back together again.

To an editor in 1959, Ginsberg wrote that 'Kaddish' 'takes off' from
a long poem by Edward Marshall, 'Leave the Word Alone', which
had appeared in *Black Mountain Review*, no 7. Marshall's poem is
about his mother, Lena, who entered an insane asylum at the age of
thirty-five, having just delivered her baby, the poet.

> That was twenty-three years ago and now she is in an
> insane asylum because she wanted
> to read the bible   and her
> health book
> She reads nothing, for she is   catatonic, dementia-
> praecox among the wolverine
> gang of girls

Like Ginsberg, Marshall, too, had had a spell in the mental hospital,
remaining there for five months. The poem spins various family
anecdotes, as it unravels the tangle of relationships among aunts,

uncles, grandparents, much as 'Kaddish' does. For Marshall, who wrote 'Leave the Word Alone' in 1955, the year Ginsberg was liberated by his psychiatrist, writing the poem was 'a process I must go thru / to stay out of the asylum'.

The next issue of the *Chicago Review*, Winter 1958–9, was in preparation. The editors, Rosenthal and Carroll, planned to devote it to four authors only. There would be a long, improvisatory paean to Carr by Kerouac, entitled 'Lucien Midnight', three poems by Corso, and ten further chapters from *Naked Lunch*, all to be set beside a work by the avant-gardist elder, Edward Dahlberg. However, the previous issue, which contained the 'invisible hierarchies' section, had provoked a journalist on the *Chicago Daily News*, Jack Mabley, to write a column about the magazine and its new coterie:

> Do you ever wonder what happens to little boys who scratch dirty words on railroad underpasses? They go to college and scrawl obscenities in the college literary magazines ... A magazine published by the University of Chicago is distributing one of the foulest collections of printed filth I've seen publicly circulated ... The 'beat' generation has quite a representation on the Midway. I haven't had much personal contact with these people but I get the impression they are young, intellectual, need baths, and have extreme contempt for the less fortunate than themselves, which is almost everybody ...

Mabley went on to say that the material in the *Chicago Review*, if read as a public performance, would result in criminal charges of indecency. The trustees of the University, he concluded, 'should take a long hard look at what is being circulated under this sponsorship'.

The Winter issue ought to have gone to bed at the end of September, but delays in gathering the material, together with a request from the still cautious Carr to cast an eye over the Kerouac piece, meant that the process was still stalled at the beginning of November. This left time for the University authorities to do as the journalist Mabley had suggested, and take a long hard look at what was going into the next issue. A showdown followed. According to Rosenthal, he and Carroll were told by the Chancellor that the contents of the magazine should be 'innocuous'. Anything more,

Rosenthal told Ginsberg, and the *Chicago Review* would be shut down.

Ignoring this injunction, Rosenthal went ahead with his preparation of the Burroughs material, and 'best piece I ever saw of Jack's'. When Chancellor Kimpton realized that the editorial policy had not been altered, as instructed, he carried out his threat, and halted production of the magazine. Carroll was sacked, the reason given being that he was not enrolled at the University and therefore had no proper claim on the office of poetry editor of a University publication. Rosenthal resigned. Corso wrote him a letter:

> Dear Irving,
>
> What? Suppression? Chicago? Are you weeping? I hear from Ginsberg that you are tiny, wet-eyed, low-voiced, a rose in a terrible giant's land; do you wet the bed? ... I always heard University of Chicago was a great happy free institute of soulful sparkle and joy. Is it because of Burroughs? Poor Bill, the Elysium of Al Capone tommy guns his scathless soul ... What happens to you now? Do you flee?
>
> Death to Van Gogh's Ear! Long live Fried Shoes!

The two editors did not flee. Instead, they went off to found their own magazine. At Kerouac's suggestion, they called it *Big Table*, and the first issue was to be subtitled 'The complete contents of the suppressed winter 1959 issue of the *Chicago Review*' – a guarantee of success. They prepared a cover-design showing the Stars and Stripes, which could be seen either as an ironic joke or as a visual plea for the defence of freedom of speech.

The editors asked the author of *Naked Lunch*, still in Paris, for an updated biographical note.

'Who are you?'

'An expert marksman and a student of Mayan codices.'

★

Ferlinghetti waited patiently for the material for a second volume of poems by Ginsberg, with which to crown his success in the courts; but he had no intention of taking on himself the task of publishing, unquestioningly, everything that emanated from the newly famous Beat Generation.

At Ginsberg's suggestion, back in the spring, Burroughs had submitted 200 typewritten pages to City Lights, under the title 'Interzone'. Ferlinghetti rejected it. 'I didn't like that kind of writing', he said later. 'Burroughs's trip was death' (this, Burroughs would not have denied). Ginsberg attempted to persuade him, but Ferlinghetti remained independent of the opinions of others as to what City Lights should publish, just as he declined to pay attention when Customs and police told him what not to publish. He turned down Kerouac's book of poems, *Mexico City Blues*, even as *On the Road* and its author continued their ascent to fame. Ferlinghetti also refused a second volume of poems by Corso, who then struck a deal with James Laughlin, owner of New Directions. Snyder did the same, when City Lights turned down his long poem *Myths and Texts* ('Well well' – Snyder to Ginsberg). Other San Francisco poets, such as McClure and Whalen, never published books under the City Lights imprint.

When the University of Chicago closed down the *Chicago Review*, Ginsberg advised Rosenthal and Carroll to take the material to San Francisco, expecting City Lights to rise to the challenge of *Naked Lunch* this time, and take up the cause of free speech once again. But Ferlinghetti maintained his lack of interest in Burroughs. He saw no reason to publish work simply because it had been banned.

After Ginsberg had set sail on the *Liberté*, Burroughs remained at the Beat Hotel, room 15, bare lightbulb, no chairs, guests invited to sit on the bed beside the three-piece-suited writer, surrounded by stray pages of *Naked Lunch* in various stages of decay. He made a foray to Tangiers to sort out his Interzone affairs, though his affairs anywhere beyond the zone of art were minimal. The outward accoutrements of life had been reduced to fit into any hotel drawer. The metal typewriter case was his valise.

Heroin, the old friend and enemy which he thought he had shaken off for good with the help of Dr John Dent in London, had returned to comfort him. Ginsberg used heroin on and off throughout the 1950s without ever acquiring a habit, but Burroughs was psychologically and metabolically an addict. Though he could stay clean for up to a year at a time, he would relent eventually and begin the beguiling ritual, so enticing in itself, so thrilling, so

familiar, and become hooked again. Then he would kick again –
'Have been in bed the last week with the cure', he wrote to
Ginsberg in August 1959, one of many 'cures' (the idea of this one
being to remain indoors for as long as possible, while asking a friend
to hide his clothes); then, sooner or later, he would, as he put it,
'take a fall'. In *Junkie*, he gave a description of a cure undertaken in
Mexico City with the help of Benzedrine, black coffee, and tequila:

> After ten days of the cure, I had deteriorated shockingly. My clothes
> were spotted and stiff from the drinks I had spilled all over myself. I
> never bathed. I had lost weight, my hands shook, I was always . . .
> knocking over chairs, and falling down. But I seemed to have unlimited
> energy and a capacity for liquor I never had before. My emotions spilled
> out everywhere.

Other drugs were more agreeable. Marihuana was a daily staple (as
was hard liquor), and Burroughs found to his satisfaction that the old
standby, Paregoric, an elixir of opiate he had been using as a cheap
junk-substitute over the years, was available across the counter at any
chemist's shop in Paris. He was undergoing psychoanalysis, and was
of the opinion now that the 'bad thing' he had witnessed in the
woods as a child was a miscarriage, and that the results had been
burnt by his governess, Mary, and her lover. Was this the original
moment of possession by the Ugly Spirit, from which all future
occupants were descended? Burroughs believed in his 'possession' in
a pre-Freudian, almost medieval sense.

With Allen gone, there was space for a new (corporeal) intimate
in Burroughs's hermetic existence. It was taken by Brion Gysin, a
shape-changing trickster-figure whom Burroughs had first known as
the proprietor of the 1001 Nights Café in Tangiers. Gysin had also
quit the Interzone, which was in political turmoil and less safe now
for foreigners. On hearing that he was in need of accommodation,
after a chance meeting on the boulevard St Michel, Burroughs fixed
him up at Madame Rachou's hotel, room 25. There, Gysin found
'Naked Lunch served at all hours in a dark, airless transitional room
full of transformations and metamorphoses. Kafka's cockroach fled in
terror.'

The two men had not got along well in Tangiers, but now
Burroughs fell under Gysin's influence. He was a nomad: part Swiss,

part Canadian, English-educated, homosexual (he and Burroughs did not become lovers), with a Greek wife to boot. In Tangiers, Gysin had moved through the medina in Arab dress. He despised Burroughs at the beginning of their acquaintance for being a drug-addict and (he thought) a layabout. Burroughs lived in the 'Spanish' style (the reference was to his choice of boyfriends), whereas he, Gysin, had chosen the traditional Moroccan way (i.e., Moroccan boyfriends). He had lost the 1001 Nights, he told people, not because of anything as mundane as money troubles, but because of a magic spell. During a routine check on a kitchen ventilator, Gysin found 'the Mare's Nest': a collection of pebbles, shards of mirror, seeds, and a piece of paper with a message written from left to right, then top to bottom, calling on the devil of smoke to 'make Massa Brahim [Brion] leave the house as the smoke leaves this fire, never to return'. A few days later, Gysin lost the business to a swindler. It was the kind of story Burroughs believed in utterly – offering a peep into a reality that was beyond explanation – and it would have shaped his new respect for, and faith in, Gysin.

Gysin was a painter who, at the age of nineteen, had associated with the Surrealists in Paris. He brought to the Beat Hotel theories of chance and prophecy in art, in which Burroughs foresaw the possibility of extending a form of writing that appeared to have reached an impasse in the maw of *Naked Lunch*. Gysin would toss out a theory – 'Writing is fifty years behind painting' – and Burroughs would pounce on it, sensing scope for investing his own work with new urgency. Together with Gysin he began to experiment with montage, pasting photographs, illustrations from magazines, news-paper-clippings, and scraps of original writing, into notebooks, to form new 'intersections' – a key word, from now on, in Burroughs's technique.

To some people, the camp, confident Gysin was self-centred as only a child can be, but he was to guide Burroughs on to a new path. The writing in *Naked Lunch*, which was currently mortifying the Chicago academic establishment, Burroughs now regarded as too tame and too limited for his purposes. As he told his loyal confessor, Ginsberg: 'Unless I can reach a point where my writing has the . . . urgency of bullfighting, it is nowhere and I must look for another way.' And he introduced his new mentor:

He has undergone a similar conversion to mine and doing GREAT painting ... He is doing in painting what I try to do in writing. He regards painting as a hole in the texture of the so-called 'reality', through which he is exploring an actual place existing in outer space.

Other theories propounded by Gysin had a similar effect on Burroughs. Like Ginsberg, Burroughs was disaffected from orthodox political and economic systems; but as Ginsberg limbered up for the role which he was to occupy in the coming decade, of activist on behalf of alternative politics, Burroughs moved in the opposite direction. It sounded far, far out, but he meant it:

the whole existing system can be dreamed away if we get enough people dreaming on the Gysin level. There is nothing to stop the power of a real dream. I mean this literally. You know, I can dream money into my pocket.

These and other Surrealist-inspired suggestions were to provide a hunting-ground for Burroughs, as he sought to find The Answer once again. He was for ever in search of it − heroin, crime, yagé, orgone boxes, Reichian analysis and other drugs and systems, had all been utilized to try to break through to the other side of the so-called reality. What Gysin introduced into the problem-solving process, on which Burroughs had been engaged for most of his life, was the revelation that 'Words are the principal instruments of control'. Rub out the Word!

Gysin himself remained bitter at his exclusion from the Surrealist group, which had occurred in Paris in 1935, when Gysin was only nineteen. On the eve of a Surrealist show, Breton had ordered Gysin's paintings to be taken down. No explanation was given. However, he could claim to share his distinction with Tristan Tzara who, twenty years before Gysin's demise, had roused the Surrealist general's anger by cutting up a sheet of paper with words written on it, then picking the separate pieces out of a hat and calling the result a poem.

10

The birth of the beatnik

Q: What do you think of being King of the Beatniks?

A: Well, you know I never was a beatnik, doncha?

Q: How did the word evolve?

A: Well, first it was Beat Generation ... then Sputnik went up, remember? Then they called it beatnik.

Sputnik 1 went into orbit on 4 October 1957, the day after 'Howl' was cleared by Judge Horn in San Francisco, and one month after the publication of *On the Road*. A week or two later, a columnist on the *San Francisco Chronicle*, Herb Caen, wrote that the mad young bohemians skulking round North Beach and hanging out in its proliferating espresso bars were as 'far out' as Sputnik. Their window display was 'beat', but Caen redesigned them: from now on they were 'beatniks'.

The suffix waved an unwashed hand in the direction of beardedness, idleness, hoboism, non-patriotism, and, the ultimate, communism. So began, ironically, the commercialization of, and capitalization on, the rebellious image. Beatnik turned 'beat' into kitsch.

The Beats disliked the appropriation of 'beat', and its melding into 'beatnik'. 'The foul word is used several times', wrote Ginsberg in a letter to the *New York Times Book Review* (respecting the notion of taboo utterance, for once), in response to an uncomplimentary article about Kerouac;

But the 'beatnik' of mad critics is a piece of their own ignoble poetry. And if 'beatniks', and not illuminated Beat poets, overrun this country they will have been created not by Kerouac but by industries of mass communication which continue to brainwash Man . . .

He signed off: 'Prophetically, Allen Ginsberg'. 'Beat' was a state of being, said the prophet; 'beatnik' was fancy dress. Beat was identity; beatnik was image.

It had been on its way for some time, and others less eager than Ginsberg to believe in a wholesale revolution in 'mind' ('illuminated Beat poets' overrunning the country, etc) had seen it coming. One evening in Tangiers, Kerouac had been summoned to a party by Ginsberg, who was entertaining a 'big bunch of hipsters and chicks' whom he had met in the medina. As Kerouac sat and listened to their 'awful "likes" and "like you know" and "wow crazy" and "a wig man, a real gas" ', he was gripped by an overpowering nausea at the false consciousness of hip, which he himself had helped to create. 'Whither goest thou, America, in thy shiny car in the night?' he asked on the long-ago holiday with *Überbeatmensch*, super-man double-man. Dean–Neal. Here? To be crowded out by a bunch of weekend beatniks? This dispiriting insight occurred in the spring of 1957, the very moment at which *On the Road* was at last being set in type, and there was he, 'already sick of the whole subject'.

By the middle of 1959, it seemed as though you could hardly open a magazine without encountering a photograph or a caricature – in the fashion department as much as in the feature pages – of the typical beatnik: loose-fitting hooped T-shirt, beret, goatee beard, sunglasses, poetry book in hand; for chicks, subtract the beard and add deep fringe and heavy eye make-up. *Playboy* ran a version of an address Kerouac had given to students at Brandeis College late in 1958, 'Origins of the Beat Generation'. Much though he disliked its current manifestation, Kerouac still laid claim to being the founder of the Beat Generation. He explained to his audience that, yes, 'beat' had originally meant low, down on your luck, but then he had had a revelation one afternoon in a church in his hometown, Lowell: suddenly, with tears in his eyes, he had 'a vision of what I must have really meant with "Beat" . . . as being to mean "beatific" '.

Playboy had no interest in beatific, but went all out for beatnik.

246

The December issue contained 'Before the Road: The earlier adventures of Dean Moriarty', an account of Neal's poolroom days in Denver during the Second World War. The editorial column, 'Playbill', introduced Kerouac and three other writers featured in the magazine:

> a foursome of fiction by the ever-beat Jack Kerouac, the sometimes beat Alberto Moravia, the rarely beat Max Shulman, and the never-beat Roald Dahl.

There was a 'Beat Playmate', Yvette, 'a beatnik found in a coffee-house'. She was blonde, crop-haired, and anything but down on her luck: 'She's interested in serious acting, ballet, the poetry of Dylan Thomas, classical music ("Prokoviev drives me out of my *skull!*").' Yvette was also 'restless and uninhibited enough to drive a Jag in the desert for kicks'.

Life took the anti-Americanism encrypted in the Soviet-sounding suffix more to heart than most other magazines. In September 1959, *Life* ran a feature entitled 'Squaresville USA vs Beatsville'. It was prompted by the news that three teenage girls in the Midwestern town of Hutchinson, Kansas, had sent an invitation to Lawrence Lipton, author of the recently published *Holy Barbarians*, an account of beatnik life in Venice, California. When word went round Hutchinson that the place was on the brink of invasion by beatniks, a parents' revolt took place, and they called in the law. A spokesman for the police department told *Life* that a beatnik was someone who 'doesn't like work, any man who doesn't like work is a vagrant, and a vagrant goes to jail around here'. Lipton was hastily uninvited, and the trio of girls who had innocently contacted him had their Americanness – and what Ginsberg might have called their 'psychic virginity' – protected by being 'whisked away to seclusion by their distressed parents'. Before they disappeared, the journalist from *Life* elicited a quote from one of them, Luetta Peters: 'We know beatniks aren't good', she said, 'but we thought they just dressed sloppy and talked funny. Now we know that they get married without licenses and things like that.'

Things like that? Even if they had not read the uncensored version of what still appeared on the printed page as 'who were . . . in the . . . by saintly motorcyclists and screamed with joy', their intuition –

or their parents', or the local policeman's intuition – read the dotted runes and understood the threat to the Hutchinsonian way of life. 'Now we know . . .': that Ginsberg, Corso and Orlovsky all sleep in the same bed; that Ginsberg and Orlovsky share both boyfriends and girlfriends; that they performed oral sex on each other in the grounds of a church in Assisi; that they wrote separate accounts of their 'experiments' (Peter fellating Allen while Allen writes a poem); that they inject heroin; that Ginsberg had left the Cassady household because Mrs Cassady had surprised him with Mr Cassady's penis in his mouth; that Mr Cassady – the same Cassady who was the hero of the current beatnik novel – was in the habit of sleeping with several women in the same day (though not now, because he was in prison), and much more. The long hair, the loose clothes, the beards, contained the answers if you asked questions of them that were tough enough. Luetta Peters and her friends were probably also unable to admit that part of the beatniks' original appeal for them had been their own literally unspeakable (in the town of Hutchinson) interest in the subject of sex.

Life printed a picture of a 'happy home in Kansas' – a living-room where the four-square family congregated for a 'TV session', or gathered round the photograph album ('unfailing fun'). This was contrasted with a 'hip family's cool pad' in Venice, California, where the 'emphasis is all on "creativity" with no interest in physical surroundings'. The occupants were shown sprawled on mattresses on the floor, with empty beercans lying around.

Soon there was Rent-a-Beatnik, *The Beat Generation Cookbook*, and a *MAD* magazine special, featuring mock advertisements for 'Paint Smears – all colors, paste on easily' and 'Oversize Sweaters for Beatnik chicks – one size only (too big)'. There was a glossary of 'Square Terms' ('*Daddy* – the tag a square pegs his old man with') and a gallery of 'Hipsters', complete with their philosophies. One was Wanda Kuhl, who used to 'sit around at home nights with nothing to do', until she became a beatnik. 'Now every night I go to some coffee house and sit around and listen to jazz records. I'm leading a real wild life now.'

The Beat Generation Cookbook offered recipes for 'Ginsburgers' ('half-cup chopped Pickled Beats, 1 cup cooked Square potatoes'), 'Subterranean Spudniks' ('This bit was supplied by a young Beat doll who is also the mother of three Beatlets'), and 'Haiku Hash' ('The only one that is anywhere near as popular as the Pablo Picasserole').

Rent-a-Beatnik was the brainchild of Fred McDarragh, a photographer who was making a speciality of beat (and beatnik) scenes. McDarragh placed an ad in the *Village Voice*:

RENT genuine BEATNIKS
Badly groomed but brilliant
(male and female)

The rental price was $40 nightly. (*MAD* countered with 'Rent a SQUARE for your next Beatnik Party'.) Props, such as bongo drums and guitars, were extra.

One of McDarragh's rentable beatniks was the poet Jack Micheline, 'an intense, beardless New Yorker of 29', according to the *New York Herald Tribune*, which ran a story about these glimmers of the spirit of free enterprise among the indolent hip. 'It's sad', Micheline told the *Herald Tribune*'s reporter, 'that a poet of my reputation has to do a whole lot of gigs just to make a buck.'

Another rentable beatnik was Ted Joans, 'an ebullient Negro bard and painter who came to New York from Indiana'. Joans was rented out to a party in the affluent New York suburb of Scarsdale, to read his poetry. When it came time for the recital, however, the guests were too drunk to want to listen. 'But he was there', the host, Lawrence Barken, told the *Trib*, 'resplendent in his beret and his slightly torn black sweater. It worked out wonderfully. People in Westchester are still talking about it.' The Hipikat had come a long way.

Early in 1959, Ginsberg, Corso and Orlovsky set up a travelling circus. Ostensibly to raise money for the first issue of *Big Table*, it was also the opportunity to proselytize on behalf of beat poetry and beatitude, to tarnish the gold standard of American moneymaking values, to wake up the 'fabled damned' for a moment. If the discussion appeared to be reverting to normality, just throw in a 'Death to Van Gogh's Ear', or 'Poetry is a wose'. Ginsberg and Corso made an effective double-act, with Orlovsky in the middle as Harpo Marx. On his radio programme on WFMT in Chicago, Studs Terkel, introducing them as 'two certainly very alive young poets', had to be interrupted and alerted to the fact that Orlovsky was there at all. 'We've brought an angel along!' cried Ginsberg into the mike. Then, while Terkel and Ginsberg were carrying on a conversation about the 'philosophy of beat' – it's only a label, Ginsberg explained, but 'actually quite a beautiful label . . . it's poetically interesting . . . everybody's so worn down to a point where they'd be able to receive God . . .' – Corso struggled free of his leash. Suddenly he said that he didn't like 'all these people'. Which people? asked Terkel. Corso turned coy and wouldn't say, though the conversation had been about beatniks. 'I hate them', Corso repeated. Then, under prompting from Terkel, he admitted that he loved them. 'I can't make up my mind. You're making me paranoid.'

Orlovsky broke in to add, in a frail voice, that 'beat' came from Fra Angelico, 'who used to cry a lot. He would cry for four hours at a time before he painted Christ.' Orlovsky sounded close to tears himself. 'Before he painted the Virgin', corrected Ginsberg. Corso butted in again to say that he had just written a poem about his hair. Could he read it?

> It was lovely hair once
> it was
> Hours before shop-windows   gum-machine mirrors   with great
> > combs
> Washed hair I hated
> With dirt the waves came easier and stayed . . .

Still in Chicago, the trio gave a reading in the home of a local banker. Representatives of the press were invited. *Time* devoted most of a page to the event.

At length Poet Ginsberg arrived, wearing blue jeans and a checked black-and-red lumber shirt with black patches. With him were two other shabbily dressed Beatniks. One was Ginsberg's intimate friend, a mental-hospital attendant named Peter Orlovsky, 25, who writes poetry (*I talk to the fire hydrant, asking: 'Do you have bigger tears than I do?'*); the other was Gregory Corso, 28, a shaggy, dark little man who boasts that he has never combed his hair – and never gets an argument . . .

As the formalities began, somebody shoved a microphone in view.

'I'm Peter Orlovsky', said Peter Orlovsky. 'I'm very fine and happy and crazy as a wild flower.'

'I'm Allen Ginsberg', said Allen Ginsberg, 'and I'm crazy like a daisy.'
'I'm Gregory Corso', said Gregory Corso, 'and I'm not crazy at all.'
Would they like to make any comment? 'Yes,' said Corso. 'Fried shoes.'

★

Emerging from the timid, nervy, repressed Ginsberg of a decade earlier was a bright, haloed creature. Ginsberg was saved through faith – faith in his own visions. 'Not for nothing did I hear Blake's voice ten years ago', he told a literary editor, Max Gartenberg, 'his actual voice I mean.' Get this straight: Blake talks to me, not you. Nine months later, Ginsberg repeated to the same correspondent that there was no doubt that the voice he heard was Blake's voice, 'I mean heard, aurally, literally.' Spun through successive retellings, his Harlem experience had become the ceremony of his election to the circle of prophetic poets. He belonged, he told Gartenberg, 'to the *Church of Poetry*'.

He had no hesitation about telling audiences the same thing. At a reading at City Lights in 1959, Ginsberg prepared the crowd for what they were about to hear by saying that, when he wrote, he got a rhythm going and then improvised with the help of what sometimes 'appears to be Divine Inspiration'. When so possessed, he arrived at the feeling that 'the world can be entered and Prophesied by a Single Soul'. At another reading the same year, at New York University, he announced that he was writing for 'God's ear'.

It was also within the realm of the Prophet to spit fire and brimstone, and Ginsberg's assaults on what he called 'standard American values' and all those that had been corrupted by them, became more vitriolic as they became more public. He had always linked the personal and the political. For Burroughs and Kerouac, 'beat' was body politics: freedom from police interference, from moral interference (whose morals anyway?), freedom to move to different latitudes and freedom to mutilate oneself, or mutilate one's text; for Ginsberg, it became, as he became more famous, a spiritual pressure group. From having been content to work on changing the subject of his own psyche, he all of a sudden wanted to change the world.

251

The letter to the *NYTBR* (a response to a review of *The Subterraneans*), in which he berated 'mad critics' and 'industries of mass communication which continue to brainwash man', was followed by an essay in the *San Francisco Chronicle*, which began from the premiss that 'America is having a nervous breakdown'. Ginsberg prophesied a police state, the apparatus of which was already in place. Although San Francisco was a city where a few poets 'have had the luck and courage and fate to glimpse . . . the nature of God', nevertheless 'the police and newspapers have moved in, mad movie manufacturers from Hollywood are at this moment preparing bestial stereotypes of the scene'. Those who chose to use heroin, like Ginsberg himself, found themselves 'threatened with permanent jail and death'. Worse than that, he shrieked, sense finally strangled by rhetoric, to be a junkie in America 'is like having been a Jew in Nazi Germany'.

In the author's note to his forthcoming book of poems, *Kaddish*, Ginsberg declared that 'the established literary quarterlies of my day are bankrupt poetically thru their own hatred, dull ambition or loudmouthed obtuseness'. A letter to the anthologist Gartenberg, who was compiling a collection of writing by both the Beats and the Angry Young Men, issued a warning to mind what he said in public about the Beat Generation. It was ornamented by a half-page illustration of a skull and crossbones.

Another skull and crossbones for another era. One of the most successful campaigns of 1959 was fought at Columbia University, where, fifteen years earlier, a different Ginsberg had etched a skull and crossbones on a dormitory window, and found himself suspended from the College, beginning the painful process which led eventually to the Psychiatric Institute.

In February, together with Corso and Orlovsky, Ginsberg read at the McMillin Theater on campus, at the invitation of a student club. Members of the English department, including Trilling, declined to sponsor the occasion in any way, and made public their rejection of it. When Ginsberg and friends stepped on to the podium before a large collection of students, there were only a few 'faculty wives' present from within the University to witness the triumphant return.

One of the faculty wives was Diana Trilling, who intended to write about it for *Partisan Review*. Like her husband, their friend and colleague Auden boycotted the meeting ('I'm ashamed of you', he gently chided Diana); her editor William Phillips also stayed away, though he welcomed her thoughts on the event. She was curious to know what had become of Ginsberg, with his annoying 'sensation-seeking', his 'lurid boasts' about being the confidant of Blake, his poems which were 'never quite good enough', who had, at one stage, been painfully involved with her family. She was proud that it was not just anyone to whom Ginsberg had gone in his trouble; 'it was Lionel'. She and her husband, she wrote, were forced to regard Ginsberg as 'a case' – a gifted and sad case, a nuisance case, even a guilt-provoking case, but above all a 'case'.

On the platform at McMillin, before a large audience of newly long-haired, bearded, unnecktied students, Ginsberg read part of 'Kaddish', and as he read 'he choked and cried'. He read another poem, also bound for his new collection, 'The Lion for Real' – 'I came home and found a lion in my living room' – which Mrs Trilling understood as a tribute to her husband. She heard it as 'a passionate love poem', and when she got home to the Trillings' apartment on Riverside Drive, where a meeting was in progress among her husband and his colleagues, she announced, in the presence of the assembled company, 'Allen Ginsberg read a love-poem to you, Lionel'. She felt sure that the wild poet's tame old teacher would understand why.

Except that she was wrong. She had misheard. 'The Lion for Real' is about Ginsberg's Blake experience; the 'lion' in the living-room is not 'Lionel' but a force, an emissary from God. The spiritual dynamic of the poem propels it in exactly the opposite direction to the one recommended to Ginsberg by Trilling. If Ginsberg dedicated it to his former teacher on the night, it could only have been as an ironic riposte to the sensible but (Ginsberg now firmly believed) wasteful advice encapsulated in the word *adjust*.

Diana Trilling's article, 'The Other Night at Columbia', came out in the Spring issue of *Partisan Review*. Ginsberg's brother Eugene Brooks wrote to him to say that he had read it, and that he found it 'sensitive and modest'. Not, as Ginsberg did, 'self-smug or bitchy'. Allen pointed to the misunderstanding of 'The Lion for Real', and threatened to write to the magazine with another assault on the 'mad critics' of 'ignoble poetry' who couldn't even listen straight. His brother gently suggested that Mrs Trilling be allowed to put that interpretation on it if she wished.

At the same time that he was fuming to Eugene, Ginsberg heard from Kerouac's ex-girlfriend, Joyce Glassman, who was working as a secretary at *Partisan Review* (in succession to LeRoi Jones's wife). She said that the editor was hoping Ginsberg would reply to the article in a letter. 'Various wrathful ones have already come in', she added.

The wrath was doubtless stirred by Mrs Trilling's sympathetic attitude towards the beat prophet (which Eugene could see but Allen could not). When, during the question-and-answer session, someone in the audience had asked Ginsberg to state his philosophy, Mrs Trilling had thought: 'Here we go, he'll tell us how he's crazy like a daisy', or else utter one of the other beat wisecracks she had read in *Time*. But, instead of saying he was crazy-daisy, Ginsberg replied that he had no philosophy; 'he spoke of inspiration, or . . . ecstatic illumination, as the source of his poetry', which surprised and pleased Mrs Trilling.

Ginsberg decided to take up *Partisan's* offer to respond to the article. His letter appeared in the Summer issue. There were no 'wrathful' letters, only his: 'The universe is a new flower. Allen Ginsberg.'

The first issue of *Big Table* came off the press, at last, in March, sporting the Stars and Stripes on the cover. 'Will you guys promise to visit me if I go to jail for printing this mag?' Irving Rosenthal worried in a letter to Ginsberg and Kerouac. *Big Table* had become a cause. Its defiance of the academic establishment, which had attempted to wish away the contents of the *Chicago Review*, placed it instantly in the best tradition of twentieth-century little-magazine publishing. Rosenthal and Carroll could proclaim themselves the heirs of Jane Heap and Margaret Anderson, whose *Little Review* had carried portions of an earlier banned book, *Ulysses*, and as a result had been burnt on four separate occasions. Warned by Ezra Pound (who sent them the manuscript) that to print Joyce's work was certain to land them in a censorship struggle, Miss Anderson replied: 'This is the most beautiful thing we'll ever have . . . We'll print it if it's the last effort of our lives.' Rosenthal and Carroll felt the same way. Who would give two cents now for Isaac Rosenfeld's lament for the avant-garde?

Four hundred copies which had been deposited in the mail for subscribers were promptly impounded by the Post Office. They neglected to tell the publishers, however, and Rosenthal and Carroll only discovered that *Big Table* 1 had been deemed 'unfit to go through the mail' when subscribers wrote in to complain that their copies had failed to arrive.

The Post Office beheld indecency not only in the latest helpings of *Naked Lunch* – the largest and strongest yet – but also in the long prose piece, divided into fifty sections, by Kerouac. Its original title was 'Lucien Midnight', and it was meant as a tribute to the mercurial nature of the founding member of the libertine circle; but, after seeing galley proofs, Carr requested that the title be changed – his disguise was still self-effacement – and Kerouac renamed it 'Old Angel Midnight'.

The Post Office's concern was with obscenity. The Chancellor of the University and others interested in the fate of the *Chicago Review* objected on aesthetic grounds. They claimed that the writing selected by the editorial team of Rosenthal and Carroll was 'half-literate'. This was becoming a common criticism of the work of Kerouac and Co, and it was reiterated in unexpected places. William Carlos Williams, who had endorsed Ginsberg's book (though in obtuse terms, remembering Ginsberg as someone he had known after the First World War), wrote to Joseph Renard in 1958 asking if he was familiar with the work of the 'San Francisco gang'. Renard's own poems, Williams wished to stress, 'are not an offshoot from that impetus – which is really illiterate, though I should be strung up [if] it were known . . .'

In his most recent prose experiment, Kerouac granted himself the right to say 'anything I want, absolutely anything'. And he stuck to that right:

> 2. Flaki – amete – interrupted chain saw sting eucalyptus words inside the outside void that good God we cant believe anything is arsaphallawy any the pranaraja of madore with his bloody arse kegs, shit – go to three.

'Old Angel Midnight' begins on the path of spontaneous composition and ends in the Tower of Babel. The cause of comprehensibility was finally dropped. Here was the verbal jazz master willing to forget everything he had ever learned – including the relationship between words and things, words and actions – and to leave it all in the hands of his genius. Close your eyes and just hit the keys. Kerouac's current favourite pianist, Cecil Taylor, was doing something similar in music – he would become known for clambering on top of the piano and playing upside-down, and for climbing inside and plucking the wires. And now here was Kerouac, plucking the wires of verbal facility, writing upside-down. Not forgetting to stir in a little chopped-up Buddhism:

> Pirilee, pirilee, tzwé tzwi tzwa – tack tick – birds & firewood. The dream is already ended and we're already awake in the golden eternity.

Since the early 1950s, following the composition of *The Town and the City*, and the first version of *On the Road*, Kerouac had moved his method of composition ever closer to the area of music. He 'blew' on his typewriter as a jazz musician blew on his instrument. It wasn't cool jazz, it was bebop, hard and fast, the faster the better, until the melody was lost in a blur of notes. Kerouac could type faster than anyone else, according to Philip Whalen:

> The most noise that you heard while he was typing was the carriage return, slamming back again, and again. The little bell would bing-bang, bing-bang, bing-bang! And he'd laugh and say, 'Look at this!' And he'd type, and he'd laugh. Then he'd make a mistake, and this would lead him off into a possible part of a new paragraph, into a funny riff of some kind . . .

His old friend from Horace Mann Prep School, Jerry Newman, had progressed from his days as an amateur collector of live recordings in the 52nd Street clubs to become a professional recording engineer. One day, Newman set up a session with the pianist Ralph Burns, to be produced by Leonard Feather. Knowing of Kerouac's excitement at being close to jazz musicians, Newman invited him to attend. But Kerouac brought along a bottle, and proceeded to get plastered. As the session got under way, he kept on telling Newman that the only pianist worth listening to in New York was Cecil Taylor. Newman had worked with Taylor in the past, and admired him, but his mind was on the present session with Burns. While Newman was setting up the microphones, however,

> Jack got on the phone and invited, at his own initiative, Cecil Taylor to come over and play . . . The trouble I had shooing Jack away from the piano (by this time he was himself playing on the Steinway) ruined the rest of the session, and I finally flipped . . .
>
> At this point he called me a 'dirty Jew bastard'.

★

'My contract includes a Hollywood clause – what? Lana Turner and me?' That was to a friend ten years before, in the first flush of excitement at having sold *The Town and the City* to Harcourt Brace for $1,000. Ever since, Kerouac had nursed hopes of seeing something of his in the movies, and of seeing some movie money. Through the late 1940s and into the 50s, Kerouac's fantasies of buying a ranch, growing alfalfa, raising a small herd, cosying down with Neal (and Carolyn, if necessary), had lacked financial back-up. The sale of a book to Hollywood was the answer.

There had been cause for optimism following the publication of *On the Road*. An offer of $100,000 was reportedly placed on the table by Warner Bros . . . Paramount entered the bidding . . . Brando was still interested . . . Kerouac's agent was holding out for $150,000 . . .

It was pie in the sky, and the rights to the book remained unsold.

The only one of his novels to be made into a film was *The Subterraneans*, which Grove Press had published in February 1958. The sum paid for the rights was one-tenth of what he had hoped to receive for *On the Road*, and the film version turned out to be a parody of the original book. An interracial love affair on the screen posed moral and commercial questions which MGM was unwilling, or simply unable, to consider; and so Mardou Fox, the 'brown mistress', the 'child of Bop', was played by the ultra-fair Leslie Caron. The underground spirit of the book was swept out and a topical weird-beatnik phantom inserted in its place. The Kerouac character, Leo Percepied, was portrayed as a vicious roughneck by George Peppard, and the script had great fun with this tough guy's dependence on his mother.

The opening scene involves a conversation among four characters, the Corso figure Yuri, Arial Lavalina (whose role was upgraded for the screen, possibly because the scriptwriter had heard that he was based on Gore Vidal), Adam (Ginsberg), and the far-out beat-chick Roxanne. They talk nonsense. It is parody Beat nonsense. And yet, as it goes on, it becomes apparent that it is not, really, that far removed from 'Fried shoes' and 'Crazy as a daisy'.

> Yuri (to Arial): If I were you, man, I'd go to the moon – I mean it's like conk-coo-coo-cool up there, but private man, like now anyway. Later on it'll be the new Miami Beach but now it's still away, and if I were you I'd go to the moon . . .

> Adam (to Roxanne): If I were you . . . and I *am* . . . why then we'd be each other. And if I knew what that meant I'd know everything. I'd know *you*.

Roxanne rises, and begins a strange dance routine, chanting her own accompaniment all the while, her voice rising to a crescendo: 'There's a tiger in my bones! I'm filled up with him! he's coming out! Tiger, tiger, burning bright!' In a token acknowledgement of the Harlem vision, Adam pipes up: 'In the forest of the night.'

The film's single consolation was a soundtrack by Gerry Mulligan, Carmen McCrae and Shelly Manne, among others. Kerouac was angry and embarrassed at seeing his work travestied. He could only protest that he had not even been paid a decent price for selling out.

A desperately ironic reversal of the original ethos of *beat* took place around the alternative title for *On the Road*, 'Beat Generation'. Over the course of a weekend in 1957, Kerouac had written a three-act play, for which he had used his own old favourite title – since his novel was finally settled, he decided to call the play 'The Beat Generation'. The substance of it was drawn from an evening at the Cassadys' home in Los Gatos in 1955, when a visit of the local bishop and his elderly mother and aunt coincided with the unexpected arrival of Kerouac, Ginsberg and Orlovsky. The visit turned into a nightmare for Carolyn. After tea had been served, Ginsberg sat between the two elderly women and asked brightly: 'Now, what about sex?' Caressing a bottle of wine, Kerouac slouched down on the floor by the bishop's legs and fell into a drunken sleep. As Carolyn endeavoured to carry on a normal conversation with her guests, Kerouac would wake up now and then, look at the bishop and say: 'I love you', then go back to sleep. When Neal arrived home from work, he took the side of his wild-man buddies over that of his wife and her clergyman.

In 1959, Kerouac, Ginsberg, and some Greenwich Village friends hatched a plan to make a short film, using the third act of Kerouac's play, which dramatized the bishop's visit, as the central event. They wanted to call it 'The Beat Generation'. However, it was discovered that MGM had copyrighted the title, and were about to give it to a B-movie featuring a rapist on the run from the police. When not terrorizing women, the villainous hero of the film *The Beat Generation* hangs out in espresso bars and at beatnik parties, where strange dances are performed by men with goatee beards and dyed-blonde beat-chicks to the rhythm of the bongo drums.

The alternative film went ahead. It was called *Pull My Daisy*, a title borrowed from the early poem by Ginsberg which had appeared in the magazine *Neurotica*. The director was the Swiss photographer Robert Frank. Ginsberg, Orlovsky and Corso were given parts, the former pair to play themselves, and Corso to move between himself and Kerouac, who did not wish to appear. They used a loft at the corner of Fourth Avenue and 12th Street as the set; there was one camera, one spotlight, one professional performer – the French actress Delphine Seyrig, who took the role of that other outsider, Carolyn Cassady – and an impromptu voice-over by Kerouac. The composer David Amram, well-known around the Village, was enlisted to write some music, but the technique and spirit of the film were improvisatory; it was a jazz movie, a boy-gang reunion, a homage to the still imprisoned Neal Cassady, and a jeer at his wife.

Pull My Daisy begins with the Carolyn-figure (unnamed) letting in the dawn. Kerouac's narration (which was recorded in one sitting, after he had watched the film twice) is warm and plangent:

Early morning in the universe. The wife is getting up, opening the windows, in this loft that's in the bowery in the lower east side, New York. She's a painter and her husband's a railroad brakeman, and he's coming home in a couple hours, about five hours, from the local. 'Course the room's in a mess. That's her husband's coat on a chair – been there for three days – neckties and his tortured socks.

Before her husband, Milo, returns from work, the poets bounce into the room, 'laying their beercans out on the table . . . bursting with poetry'. Milo gets home shortly before the arrival of the bishop and his womenfolk. After the disastrous encounter has taken place, Milo is nagged by his wife, who had so badly wanted the visit to be a success, and, now that the guests have gone, feels humiliated and let down by Milo and all his friends. Tired of her bleating complaints, the boys get up and leave. Milo remonstrates:

> Ah, shut up, I didn't do nothing, you know I didn't do nothing and it's not bad. These are nice fellas. They're just sitting – now they're getting up and they're leaving. I don't blame them for leaving.
>
> You don't understand . . .
>
> Come on there, Peter, Gregory, Allen, come, let's go. Come on down these steps. Let's go. We'll go somewhere; we'll find something. Maybe we'll play by fires in the Bowery.
>
> She's crying.

While Milo prepares to leave with the boys and the camera lingers on a lonely woman in an empty room, the narrator adds blithely: 'She'll get over it.'

They bound down the stairs towards the front door and the open streets, the Territory, away from churchly decorum, wifely rectitude, domestic drear. 'Here comes sweet Milo, beautiful Milo. Hello gang. Da da da da da.' The boys start the rap: 'Let's go! 'sgo! 'sgo! Off – they – go.'

All the essential elements of the boy-gang are there: anti-authoritarianism, jazz, bop-prose narration, girls-in-dresses-better-left-at-home spilling into misogyny, boys' adventure spilling into homosexuality. It is the emblematic Beat Generation film. At the close, Kerouac even had them going on the road again. But that was only wishful thinking.

By this time, Kerouac felt confident about applying his technique of verbal spontaneity to practically any genre: novel, poem, drama, filmscript. Spontaneity, after all, had scriptural backing. When Gary Snyder suggested that he try his hand at writing sutra – the classical form, purporting to convey the thoughts of the Buddha himself – it seemed like a logical extension, and Kerouac didn't hesitate. He produced *The Scripture of the Golden Eternity*, sixty-six sections of spiritual bromide.

> When you've understood this scripture, throw it
> away. If you can't understand this scripture,
> throw it away. I insist on your freedom.

While Ginsberg and Burroughs continued to overreach themselves to catch the fleeting vision, Kerouac's natural skills turned inwards, regarded no other, and wasted. By the middle of 1959, he was being seen by a fascinated public as an ex-hobo, a bohemian institution, or as just the latest gimmick. To himself, he was a genius. His declarations about his own stature and ability became more and more uncoordinated and wayward. On a radio programme broadcast from Lowell, Kerouac rambled, giggled, and burst into tears by turns, while a befuddled host attempted to keep up the theme of local boy made good. He was questioned about his by-now famous refusal to revise his prose. 'Once God moves the hand', intoned Kerouac solemnly, 'to go back and revise is a *sin*!' Uh-huh, said the interviewer, 'that's great, Jack.' Asked if he felt he had accomplished what he set out to do in writing, the audibly drunk writer shot back: 'I accomplish anything.' Proust and Joyce were the two greatest writers of the century so far. As to the third . . .

> I read all of *The Remembrance of Things Past* by Marcel Proust, and I
> decided to do just like he did — but fast . . . James Joyce was going to sit
> by the sea and write the sounds of the sea, but he died and he didn't do
> it, so I did it for him.

Writing to LeRoi Jones on a piece of toilet paper from Paris, Ginsberg had complained that he was 'tired of being Allen Ginsberg', and that people approached him in cafés and on the street 'with all these strange ideas about who I am'. Compared to Kerouac's fame, however, Ginsberg's was still of the local variety. He had yet to publish a second collection, though by now most of what would be *Kaddish and other poems* was ready to be handed over to Ferlinghetti. Much of the work intended for the book was drug-infused — as the titles indicate: 'Mescaline', 'Lysergic Acid', 'Laughing Gas' — and while they do not live up to the title poem, they gesture towards Ginsberg's intention to make his poems include everything contained in the vertical figure, 'I'.

On a different continent, in a different genre, one he invented as he went along, Burroughs was engaged in a comparable project, with this paradox: that his inclusiveness had the aim of invisibility. As he was always attempting to kick narcotics, so he was always in the process of trying to kick his own fleshless features, and move beyond 'the so-called reality' by disappearing through a hole in the texture of a painting by Brion Gysin, or a painting by Gysin's disciple – himself.

The expansionist project was not joined by Kerouac. His drug was drink. People who saw him at social gatherings were spellbound by his party-trick of falling flat on his face, like a felled tree, in the middle of a sentence.

Increasingly disaffected from his earlier role as 'father of the Beats', Kenneth Rexroth responded to 'Fried shoes', 'Poetry is a wose', Ginsberg's habit of taking off his clothes while reciting his poems, Corso's uncombed hair, Kerouac's ever more uncombed mind, by doing what radicals of his generation always did when they wanted to make a protest: he wrote an article. In 'The Commercialization of the Image of Revolt', Rexroth expressed the view that the most deplorable thing about the rise of the beatnik was that it eclipsed a dissident movement which had the potential to create actual change.

He began by paying homage to the 'great *aliénés*' of the past. There had been writers in every period who were dissidents. Baudelaire synthesized the various types of nonconformity into one person: 'There's hardly . . . a fad taken up every five years by a new bohemian generation which Baudelaire didn't push to its limits. He would have been perfectly at home in Greenwich Village.' Rexroth meant the Greenwich Village of the 1920s, or even of the early 50s; but as for the present, 'what has happened in the past four or five years is that dissent has become a hot commodity'.

The word 'commodity' was a signal for radical disgust. The capitalist system – incorporating the 'industries of mass communication' against which Ginsberg had fulminated in his letter to the *New York Times* – was going through its customary motions of assimilating its critics, turning them into cute dolls with berets and T-shirts, and selling them through the mass-market magazines as court jesters to the bourgeoisie. Dissent, a university professor told Rexroth, 'is the hottest thing around'. The anarchist essence of *beat* was being siphoned off and used to fuel the same old superstructure. Beat? Sure, we can sell it. Subversive? They'll be queuing round the block. The final result of the anarchist-based San Francisco Renaissance was 'Rent-a-Beatnik' in a posh New York suburb. Baudelaire's injunction to artists to 'épater les bourgeois' had become *amuser les bourgeois*. When the beatnik turns up at a party in Scarsdale with his bearded vocabulary and his bereted verse, they are tickled to be *épaté*; they have a ball, he takes their money, everyone goes home happy. Remark the difference: in 1957, Allen Ginsberg's poem was under investigation as a criminal act, while in 1959 Jack Kerouac was publishing his latest discourse on hip to *Playboy*, or some other girlie magazine. 'Well', sighed the old anarchist Rexroth, 'it sells books.'

Kerouac, in particular, became the target of Rexroth's disgust. When *On the Road* was unpublished and an underground cult, Rexroth compared its author to Céline and Beckett, the two great *aliénés* of postwar literature; now that Kerouac's books were coming out one after another, in a fog of obfuscating publicity, Rexroth changed his mind and took every opportunity to say how bad he thought they were. Suddenly, the cult writer was a self-styled bop poetaster who knew nothing about jazz (he had the 'time sense of May flies', Rexroth said); the same went for his 'sophomoric Buddhism'.

Rexroth's assault began with an unfavourable review of *On the Road* in the *San Francisco Chronicle*. It was followed by a second piece in the same paper, six months later, when *The Subterraneans* appeared, headlined: 'The Voice of the Beat Generation has some Square Delusions'. *The Subterraneans*, Rexroth concluded, was a story about 'jazz and Negroes . . . two things Jack Kerouac knows nothing about'. He could think of no better put-down than to say that the King of the Beats was 'a furious square'.

Still, Rexroth felt that one good poem was worth a great many berets and beards, and when Ginsberg applied to the Guggenheim Foundation for a grant in October 1959, Rexroth agreed to sponsor him. 'Of course I will be happy to recommend you for a

Guggenheim', Rexroth replied to Ginsberg's request, 'you deserve it, you are a good poet.' But, he added, in a reference back to dissent as a commodity,

> don't expect me to approve of all your activities and friends, nor your and their childish boasting about narcotics and . . . evil parody of the sane and uncompromising way of life some of us have worked out here in San Francisco. Nor can I accept their habit of identifying themselves to the gutter press on Madison Avenue, Fleet Street or Paris.

At a soirée at Rexroth's house a year or so earlier, Kerouac had got noisily drunk and started jabbing, 'I'm a better poet than you are, Rexroth', every time his host began to speak. Rexroth responded by calling him a 'punk'. On another occasion, Ginsberg had taken off his clothes and leapt on Rexroth, kissing him all over and squealing: 'I love you!'

The activities of the Beats and their friends could be more seriously disruptive than that. Robert Creeley, the editor of the *Black Mountain Review* and a close friend of Ginsberg, also attended Rexroth's literary evenings, and soon began an affair with Rexroth's wife, which effectively ended the marriage. In *The Dharma Bums*, Kerouac attempted to take revenge for Rexroth's attack on him by giving the older writer the name 'Rheinhold Cacoethes', disinterring Carr's favourite word − a desire for something harmful − from the Columbia days. Cacoethes − who acted as MC at the Six Gallery reading in Kerouac's novel, as Rexroth did in life − was 'a bow-tied old anarchist fud'. But no matter, Ginsberg was still a good poet, and Rexroth told him: 'I hope you get the Guggenheim.'

If it occurred to him that Ginsberg's cap-in-hand request for Guggenheim money conflicted with his increasingly shrill anti-establishment public stance, that it might be another example of the system gobbling up its critics, Rexroth refrained from saying so. However, another poet whom Ginsberg approached, Richard Eberhart, was quick to make the point. 'How can you do it?' he wrote back. 'The idea is that America is against you, offering only the gutter and madness.' Eberhart still backed the application, but the administrators of the Guggenheim fellowships may have shared his doubts, for Ginsberg's request for an award was turned down.

★

In Chicago, the Post Office arranged a hearing to discuss the seizure of *Big Table* 1. The magazine was invited to defend its alleged seriousness of purpose. Several literary figures approached by Rosenthal and Carroll agreed to speak or submit written depositions, including some who had refused any close association with the Beat Generation, such as John Ciardi, the editor of the *Saturday Review of Literature*, and the much put-upon Lionel Trilling. They defended the right to publish descriptions of the alarming medical techniques of Burroughs's Dr Benway, who performs open-heart surgery with a lavatory suction-pump (sterilized by swishing it around the toilet bowl), and Kerouac's experimental and occasionally expletive-loaded 'babbling world tongues' in 'Old Angel Midnight'.

The Post Office's position, as stated by their attorney, was that

> this magazine, *Big Table* 1, is obscene and filthy. And it has no redeeming value. It is conceivable that certain literary critics would state that certain essays and poems contained in this magazine have some literary merit. Such people, however, are not able to speak for the average member of the community. It is inconceivable that [they] would find in this magazine anything but filth, and it is the effect this magazine has on the average member of the community that the Law is concerned with.

At the hearing, Paul Carroll tried to read from *Naked Lunch*, but the examiner, William A. Duvall, put a stop to it. The validity of the seizure was upheld, and *Big Table* 1 was declared unfit to go through the mail. The 400 impounded copies were staying put, in the Chicago post office in which they had been deposited for mailing some months earlier. In theory, the decision meant that, as publishers of the magazine, Rosenthal and Carroll could be tried and sent to prison; however, they went on the counterattack and filed suit in the District Court of Chicago, with the help of the ACLU, on the basis that the ban was unconstitutional and that the magazine represented a 'legitimate literary effort'.

Ciardi extended his defence of *Big Table* to the pages of the *Saturday Review*. He was much impressed by what he read of *Naked Lunch*, which he described as 'not only a masterpiece in its own genre, but ... a monumentally moral descent into the hell of narcotic addiction'. This comment, appearing in the 27 June 1959 issue of the *Saturday Review*, was the first independent critical reaction to any of Burroughs's work anywhere. To 'Old Angel Midnight', however, Ciardi had a different response: he thought it unlikely that the judges in the forthcoming court hearing would pronounce it obscene: 'It is impossible to conceive how any average man can go on reading the stuff, let alone be corrupted by it.'

Ciardi's article, 'The Book Burners and Sweet Sixteen', was severely critical of Chancellor Kimpton's instruction to Rosenthal to make the contents of the *Chicago Review* 'innocuous and uncontroversial', and to ensure that they contained 'nothing that would offend a sixteen-year-old girl'. When, asked Ciardi sardonically, 'has the true role of the American university been more profoundly enunciated?' He predicted that *Big Table* 1, already a cause célèbre, would be released sooner rather than later. But, then, what assurances did the editors have that the harassment would not begin all over again with *Big Table* 2? Ciardi pointed out that this act of literary suppression involved an unseen tool: the financial pinch. 'Who pays for the trip to Washington and for the counsel?' asked Ciardi.

> Is this the true intent of the Post Office: to force a safe and sane sixteen-year-old sweetheart conformity upon all writing, by making it financially disastrous to venture beyond the literary standards of a postal inspector who yet seems to enjoy peeking into other people's more promising mail?

The article drew forth a spate of letters, including one from Chancellor Kimpton, who insisted he had never told Rosenthal to make the magazine 'innocuous', and another from Richard Stern, a writer and professor who was part of the Advisory Board to the *Chicago Review*, denying that the University's action amounted to censorship. Stern claimed, rather, that the Board merely disapproved of the editors' choice of material, as it was entitled to do, and had wanted the *Chicago Review* to contain more student writing. In its fixation on a particular literary movement, which had nothing to do with the University or with Chicago, he argued, the *Chicago Review* under Rosenthal and Carroll was neglecting its recognized function.

In September, almost a year on from the original brouhaha, started by Jack Mabley's column in the *Daily News*, Judge Julius Hoffman concluded that *Big Table* 1 was 'not obscene'. Commenting on the articles by Burroughs and Kerouac to which the Post Office had objected, Judge Hoffman ruled that both were in the 'broad field' of serious literature. Concerning the selections from *Naked Lunch*, he said he realized that they were intended to 'shock the contemporary society', but this was, perhaps, 'to better point out its flaws and weaknesses'. In other words, he appreciated the satirical nature of the work. Burroughs had now received a second critical notice – from a judge – and, like the first, it was favourable. As for the alleged obscenity, Judge Hoffman understood that many readers would seek out *Naked Lunch* for the thrill of seeing taboo words in print, but he stated that 'clinical appeal is not akin to lustful thoughts'. There were no grounds for assuming that it was the author's intention to corrupt. Judge Hoffman could likewise find no reason for sustaining the objection to 'Old Angel Midnight', and he recommended the ban be 'vacated and set aside'. For the second time in two years, the law had come to the rescue of the Beat Generation.

Beatniks and other rough beasts from beyond the domestic frontier continued to slouch through the American living-room, courtesy of the press. Ginsberg told a reporter from the *New York Post* that 'the whole Beat Generation thing, if it's anything, is prophets howling in the wilderness against a crazy civilization'. The journalists, in turn, obliged this creation, depicting him as a new sub-species: the voluntary drop-out, hidden by hair, babble-tongued, 'howling' at the gate, though less as a prophet than a barbarian.

The *Post* published a twelve-part series about the Beat Generation, on consecutive days in March 1959. It was more thorough and sympathetic than any other report to date, but as a popular daily, the *Post* could not help being trite:

> Those who were drinking did so from quart bottles of beer, assorted mugs and cups, and two jugs of yellow wine that stood on the corner of a table along with a bowlful of salted peanuts and two equally seasoned cockroaches.
> 'Who invited THEM?' asked a guest.
> 'Man, they LIVE here', replied another.

And it offered sensationalism that was not really sensationalism, but a simple recording of the facts:

> The poet lays aside his manuscript, unzips his pants and takes off, amid some screams and a few gasps, all his clothes. Then he retrieves his manuscripts and resumes reading.

The journalist, Alfred G. Aronowitz, quoted definitions of beatness, mission statements, aesthetic creeds, which, novelties to the general public only months earlier, already sounded worn out by dint of repetition. 'The point of beat is that you get beat down to a certain nakedness', said Ginsberg, for the ninety-ninth time. Kerouac also did his act: 'Neal is more like Dostoevski than anybody I know', he said, adding: 'Neal Cassady and I love each other greatly.'

(A sidelight on Ginsberg's growing confidence in himself and in the revolution he co-led is provided by a letter written by Aronowitz nine months after the series had appeared in the *Post*. Aspiring to write poetry and a play – about the Beat Generation – Aronowitz appealed to Ginsberg for encouragement. He received a scolding letter in reply – Ginsberg was getting better at the scold. 'naturally your letter depressed me', Aronowitz wrote back, probably hoping that his refusal of conventional upper-case would further his cause, 'it got to the heart of things. the only way i know how to express myself is through contemporary journalism (i could be a very happy man within this framework if i hadn't met you)'.)

Time magazine continued to print reports on beat, or beatnik, life, always with chirpy titles: 'Bam; Roll On with Bam!' went one; 'Bang Bong Bing' said another; and, sprightliest of all, 'BONGO, BONGO, BONGO, bingo'. *Life* followed up its earlier pieces on the 'Howl' trial and on 'Square vs Hip' with 'The Only Rebellion Around', a long, hostile article by a staff writer called Paul O'Neil. 'They are loafers', wrote O'Neil of the Beats and the beatniks,

> passive little con men, lonely eccentrics, mom-haters, cop-haters, exhibitionists with abused smiles and second mortgages on a bongo drum – writers who cannot write, painters who cannot paint, dancers with unfortunate malfunctions of the fetlocks.

Having thoroughly dusted up his subjects for starters, O'Neil followed through with the lethal thrust: 'People very like them distributed pamphlets for the Communists in the 1930s.'

Whatever the flavour of his judgments (listening to Ginsberg talk was 'an experience very much like sharing a room with a wind machine'), O'Neil had done his homework. He profiled all the leading figures in New York, travelled to San Francisco to talk to Michael McClure and Philip Lamantia ('a delightful conversationalist, but his poetry is close to gibberish'), and dispatched a researcher to Paris to report on the daily life of the scion of the famous adding-machine inventor. Based on reports sent back, O'Neil described the horror of Burroughs's existence on rue Gît-le-Coeur: 'now 45, a pale, cadaverous and bespectacled being who has devoted most of his life to a lonely pursuit of drugs and debauchery'. This evocation was illustrated by a picture of Burroughs sitting on a brass bed under a dim light at the Beat Hotel, contemplating his appalling life.

The photographer was Loomis Dean, who, together with the researcher David Snell, had visited Burroughs at the hotel on O'Neil's behalf. They made a good impression right away, by greeting the author with a line adapted from the double-act detectives, Hauser and O'Brien, in *Naked Lunch*: 'Have an Old Gold, Mr Burroughs.' ('Hauser had a way of hitting you before he said anything just to break the ice. Then O'Brien gives you an Old Gold.')

Snell and Dean wined and dined Burroughs, stoked him up not with Old Golds but with the finest Havana cigars ('from Mr Luce's private stock', they enjoyed telling him, and he enjoyed telling others), and he took a liking to them: 'Very amusing and knowledgeable characters', he called them in a letter to Ginsberg. He admired Dean's assiduous photographic method: five rolls of film were devoted to the subject in his room ('lighted by a single forty-watt bulb, maximum allowed by the management'), at the downstairs bistro having coffee, and in Brion Gysin's room looking at Gysin's paintings through strange magnifying spectacles, the better 'to see depth and detail'. They spent two days interviewing him in cafés and restaurants.

It was scarcely Snell and Dean's fault if Paul O'Neil, bent on ridiculing and damning everything beat, devoted two short paragraphs to *Naked Lunch*, described Burroughs as debauched, and, from Dean's five rolls of film, selected a picture that made him resemble a sat-up corpse.

At the very hour at which Burroughs was being entertained by the double act of Snell and Dean in a Left Bank bistro, Brion Gysin was back at the Beat Hotel preparing a mount for one of his drawings. His Stanley knife slipped and sliced through a pile of old newspapers. Gysin playfully pieced together the strips to form a mosaic of *Herald Tribune*, London *Observer*, *Continental Daily Mail*, and (of all things) *Life*. It was amusing. It yielded strange meanings, with the hint, even (remembering Tristan Tzara pulling pieces of paper out of a hat forty years before), of surrealism.

When Burroughs returned to the hotel from his expenses-paid junket, Gysin showed off his latest trick:

> To protect this art the right way, clout first Woman and believers in their look of things. Fourteen-year-old boy has many of her belongings.

> Swiss boys were absolutely free from producers of outboard spiritual homes.

> I, Sekuin, perfected this art 'along the Tang dynasty'.
> Might be just what I am look.

Burroughs immediately saw in Gysin's serendipitous discovery the chance to unlock his own strange meaning, by cutting through the language horde – 'someone else's rusty load of continuity'. It offered the possibility, for a writer who understood that he was controlled by words, more than he controlled them, of slicing through the reality narrative, while continuing to construct artefacts out of words. He adopted the cut-up as the next logical step in his continuing quest for the secret of telepathic communication – 'If you cut into the present, the future leaks out' – and he saw that the little accident also had the potential to project him beyond whatever ugly words were printed about him in magazines such as *Life*. 'I pass along one of my specialized bits of wisdom', he had once written to Ginsberg. 'Always use poultry shears to cut off fingers.' The cut-up allowed him to feel (momentarily) as the protagonist in his story 'The Finger' had felt many years before, that 'a lifetime of defensive hostility had fallen from him'. And it placed him beyond the antics of vacation beatniks who had infested his old haunts, from Tangiers to St Louis. 'Rent-a-cut-up'? It just wouldn't swing.

Behind the beat

as he leaps Updike swing

The *New Yorker* published a parody of *On the Road*, on 21 February 1959, entitled 'On the Sidewalk', using mock bop prosody portmanteau words (eyes 'tightshut' etc), repeating the word 'sad' every few lines, and depicting the narrator and his friends as little children. The author was John Updike, a rising star of the magazine, whose first novel, *The Poorhouse Fair*, came out that year. 'On the Sidewalk' included a Ginsberg character called Gogi Himmelman, who shouts 'This is IT', as he leaps on to his kiddies' scooter and races down the street at 'thirtyrevolutionsasecond' in the direction of the narrator's mother's house. The piece ends:

> I was not allowed to cross the street. I stood on the gray curb thinking, they said I could cross it when I grew up, but what do they mean grown up? I'm thirty-nine now, and I felt sad.

To see how Updike would fend for himself in the Burroughsian jungle of chance, the above paragraph and quotation, together with the final paragraph of the previous chapter, were cut up according to Brion Gysin's instructions: 'Pick a book   any book   cut it up . . . slice down the middle   dice into sections . . . pour on some Madison Avenue prose   shuffle like cards'. It produced the following result (a little editing is permitted within the framework of chance).

It offered immediately words more than Tangiers   his friends of unlocking reality artefacts   of next step   defensive hostility

on to his language horde   next step in his communication out −
down the street at his own strange rising star

old haunts, my specialized bits of wisdom *New Yorker,* load of
beatniks as little Himmelman now allowed to cross the present, the
little accident   Always use poultry shears in the direction of
someone else's rusty narrator and the cut-up as the logical for the
secret of telepathic   of the narrator's writer who understood he
had infested words. He adopted continuing quest

If you cut into   and he saw that the him in magazines
whatever ugly words   to project him beyond the antics of
narrative fingers, while repeating vacation   he was controlled by
continuing to construct mock bop   the possibility for a slicing
through as *Life* sad Sidewalk using Ginsberg character as he leaps
Updike swing   wouldn't revolutionsasecond *On the Road*
    'This is IT' tightshut cutting 'sad' every few   word leaks
John 'Rent-a-cut-up?'   discovery controlled them, portmanteau
entitled 'On the eyes Burroughs the chance through the continuity'

11

Terminal cut-up

certainly language chopped into slices
will never release in you the stream which
employs white methods
   – Tristan Tzara, *Le Coeur à gaz* (1920)

In the fall of 1958, Burroughs wrote to Ginsberg that he was 'dissatisfied with all the work I have done in writing'. A few months later, he was wondering 'if any writing now has much raison d'être'. For good measure, he added: 'Just can't dig the natives on this planet.'

He refused Ginsberg's offer of help to find a publisher for *Queer*, which had languished, untouched, since 1952. As a straightforward, sequential-narrative account of a love-affair, it was 'not representative' of what he was doing now. Even *Naked Lunch* was set in too constricting a form, limited by semantic signals from the world outside, the world of 'sense' which made no sense, which was controlled by con men – not the low-down, scrofulous con men he had first observed with Huncke on Henry Street, but plausible con men in office blocks on Madison Avenue, or conning in the White House.

Nevertheless, Burroughs shared the conventional writer's desire to get his latest book up on its feet and walking. The issue of *Big Table* containing 'Ten Episodes from *Naked Lunch*' had at last arrived in Paris, and, at the same time, word of the Post Office banning order had reached the office of Maurice Girodias, the proprietor of

274

Olympia Press. He had turned down *Naked Lunch* eighteen months before, claiming that it was a mess; now that it had a reputation for obscenity, however, the mess was becoming clearer, and he was interested again. Girodias arranged an introduction to Burroughs (on the previous occasion, he had dealt with Ginsberg) through a young South African poet named Sinclair Beiles, who lived at the Beat Hotel and who had written an Oriental pot-boiler for Olympia, *Houses of Joy*, under the pseudonym Wu Wu Weng. When Burroughs went along to meet the publisher, he found himself treated with all the deference due to an author capable of generating a scandal (and a profit).

Girodias had suddenly become quite wealthy. An earlier pot-boiler, *Lolita*, had been sold to an American publisher and proved an immense *succès de scandale*; as Girodias retained a significant stake in the edition, he had made a tidy fortune. The thought of hoarding it never entered his mind. Girodias treated money like confetti: it was capable of transforming a dull situation – everyday life, for example – into something gay. Out of the fluent profits from the Putnam edition of *Lolita*, he had bought a building in the street where he had his office, rue St Séverin, and transformed it into a honeycomb of restaurants and nightclubs. After toying mischievously with the idea of naming the enterprise after Nabokov's novel, Girodias settled on 'La Grande Séverine'. It was a financial disaster.

Girodias also treated authors like confetti: capable of giving brightness to a grey day, but disposable and cheap. As a publisher, he abhorred contracts. As a businessman, he curried favour with a wad of notes. As a gentleman, he wished to be thought as good as his word. As a rascal, he frequently went back on it. Most of the books issued by his firm were written in a matter of weeks, or even days, and the authors – Alexander Trocchi, John Stevenson and Iris Owens were among the most prolific, producing *School for Wives*, *Roman Orgy*, *Rape* and *Innocence*, among many others – usually considered themselves well rewarded. They received $200 for each erotic adventure, enough to live modestly in Paris for several months. When it came to more serious books, though, Girodias wished to adopt the same line.

With Burroughs, his charm and resolution gained him a firm footing. First of all, he explained over fine wines at La Grande

Séverine, he intended to publish the novel (called *The Naked Lunch* in the Olympia edition and subsequent British editions; *Naked Lunch* in the American edition) within a month of buying it. Author and publisher shook hands. Girodias also told Burroughs that he would offer $800. Burroughs accepted, they shook hands again, and the money was forthcoming. When Burroughs insisted on a contract, Girodias hesitated, then offered his hand; Burroughs shook, and received his piece of paper.

Naked Lunch duly came out in July 1959, no. 76 in the Traveller's Companion series, in an edition of 5,000 copies, quickly followed by a reprint of the same amount. There was immediate interest from American publishers, and from other sources, so that within a month of publication Girodias could entertain Burroughs at La Grand Séverine once again, to outline a series of tax-avoidance schemes, bewitching him with percentages and plans for foreign residency. 'Girodias thinks we are going to make that kind of money', Burroughs told Ginsberg. He was correct in all but his use of the plural pronoun. 'As he put it to me straight . . . (and he does come on straight), "This is a complicated business full of angles. I know them – you don't. Let me handle it. You will have to trust me." '

Burroughs relished that kind of talk. He filed his contract in a safe place, and let Girodias handle things – the first offer on the table was $3,000 from Grove Press for the American rights – and was swindled out of thousands of dollars in US and European royalties. Girodias later expressed remorse for his theft; and Burroughs publicly stated his forgiveness. The Frenchman had, after all, published a book which even the author had regarded as unpublishable.

There was another favour to be grateful for. On the eve of the book's appearance, Burroughs received a publication present in the form of a warrant from the Paris drugs squad.

'Eight am. tap tap tap.' He spent 'a horrible junk-sick day' in detention, he told Ginsberg, while the officers typed out forms and took his photograph; 'and when they went to develop the picture there was nothing on the plate . . . not for nothing am I known as "the Invisible Man" '.

Burroughs's scent had been picked up from letters written to others by an old Tangiers connection. While he was free on bail and waiting for the case to come before the court, Girodias offered his help. He put Burroughs in touch with his lawyer, who advised him to write something that would convince the judge that he was a serious *homme de lettres*, and would also present him as a writer on the verge of a great career and engaged in a struggle to overcome the addiction which, until now, had hindered him.

Burroughs produced 'deposition: testimony concerning a sickness'. Girodias had his brother translate it into French, and they placed it in *La Nouvelle Revue Française*. The deposition would serve as the introduction to future editions of *Naked Lunch*:

> I awoke from The Sickness at the age of forty-five, calm and sane, and in reasonably good health except for a weakened liver and the look of borrowed flesh common to all who survive The Sickness . . . I have no precise memory of writing the notes which have now been published under the title *Naked Lunch*.

When he appeared in court, he was handed a suspended sentence and was made to pay a small fine, but almost all the money he had made out of his publishing success went into paying the lawyer's fee.

Naked Lunch is a tour de force of ventriloquism: from the hard-boiled *Junkie* mode of the first and penultimate chapters ('When he walked in on me that morning at eight o'clock, I knew it was my last chance'), through the science-fiction scenarios involving the Mugwump ('sits naked on a bar stool covered in pink silk. He licks honey from a crystal goblet with a long black tongue. His genitals are perfectly formed . . . The Mugwump has no liver, maintaining himself exclusively on sweets'), to the porno pranks of 'A. J.'s Annual Party':

> Mark's lips are drawn back in a tight snarl. 'All right, Johnny boy.' He contracts his body, slow and steady as an oiled machine, push his cock up Johnny's ass . . .
>
> They push Johnny forward onto the gallows platform covered with moldy jackstraps and sweat shirts. Mark is adjusting the noose. 'Well, here you go.' . . .
>
> Johnny douses Mary with gasoline from an obscene China jar of white jade . . . He anoints his own body . . . They embrace, fall to the floor and roll under a great magnifying glass set in the roof . . . burst into

flame with a cry that shatters the glass wall, roll into space, fucking and screaming through the air . . .

The book's twenty-two chapters were arranged in random sequence. Burroughs had resisted Ginsberg's suggestion to impose a semblance of narrative order, keeping faith with his own convulsive aesthetic. A large amount of *Naked Lunch* was composed of 'routines', Burroughs's term for writing that he hoped would 'come off the page' and affect the reader with an urgency like 'the urgency of bullfighting'. It is a shocking book, but the shock frequently takes the form of purgative laughter. Its satire is in places prophetic. The opportunist Arab fundamentalists of Islam Inc shuffle for space with a political party called the Divisionists, who accumulate members by cloning:

> They cut off tiny bits of their flesh and grow exact replicas of themselves in embryo jelly. It seems probable, unless the process of division is halted, that eventually there will be only one replica of one sex on the planet: that is one person in the world with millions of separate bodies . . .

And the hidden agenda: 'We must strictly control the division of Undesirables . . .'

The routines had their origin in letters written to Ginsberg since the early 1950s, which form the backbone of *Naked Lunch*. Stories about Tangiers and its inhabitants found their way in – Paul Bowles is given the name Andrew Keif in the 'Interzone' section of the novel ('Keif the brilliant, decadent young novelist who lives in a remodelled pissoir in the red light district') – as did rum characters from Burroughs's underworld days, such as Phil White, his pickpocketing tutor, nicknamed 'The Sailor': 'He laughed black insect laughter that seemed to serve some obscure function or orientation like a bat's squeak. The Sailor laughed three times. He stopped laughing and hung there motionless listening down into himself. He had picked up the silent frequency of junk.'

Suddenly, for Burroughs, who had no precise memory of writing *Naked Lunch*, who had yet again slithered out of jail, all roads were open. He had begun work on a sequel (it went through a number of transformations and became *The Soft Machine*). A French translation of *Naked Lunch* was already under way, by Eric Kahane, Girodias's brother. There were plans to dramatize the book in London (they came to nothing). His interest in the graphic arts was deepening under Gysin's influence, and he was thinking of mounting an exhibition (one of his drawings was used on the jacket of *Naked Lunch*). 'I have been outside', he told Ginsberg, friend, inamorata, audience ('receptor'), one-time agent. 'I have come up from the area of total humiliation and failure, climbed up cell by cell with a million setbacks and debacles. I don't figure to go back.'

The most dangerous thing, said Burroughs, whose main occupation in Tangiers had been to 'look at the end of my shoe for eight hours', was to 'STAND STILL'.

Some of the greatest movers were standing still. Cassady, who was himself the frontier, as well as the machine moving towards it, stayed in prison until the middle of 1960. At Christmas 1959, he wrote to Carolyn that marriage was a 'Karmic Kutup'. On his release, she attempted to enchant him once again with the gentle joys of domestic calm, but Cassady stumbled in and out as before, in and out of marriage and employment, as, thirty years earlier, his Pa had stumbled in and out of Denver flophouses, his job a joke, his address unknown, and nothing to his name but Neal junior. Eventually, Cassady increased his legendary speed again, and became the hero of another Wild West Show, the Magic Bus, with another writer, Ken Kesey, in the passenger seat. Early one morning in Mexico in 1968, his heart gave out and he died, in a last attempt to grasp meaning, at the side of a railroad track.

At the end of 1950s, Huncke was released from a five-year prison sentence, after which he gradually insinuated himself into the new scene, where 'beat', as he knew it, wasn't what it used to be. He stayed close to Ginsberg, who was happy to have him near, writing a little, thieving here and there, mostly from friends, doing drugs. Carl Solomon was in Pilgrim State Hospital, where he would remain for many years to come. 'A generation, one should realize', he wrote during one of his spells of lucidity, 'does not merely include its most colourful, notorious or illustrious members. It also includes the non-flamboyant ones who have lived their lives in relative obscurity.'

No one saw much of Kerouac, who was living with his mother in Long Island. She censored his mail and chased away his friends.

Holmes, on a second marriage and living in the country, had done a lot of standing still since *Go*, in 1952, constitutionally incapable of making the break from the theoretical, four-square view he took of life, including beat life. When beat became beatnik, in the late 1950s, Holmes expressed his bewilderment at it all in a letter to Kerouac, scratching his head over 'beat parties' and stopped dead in his tracks by the thought of 'how immeasurably square I would seem if I was ever caught at one'. With the vexed incomprehension of one whose time has passed while he happened to be looking the other way, he wrote: 'I thought . . . "Jesus, Jack and I thought this up out of smoke those afternoons long ago, and it suited the tang and chill of what was in the air then, and all of a sudden it's gotten completely out of hand . . ." ' He was living with his new wife in Connecticut, 'trying to keep alive and warm by foraging for article things'. A second novel, *The Horn*, came out in 1958, a paean to jazz, structured round the harsh life of a black tenor saxophonist called Edgar Pool. It received a warm reception from Kenneth Rexroth, who could issue no greater compliment than to say that the depiction of blacks, music and low-down life in *The Horn* was more authentic, in every way, than that in *On the Road*.

The Gysin recipe for language chopped into slices was published in a booklet, *Minutes to Go*, put out by a small Paris press in 1960. Whereas Burroughs was forever in transit, Gysin claimed to have arrived. The cut-up was 'the method for finding the truth'. His faith in the discovery of the cut-up was absolute, his dogma concrete. 'All the religions of the "peoples of the Book", that is, the Jews, the Christians, and the Moslems, are based on the idea that in the beginning was the Word . . . Fate is written. If you want to challenge and change fate, cut up words. Make them a new world.'

Besides Gysin, there were three other cut-up artists involved in *Minutes to Go*: Burroughs, of course, the South African Sinclair Beiles, and Corso, who insisted on a postscript in which he said that he participated 'unwillingly *and* willingly . . . unwillingly because my poetry is a natural cut-up and need not be created by a pair of scissors; willingly because Mr Burroughs is a knowing man'.

(He was, but he was taken in surprisingly easily by people who said, *I know all the angles. Let me handle it.* At this time in Paris, he fell under the spell of a con man, Jacques Stern, who spun a fiction of money, a yacht in Monte Carlo, publication offers from Faber and Faber in London, and others elsewhere. 'He is the greatest writer of our time', Burroughs could say in July 1959. By September, he had rumbled Stern as a fraud.)

For his first ventures in challenging the word, rubbing it out, slicing it up to let the truth leak from the spaces, Burroughs used articles from newspapers and magazines. The publications of the Luce organization ('Have an Old Gold, Mr Burroughs') were particular favourites, being perceived as the main repositories of the controlling word horde. 'I think of words as being alive like animals', Burroughs wrote. 'They don't like to be kept in pages.' For a cut-up entitled 'Open Letter to *Life* Magazine', he took the article about the Beats by Paul O'Neil, which had described Burroughs's life in the Beat Hotel in terms of extreme wretchedness.

> Sickle moon terror nails replica in tin ginsberg. Replicas of squaresville – grey piebald pigeons – pointedly questioned, mimic each other.

Other cut-ups made use of a translation of a poem by Rimbaud, 'A Une Raison', thus linking the early Columbia libertines – 'the new men and their marching forward', in the words of Rimbaud's poem – with the endgame Beats in the Beat Hotel. The thinking behind the selection of this particular poem, from *Les Illuminations*, was not difficult to discern: 'Un coup de ton doigt sur le tambour décharge tous les sons et commence la nouvelle harmonie.' (A rap of your finger on the drum unleashes all sounds and begins a new harmony.) On Burroughs's drum, under conductor Gysin's baton, it became terminal Rimbaud:

> A rap of
> sound
> A.
>
> . . .
> Everywhere
> march
> your
> head

While talking about him least, Burroughs bore the closest

resemblance of all the group to Rimbaud, in his iron-hard individuality, his propulsion towards new systems of art and morality, the creation of a new cause and effect; they shared the same solitary nature; the same willingness to spit in the eye of the bourgeoisie, the literary in-crowd and the law; the same intensity of love for a few friends; the same gullibility, even. It is just as easy to picture Burroughs running an arms-trading station in Abyssinia, being slightly too hard on the natives one minute, too kind the next, as it is to imagine Rimbaud possessed by the idea that he can change the world by proper manipulation of a pair of scissors and an old newspaper.

In some cases, the authors of *Minutes to Go* collaborated. For one cut-up, Burroughs sliced into a prose poem by Beiles, 'Stalin': 'terminal electric voice of C . . . shift lingual . . . vibrate tourists . . . free doorways . . . tata Stalin . . .'

'Terminal' was the refrain. Gysin's contributions tended to make a more robotic sound than those of the others:

> let's not hear that noise again   and again
> that may well be   the last word   anywhere

The cut-up was terminal in the sense that it was the last word in writing, but there was a difference in the approaches of Gysin and Burroughs. Gysin's philosophy stemmed from the belief that 'everything seems to be wrong with the . . . idea that in the beginning was the Word . . . There are other ways of communication . . .' In the introductory piece which gave the booklet its title, an exposition of the method rather than an example of it in action, he launched the cut-up with a typically revolutionary claim: it provided the means by which the writer might gain access to the technology which would bring total autonomy. Like many such claims, it sounded more than a little sinister:

> be your own agent   until we deliver
> the machine   in commercially reasonable quantities

> . . . the writing machine   is for everybody
> do it yourself   until   the machine comes
> here is the system

What machine? 'I mean machines in the hands of everybody can push a button.' Did he intend to refine the technology by which he had stumbled on his method to create a machine which would compute the infinitesimal verbal possibilities it contained and 'find the truth' (another refrain from *Minutes to Go*)? The answer is yes. Gysin was full of answers, and in that respect different from his disciple, Burroughs, who found in every answer another set of questions, in every truth another tangle of untruth.

Eighty years earlier, in the town of Auburn, NY, another machine had been conceived, with the identical aim of arriving at the truth.

> William Seward Burroughs lay awake in his bed. It had been a tiring day . . . As Burroughs lay thinking, long columns of figures swam before him. For he was a bank clerk, and hence dedicated to a life of counting, checking and re-counting.

The vision that came to William S. Burroughs that sleepless night in 1882 was of a machine which would arrive at the truth of a sum by means of a system ('here is the system') of interlocking mechanisms. Naturally, it was his wish to invent a machine which could be manufactured and supplied 'in commercially reasonable quantities'. As well as bringing profit to Burroughs the inventor, the machine promised something altruistic, even pure. By reducing the amount of error in the world, Burroughs was surely increasing the degree of truth. The Burroughs Adding Machine meant the game was up for miscalculation. It was the terminal method. It was, moreover, revolutionary, shepherding countless numbers of men and women away from the mind-numbing toil of counting and checking, towards free time and its creative potential. As Gysin put it in *Minutes to Go*, the machine 'is for everybody / do it yourself'. Certain of the Beat Hotel surrealist's announcements could have come straight from the mouth of the adding machine creator himself, who, like all nineteenth-century progressives, conceived his invention in the context of social improvement, of bettering the lot of his compatriots in the nation of the future.

> we wish to announce   that . . . we esteem
> this to be truly   the American Way

The Burroughs Adding Machine went on sale in 1891 (an earlier model had been withdrawn with a fault in the crank handle). Its universal success created the Burroughs family fortune which enabled William S. Burroughs II to spend his life after Harvard graduation free from the distractions of dreary toil, to live a life devoted to concocting plans for further systems of liberation. Grandfather and grandson shared a certain cast of mind. WSB I had a favourite motto, which sounds remarkably in tune with the aphoristic turn of phrase favoured by WSB II. 'Accuracy', the inventor liked to say, 'is only truth filed to a fine point.' Burroughs the younger was addicted to fact in the way that his elder was hooked on sums. 'My advice to young writers: "You will never get anywhere sitting on your dead tail. *Go out and get that story.* Not just *any* story. *The* story." '

Like his grandfather, Burroughs was an inventor, responsible for all sorts of alluring contraptions. If some of them failed, well then, that was all in the nature of the experiment. Calculation, as William S. Burroughs I liked to say, 'is subject to many slippery errors'.

The family fund was running out. Burroughs's parents had never been wealthy. The gift shop in Cobblestone Gardens, Florida, had not prospered. Mortimer Burroughs was past retirement age. There was another son, Mortimer jr, to think of, and also Burroughs's own motherless son, Billy Burroughs III, now approaching his teens. Expensive cures had soaked up whatever surplus cash Burroughs ever had to hand, and he had sometimes fallen back on borrowing from friends. Now, at the age of forty-six, he was almost ready to support himself for the first time in his life.

Big Table, the only literary periodical to serve the first generation of Beat writers, ceased publication in the summer of 1961, after five issues. It was no longer needed. (The *Chicago Review* continued, however, under a different editorship.) By then, there were publishers in New York, San Francisco and Paris willing to take on not only Kerouac, Burroughs and Ginsberg, but also Snyder, Whalen, McClure and a host of associates. Burroughs followed *Naked Lunch* with *The Soft Machine*, and then another cut-up novel, *The Ticket that Exploded*, both published by Olympia. Girodias, the enabling old twister that he is, doesn't have a clue what Burroughs is up to, but he keeps on doing the books. 'He'd just bring in the manuscript', Girodias said, 'and I'd knock it out. I think he was doing it to pay the rent.'

He could not be more wrong. Burroughs continued to wander in private deserts, relieved by startling oases of creativity. After the death of Joan, he took on the mantle of the pariah. Even if the shooting was completely accidental (Burroughs himself returned an open verdict), it was yet as if he had wished this status on himself. As he wrote in *Naked Lunch*, the untouchables perform a 'priestly function in taking on themselves all human vileness'.

Since *On the Road*, Kerouac had published several books of prose and poetry, sometimes at the rate of three a year: *The Subterraneans*, *The Dharma Bums*, *Dr Sax*, *Maggie Cassidy*, *Tristessa*, *Lonesome Traveler*, *Mexico City Blues*, *Book of Dreams* and others had all appeared by 1961. He was never hip, and had never really tried to be. If the world laughed at the King of the Beats for wanting to live out the rest of his life with his mother, let them laugh; like Burroughs, like Ginsberg, he was only being true to himself.

Soon Ginsberg and Orlovsky would lay a new trail to the Far East, to join Gary Snyder, and in doing so would inspire a million pilgrims. Before leaving, they had taken LSD with Timothy Leary at Harvard, in controlled experiments. No one actually said so, but it was the beginning of a different phase, a post-beat world, in which Allen Ginsberg could, and did, in keening variations, chant: 'I am high and naked and I am King of the Universe'; in which he would pick up the telephone and announce to the operator: 'Hello, this is God. That's G.O.D.' God had addressed the world through Ginsberg. He had said: 'O Rose, thou art sick', and Ginsberg, from whom countless people would take succour, wished to make it well again.

As they were casting off from New York harbour for the East, Orlovsky said: 'I hope America will still be here when we get back.'

It was. And, at the same time, it wasn't.

Notes

The following abbreviations are used in the notes:

AG   Allen Ginsberg

As Ever   *As Ever: The Collected Correspondence of Allen Ginsberg and Neal Cassady*, edited by Barry Gifford, Berkeley, CA, 1977

Collected   Allen Ginsberg, *Collected Poems, 1947–1980*, London 1984

DA   Jack Kerouac, *Desolation Angels*

DB   Jack Kerouac, *The Dharma Bums*

FT   Neal Cassady, *The First Third*, San Francisco 1971

GCU   Allen Ginsberg collection, Butler Library, Columbia University

GSU   Allen Ginsberg collection, Department of Special Collections, Stanford University

Guilty   Herbert Huncke, *Guilty of Everything*, New York 1990

HO   Allen Ginsberg, *Howl: Original draft facsimile*, edited by Barry Miles, NY 1986

JCH   John Clellon Holmes

JK   Jack Kerouac

Journals   Allen Ginsberg, *Journals: Mid-Fifties, 1954–58*, edited by Gordon Ball, NY 1995

JV   Joan Vollmer

KSL   Jack Kerouac, *Selected Letters: 1940–1956*, edited by Ann Charters, NY 1964

LG   Louis Ginsberg

MCA   Malcolm Cowley Archives

NC   Neal Cassady

NL   William Burroughs, *Naked Lunch*

OR   Jack Kerouac, *On the Road*

'Report'   Carl Solomon, 'Report from the Asylum – Afterthoughts of a
            shock patient', in Solomon, *Mishaps, Perhaps*, SF 1966

WB   William Burroughs

WBL   *The Letters of William S. Burroughs, 1945 to 1959*, NY 1993

WCW   William Carlos Williams

page

4 'to see that'   Jack Kerouac [JK] to Sampas, 25 March 1943; in JK,
Selected Letters: 1940–1956, edited by Ann Charters, New York 1965
[*KSL*]. Unless otherwise stated, all citations from Kerouac's letters are
taken from this volume

4 the Navy dentist etc   these anecdotes are told in JK's memoir in the
form of a novel, *Vanity of Duluoz*, NY 1968 [*Vanity*]

5 'the crowning'   JK to Connie Murphy, n.d.

5 'My schizoid'   JK to George Apostolos, 7 April 1943

6 'without context'   William Burroughs [WB], *Early Routines*, Santa
Barbara, CA, 1982

6 poor physical   Ted Morgan, *Literary Outlaw: The life and times of
William S. Burroughs*, NY 1988

7 'The Finger' was first published in *Early Routines*; it was later included
in WB, *Interzone*, NY 1989

8 'Fog' by Louis Ginsberg [LG] was published in Louis Untermeyer's
anthology, *Modern American Poetry*, first published in 1921 and
frequently revised; it is also the source of LG's remark about 'the glory
of the commonplace'. His solo collection, *The Attic of the Past*, was
published in 1920

9 '13-year-old mercy'   Allen Ginsberg [AG], 'Kaddish', in *Kaddish and
other poems, 1958–1960*, San Francisco 1961

10 'So a sick'   *Artaud Anthology*, edited and translated by Jack Hirschman, SF 1965

10 'I was not'   Joan Vollmer [JV] to AG, October 1949, Ginsberg
collection, Butler Library, Columbia University [GCU]

12 'Know these words'   AG, journal, 1944, Ginsberg collection,
Department of Special Collections, Stanford University [GSU]

12 The definition of cacoethes is taken from *Collins English Dictionary*

12 'love of evil' . . . 'Iago'   Céline Young conveyed Mrs Carr's words
to JK in an undated letter, circa 8 Oct. 1944, GSU

13 'Violate me' AG recorded this ditty in his journal, GSU

14 'Massachusetts March' JK, *Mexico City Blues*, 89th Chorus, NY 1959

14 'ayez des' JK to Sampas, 12 March 1944

14 Young Prometheans *Vanity*

15 'Tall pines' JK to Sampas, Feb. 1943

15 'A hell of' JK to Bill Ryan, 1 Jan. 1943

16 girlfriend the girlfriend was Adele Morales, later the second Mrs Norman Mailer. The source is an interview conducted by Andrew O'Hagan in the course of making a BBC television programme on Kerouac, broadcast in 1997

16 'I miss' JK to Edie Parker, 18 Sept. 1943

16 'People in Grosse Point' these and the following remarks are from Edie Parker's memoir, 'You'll Be Okay', yet to be published in full; a section appears in *A Different Beat: Writings by women of the Beat Generation*, edited by Richard Peabody, London 1997

18 'A mischievous' *Vanity*

18 'mad ones' JK, *On the Road* [OR]

20 his parents Ted Morgan, *Literary Outlaw: The life and times of William S. Burroughs*, NY 1988

20 'kind stranger' this juvenile story is recalled by WB in 'The Name Is Burroughs', *The Adding Machine*, London 1985

20 'I liked' WB, *Cobblestone Gardens*, Cherry Valley, NY 1976

21 'Twilight's Last Gleamings' is included in *Interzone*; shorter versions have appeared in other books by WB, notably *Nova Express* (1964)

21 'evil ... gross' WB to Ted Morgan, in Morgan, op. cit.

22 'His ego' 'Essay in character analysis: Lucien Carr', AG journals, GSU

22 'Dear Allen' GSU

23 'What is art?' AG, journals

23 AG's 'squibs' appeared in the October 1943 issue of the *Columbia Jester-Review*

23 'The rose' this poem appeared in the November 1943 issue of the *Jester-Review*

24 Burroughs listened the story is told in Morgan, op. cit.

24 JK's early feelings about AG are recorded in *Vanity*

25 Céline related her reading list to JK in a letter, n.d. (circa 8 Oct. 1944), GSU

25 Trilling's novel is *The Middle of the Journey* (1947)

25 Trilling's examples of 'modern classics' are given in 'On the Teaching of Modern Literature', in *Beyond Culture: Essays on life and literature*, NY 1966

26 'the sole' from the preface to Trilling's collection of essays, *The Liberal Imagination: Essays on literature and society*, NY 1950

26 Trilling's article, 'The Mind of Youth', appeared in *Harper's Bazaar*, July 1944

27 'A Night in the Village' appeared in the May 1944 issue of the *Columbia Jester-Review*

28 Céline's views on Kammerer, and her feelings about Carr, are given in her 8 Oct. 1944 (?) letter to JK

28 Carr's state   see *Vanity*

29 'On Monday morning'   *New York Times*, 17 Aug. 1944

30 'So this'   Morgan, op. cit.

31 Carr and JK's activities on the morning after the killing are recorded in *Vanity*

32 'Puzzled'   *NY Times*, 17 Aug. 1944

32 'Good boy'   *Vanity*

32 WB's arrest was reported in the *NY Times*, 23 Aug. 1944

33 'no fairy' etc.   *Vanity*

33 Kammerer's penis   see *Vanity*, 'And his dong's still preserved.'

34 their wedding   JK to AG, Oct. 1944

36 Rimbaud's 'Notes in English' derive from his study of English while living in London with Verlaine at different times between 1872 and 1874; they are included in V. P. Underwood, *Rimbaud et l'Angleterre*, Paris 1976

36 hipikats   see Joseph E. Holloway, *Africanisms in American Culture*, Indianapolis 1990; also *Juba to Jive: A dictionary of African-American slang*, edited by Clarence Major, NY 1994. The derivations were checked with Wolof speakers at the BBC African Service in London

38 *Really the Blues*, NY 1946

40 All quotations attributed to Jack Black are from *You Can't Win*, NY 1926

40 'sincerely miserable'   JK, *The Town and the City*, NY 1950

40 Elsie-John   Herbert Huncke, *Elsie-John and Joey Martinez*, NY 1979

40 'Through the whole'   Huncke's memoirs were published in different places, in slightly varying versions, before being collected in *Guilty of Everything* [*Guilty*], NY 1990

42 strange cargo   WB, *Junkie*, NY 1953

42 'heat'   Huncke, *Guilty*

43 china Buddha etc.   *Junkie*

43 Huncke recollected etc.   ibid.

43 a 'john'   *Junkie*

43 first fix   *Guilty*

44 'jeune singe' etc. JK to AG, 23 Aug. and 9 Sept. 1945

44 Dean McKnight to LG, 17 March 1945, GSU

45 'Butler has' etc. the incident is described in both Barry Miles, *Ginsberg: A biography*, NY 1989; and Michael Schumacher, *Dharma Lion: A critical biography of Allen Ginsberg*, NY 1992

45 Dean McKnight to LG, 30 March 1945, GSU

45 'Mountains . . .' AG to WB, July 1945; see Ted Morgan, *Literary Outlaw: The life and times of William S. Burroughs*, NY 1988

46 Los Alamos and A-Bomb ibid.

46 'I feel' AG to WB, July 1945, ibid.

46 'Oh, just west' *You Can't Win*

47 Chase, 'a hero' Morgan, op. cit.

47 'that feeling' Céline to AG, n.d. (Aug. 1945?), GSU

47 the distinction between Wolfe and Fitzgerald was made in a journal entry of 16 June; brief extracts from JK's journals are to be found in *A Jack Kerouac ROMnibus*, NY 1995. Further extracts were published in the 22 & 29 June 1998 double issue of the *New Yorker*

48 'prize room' *Guilty*

48 Joan hobbling *Vanity*

49 'They informed me' Huncke, *The Evening Sun Turned Crimson*, Cherry Valley, NY 1980

50 black queen Huncke, *Guilty*

50 'They knocked' JV to Edie Parker, 24 April 1948

51 Kingsland to AG, 8 Nov. 1946, GSU

51 'sorry life' Miles, op. cit.

52 A brief tour The details of the tour have been gleaned from a number of sources, notably Bill Morgan's enjoyable guidebook, *The Beat Generation in New York*, NY 1997; *Lonesome Traveler*, *Visions of Cody* and *OR* by JK; 'Howl' by AG; *Junkie* and *Guilty*

54 I am grateful to Carolyn Cassady for allowing me to listen to a tape of Neal Cassady [NC] reading aloud

54 NC's description of Huncke is given in *The First Third* [FT], SF 1971

55 'When, in 1932' ibid.

55 'Weakened' ibid.

56 'pee-pee' ibid.

56 'Adventures in Autoeroticism ibid.

56 'crooked Grecian' *OR*

57 'from 10.30 am' NC to JK, 7 March 1947, in *FT*

58 a criminal Alan Temko expressed this view of NC in *Jack's Book*, edited by Barry Gifford and Lawrence Lee, NY 1978

58 in the nude   *OR*. In the novel, JK gave NC a pair of shorts, but he mentioned NC's nakedness in other accounts of the meeting

59 'a thousand'   JK, *Visions of Cody*, NY 1973

60 'last but not'   This unsent letter to Hal Chase was written on 19 April 1947

60 An account of JK's hitchhiking is given in Ann Charters, *Kerouac: A biography*, NY 1973

61 'somewhere'   *OR*

62 'I keep'   JK to WB, 14 July 1947

62 'long-lost'   *OR*

62 'animal'   JK to NC, 26 Aug. 1947

62 'long rapport'   ibid.

62 'The night'   ibid.

62 'I am dying to'   ibid.

63 'Thank you'   WB to AG, *The Letters of William S. Burroughs, 1945 to 1959* [WBL], NY 1993. Unless otherwise stated, all citations from Burroughs's letters are from this volume

63 'I have'   WB to AG, Sept. 1946

64 'huge rats'   WB to AG, 11 March 1947

65 'piercing'   Gifford and Lee, op. cit.

65 'upstairs'   JK to Alfred G. Aronowitz; see 'The Beat Generation', a series of twelve articles which ran in the *New York Post* between 9 and 22 March 1959

66 'flirting'   NC to JK, 3 July 1949, *FT*

66 'stark naked'   *OR*

66 'enormous'   *OR*

66 Carolyn Cassady's surprise is related in her memoir, *Off the Road: My years with Cassady, Kerouac and Ginsberg*, NY 1990

66 'disburden'   *OR*

66 'his success'   *Guilty*

67 'he came'   *OR*

68 'the same thing'   JK to NC, 13 Sept. 1947

68 The romance with 'Terry' is described in *OR*

69 'I hid'   *OR*

70 'Bullshit'   NC to AG, May 1948, in *As Ever: The Collected Correspondence of Allen Ginsberg and Neal Cassady*, edited by Barry Gifford, Berkeley, CA, 1977 [*As Ever*]

70 'in fear'   *Off the Road*

71 'I am'   NC to AG, 14 March 1947, *As Ever*

71 'I really'   NC to AG, 30 March 1947, ibid.

71 AG's confession to JK of his 'true nature', and his letter to Wilhelm

Reich (11 March 1947), are quoted in Barry Miles, *Ginsberg: A biography*, NY 1989

72 Naomi's postcard messages to AG from hospital in 1947, and the letter to AG from the Director of Pilgrim State   GCU

72 'have an apt'   NC to AG, 30 March 1947

72 'I love'   NC to AG, 7 Sept. 1948, *As Ever*

73 'Exorcise'   LG to AG, 11 July 1948, GCU

73 'Your verse'   from two undated letters to AG (Sept. and Oct. 1945)

73 'Most dear'   from 'Dakar Doldrums', in AG, *Collected Poems, 1947–1980*, London 1984. Most references are to this volume [*Collected*]; AG revised the grouping of his poems for its publication

73 'musing'   JK to AG, 26 Aug. 1947

74 'In Society'   AG, *Collected*

75 Giroux to Andrew O'Hagan, as cited

76 'Bet-a-thousand'   JK to Ed White, 29 March 1949

76 'More later'   JK, journals, *Kerouac ROMnibus*

76 'Neal is coming'   JK to AG, 15 Dec. 1948

76 'Now, now'   *Off the Road*

77 'And what a trip'   *OR*

77 'pure, abstract'   WB to AG, 30 Jan. 1949

77 'Great car'   *Off the Road*

77 'what a bastard'   *OR*

78 'beat clerk'   WB to AG, 19 Feb. 1947

78 'another fine couple'   JK to Ed White, 30 Nov. 1948; published in *Missouri Review*, no. 3, 1994

79 John Clellon Holmes [JCH] described NC as a psychopath in an undated letter to AG   GSU

79 'junkies, musicians'   JCH, 'The Name of the Game', in *Nothing More to Declare*, NY 1967

79 'goading'   ibid.

80 'something rebel'   JCH, *Go*, NY 1952

80 'frequent use'   Anatole Broyard, 'A Portrait of the Hipster', *Partisan Review*, June 1948

81 'to express all'   John Tytell, interview with JCH, in *Kerouac and the Beats: A primary sourcebook*, edited by Kit Knight, NY 1988

81 'prune-juice'   *OR*

81 'You ain't'   JK to JCH, mid-June 1952, in Knight, op. cit.

82 JK and blacks: all examples are from *OR*

82 'Mexican-Nigger'   JK to AG, 26 July 1949

82 'At lilac evening'   *OR*

83 Baldwin's short story, 'Previous Condition', first appeared in *Commentary*, October 1948; it was later collected in *Going to Meet the Man* (1965)

84 'He was asked'   Broyard, 'Portrait'

84 The phrase 'the "Hip" (the Knowing)' occurs in a synopsis for the then-unwritten *OR*, sent to JK's English publisher Eyre and Spottiswoode; see note to letter to Frank Morley, 27 July 1950, *KSL*

85 'What a terrible'   AG, journal, GSU. The entry was later transformed into the poem, 'Tonight all is well . . .', *Collected*

85 JK to hit AG   see WB to JK, 24 June 1949. JK also recorded the incident in his journal. AG initially checked into the PI in early June, only to be sent home again. His term began properly on 29 June 1949

86 'And my eye'   Tom Clark, interview with AG, *Paris Review* 37, Spring 1966

87 'lentil soup'   'Kaddish'

87 'perceptions of the moment'   Edward Lucie-Smith, *Mystery in the Universe*, London 1966

87 'Never deny'   *Paris Review* interview with AG

87 'God'   ibid.

88 'the position'   ibid.

88 Whitman's poem, 'Inscriptions', is contained in *Leaves of Grass*

90 'perhaps'   AG to NC, Sept. 1948, *As Ever*

90 'very distinct'   AG gave a full account of his arrest to Jane Kramer, who included it in her book, *Allen Ginsberg in America*, NY 1969

90 'woebegone'   *Guilty*

91 *New York Times*, 23 April 1949

91 'If I'   WB to JK, 26 June 1949

92 'Somebody had'   *Guilty*

92 'atomized amnesia'   Solomon's essay, 'Report from the Asylum. Afterthoughts of a shock patient', ['Report'], first appeared in *Neurotica* 6, Spring 1950. It was reprinted, under the author's real name, in *Mishaps, Perhaps*, SF 1966

92 The Myshkin–Kirillov exchange has been reported in a number of places, notably by Solomon in *Emergency Messages: An autobiographical Miscellany*, NY 1989

94 JCH's description of Gershon Legman is from *Nothing More to Declare*, which includes an account of the magazine and its aims. Its origins are also recalled by Jay Landesman in his memoir, *Rebel without Applause*, London 1987

94 'Murder having'   Legman's early essays were collected in *Love and Death: A study in censorship*, NY 1949

98 Solomon explains his confusion over Artaud in Paris in an interview in *Emergency Messages*

98 'bawling' Carl Solomon, 'Report from the Asylum', *Mishaps, Perhaps*, SF 1966

98 'was not mad' from 'Van Gogh: The man suicided by society'; this and other Artaud translations are from Jack Hirschman, *Artaud Anthology*, SF 1965

99 'superreal' 'Report'

100 'I fear' this and other remarks quoted are made in letters to AG and JK, dated 13 Oct., 24 Dec. 1949; 1 Jan., 5 Jan., 10 March 1950

100 'the lush' JV to AG, 31 Oct. 1949, GCU

101 Laura Lee Burroughs's three slim books on flower-arranging were published by the Coca Cola Co, 1940–42

101 'I am subject' WB to AG, 16 April 1949

101 Joan explained JV to AG, 13 March 1949, GCU

102 'I was not' JV to AG, 31 Oct. 1949, GCU

102 'croakers' 24 June 1949

102 'Convey' 16 April 1949

103 'young Tolstoy' 3 Dec. 1950

103 'I have' NC to JK, Dec. 1947, quoted in *Off the Road*

104 The death of Cannastra is described in various places (e.g., Barry Miles, *Ginsberg: A biography*, NY 1989), with slight variations. A portrait of Cannastra, as 'Agatson', is included in *Go*

104 JK's feelings about his marriage to Joan are given in letters to NC, 18 and 21 Nov. 1950

105 Joan Haverty's account of her marriage to JK, and her version of the genesis of OR, are included in her memoir, 'Nobody's Wife', which has yet to be published in full; an excerpt is included in Richard Peabody, ed., *A Different Beat: Writings by women of the Beat Generation*, London 1997

106 'Went fast' 22 May 1951

107 The extract from the three-week OR is quoted in Ann Charters's introduction to the Penguin edition of the novel (1991). The extract from the revised version is given in a letter to Solomon, 7 April 1952

108 'three new' JK to Hal Chase, 19 Oct. 1948

108 The best account to date of the genesis and development of OR is Tim Hunt's study, *Kerouac's Crooked Road*, Hamden, Conn., 1981

109 his plans JK to NC, 6 Nov. 1950

110 'Now I sit' 10 June 1951

110 'we heard' Haverty, in Peabody, op. cit.

111 'a big roll'   Giroux to Andrew O'Hagan, during the making of the latter's *Kerouac*

111 'I know'   24 June 1951

113 'A turning point'   quoted in Miles, op. cit.

113 'camp'   ibid.

114 'I can'   AG to JCH, 16 June 1949, GSU

114 'all information'   JCH to AG, 14 June 1949, GSU

115 'My "visions" '   AG to JCH, mid-July 1949, GSU

115 'Lucien tells'   WSB to AG, 1 Jan. 1951

115 'I love Helen'   quoted in Miles, op. cit.

116 'The Vestal Lady on Brattle' is the title-poem of Corso's first book (1955). It was later issued in one volume with *Gasoline*, SF 1958

117 Corso recalled his early life in 'Notes from the Other Side of April', *Esquire*, July 1964

117 'I met her'   from 'Song', in *The Vestal Lady on Brattle*

117 The story of AG's meeting with Corso is related in a number of places, including Miles, op. cit., and an interview with Corso, by Robert King, in *The Beat Vision: A primary sourcebook*, edited by Arthur and Kit Knight, NY 1987

118 'One night'   WB to AG, 5 May 1951

119 'What on earth'   WB, introduction to *Queer*, NY 1965

119 Hal Chase's remark was made to Ted Morgan, but not incorporated into Morgan's biography of WB; it was dug up by Steven Watson, author of *The Birth of the Beat Generation: Visionaries, rebels, and hipsters, 1944–60*, NY 1995. Alan Temko's remark is given in Barry Gifford and Lawrence Lee, ed., *Jack's Book*, NY 1978. WB's words are from the introduction to *Queer*

119 'four years'   JV to JK, 28 Feb. 1950

119 'She was'   *Guilty*

120 'highball glass'   WB, 'Lee's Journals', *Early Routines*

120 'whiskey'   Edward de Grazia, *Girls Lean Back Everywhere: The law of obscenity and the assault on genius*, NY 1992

120 'apple'   ibid.

120 'gin'   Ted Morgan, *Literary Outlaw: The life and times of William S. Burroughs*, NY 1988

120 'glass of gin'   Alfred G. Aronowitz, 'The Beat Generation', *New York Post*, 9–22 March 1959

121 water   Watson, op. cit.; also *Women of the Beat Generation*, edited by Brenda Knight, NY 1996

121 'six-ounce'   Barry Miles, *William Burroughs: El Hombre Invisible*, London 1993

121 'wine' Steve Turner, *Jack Kerouac: Angel Headed Hipster*, London 1996

121 'tin can' Giroux to O'Hagan, as cited

121 'she placed' William Burroughs jr, 'Life with Father', *Esquire*, Sept. 1971. A full account of the life and death of William Burroughs jr is given in Morgan, op. cit.

122 'I suspect' WB to AG, 7 Feb. 1955

123 'It's time' JCH to JK, 28 April 1950; quoted in *KSL*

125 'pryer-intoer' JK to AG, 8 April 1952

125 'smell' JK to AG, 8 Oct. 1952

127 'sequel' WB to JK, 26 March 1952

127 'switcheroo'd' WB to AG, 22 April 1952

127 'I have no idea' ibid.

127 all in jail an interview with WB, by John Tytell, in Arthur and Kit Knight, op. cit.

128 'not so bad' WB to AG, 8 March 1953

128 'what prefaces' WB to AG, 14 April 1952

130 'As for *OR*' JK's ideas for publication by Wyn are expressed in two letters to Solomon, 27 Dec. 1951 and 7 April 1952

130 'Carl read it' 11 Jan. 1952; AG's letter to JK is included in *KSL*; when, eventually, the manuscript referred to by AG was published as *Visions of Cody*, AG wrote an afterword in praise of JK and his achievement

131 Solomon's letters to JK are quoted in Gerald Nicosia, *Memory Babe: A critical biography of Jack Kerouac*, NY 1983

131 'To be blunt' WB to AG, 13 July 1952

131 'modern prose' JK to A. A. Wyn and staff, 5 Aug. 1952

131 'The Junky's Christmas' is contained in *Interzone*

132 'I don't like' WB to AG, 23 Dec. 1952

133 'OK' WB to AG, 24 Dec. 1952

134 The sources for the different descriptions of the scroll are as follows: Ann Charters, *Kerouac: A biography*, NY 1973; Nicosia, *Memory Babe*; Nicosia, 'Buddha-gate at NYU', *Beat Scene*, no. 24; AG, *Allen Verbatim: Lectures on poetry, politics, consciousness*, edited by Gordon Ball, NY 1974; Joyce Johnson, *Minor Characters*, NY 1983; Tom Clark, *Jack Kerouac: A biography*, NY 1984; Aronowitz, op. cit.; JK to NC, 22 May 1951; JK to JCH, 23 June 1957, in Arthur and Kit Knight, op. cit.; Watson, op. cit.

137 'Such great' Seymour Wyse to AG, 7 May 1952, GSU

137 *Empty Mirror: Early poems* was first published in 1961. Williams's

preface was published as a separate item in the *Black Mountain Review*, vol. 7, Autumn 1957

138 Paradise Alley is described (as 'Heavenly Lane') in *The Subterraneans*, NY 1958

138 'angel of' ibid.; Alene Lee describes the reaction of this crowd to JK, in Barry Gifford and Lawrence Lee, ed., *Jack's Book*, NY 1978; she speaks under the name 'Irene May'

139 'It's too much' *The Subterraneans*

140 'I have completely' JK to JCH, 12 March 1952

141 Cassady's letters to JK and AG are contained in, respectively, *FT* and *As Ever*

141 AG offered his explanation of Solomon's remark in a letter to JCH, 13 Dec. 1950, GSU. The words were incorporated into the poem 'I have increased power', *Collected*

141 NC's anecdote about 'a dark goat' is contained in *FT*

142 'Commie Marxist' *Vanity*

142 'POOM' Ted Berrigan, interview with JK, *Paris Review* 43, Summer 1968

142 'punk Jew' JK to JCH, June 1952, in Arthur and Kit Knight, ed., *The Beat Vision: A primary sourcebook*, NY 1987

143 'barging in' Alene Lee ('Irene May') in Gifford and Lee, op. cit.

144 'India' ibid.

144 'magazine article' *Queer*

144 WB's meeting with Schultes is described in Ted Morgan, *Literary Outlaw: The life and times of William S. Burroughs*, NY 1988

145 'baby smooth' WB to AG, 15 April 1953; this letter, and further descriptions of the effects of yagé by WB, are contained in Burroughs and Ginsberg, *The Yage Letters*, SF 1963

146 'May 12' etc ibid.

147 'violent, anarchic' James Baldwin to William Phillips, April 1949, *Partisan Review* Collection

147 'whether or not' 6 June 1958, *Arna Bontemps–Langston Hughes, Letters 1925–67*, edited by Charles H. Nicholls, NY 1980

147 'Portrait of the Inauthentic Negro' *Commentary*, July 1950

148 'Sunday Dinner in Brooklyn' was first published in *The Avon Book of Modern Writing*, no. 2, 1954; it was reprinted in *Protest: The Beat Generation and the Angry Young Men*, edited by Gene Feldman and Max Gartenberg, NY 1958

149 *Ciel de nuit*, the French edition of *Who Walk in Darkness*, published by Gallimard in 1954, poses a further mystery, as the title page gives the 'titre original' as '*Night Sky*'

150 'I had always' Broyard, *Kafka Was the Rage*, NY 1997

153 'What joy!' AG, 'Siesta in Xalba', *Collected*

153 'My mind' circa Oct. 1955, AG, *Journals: Mid-Fifties, 1954–58*, edited by Gordon Ball, NY 1995 [*Journals*]

153 'yes, yes' AG, 'Song', *Collected*

154 'book upon book' AG to NC, 14 May 1953, *As Ever*

154 'He drags' AG, 'Sakyamuni Coming out from the Mountain'; *Collected*

154 He related AG to NC, 14 May 1953, *As Ever*

156 'a blank' quoted in *Off the Road*

156 AG, 'The Green Automobile', *Collected*

156 Carolyn Cassady described her state of being frigid to the author. Other details about their sex life are contained in *Off the Road*, and Barry Miles, *Ginsberg: A biography*, NY 1989. The Cassadys' devotion to Edgar Cayce is described in *Off the Road*

157 AG's feelings of self-loathing are given in *Journals*

157 'I don't think' JCH, 'The Consciousness Widener', in *Nothing More to Declare*

158 'a dope' Miles, *Ginsberg*

158 'Oh, by the way' JCH, 'The Consciousness Widener'

158 'in the muck' AG used this phrase in 'First Thought, Best Thought', in AG, *Composed on the Tongue: Literary Conversations, 1967–1977*, SF, n.d.

158 'Who will speak' *Journals*

159 'gamblers, prostitutes' Kenneth Rexroth, *An Autobiographical Novel*, Garden City 1966

159 'Thou Shalt Not Kill' is included in Kenneth Rexroth, *In Defense of the Earth*, NY 1956

160 'The Structure of Rime 1' Robert Duncan, *The Opening of the Field*, NY 1960

160 'In the feet' ibid.

161 'The key' AG to William Carlos Williams [WCW], 9 Dec. 1955; quoted in AG, *Howl: Original draft facsimile* [*HO*], edited by Barry Miles, NY 1986

161 'I'll go' 'Love Poem on a Theme by Whitman', *Collected*

161 'I try' AG to LG, n.d., GSU

162 'aberrant' Rexroth, 'The Commercialization of the Image of Revolt', given as a talk on KPFA radio station; published in the *Dictionary of Literary Biography*, vol. 16, Part II: 'The Beats: Literary Bohemians in Postwar America' [*DLBII*], edited by Ann Charters, Detroit 1983

162 'like Elvis' John Ryan to AG, dated 14 Feb. (1956?), GSU

162 'not knowing' AG to Ryan, 9 Oct. 1955, GCU

162 'I finally' AG to JK and NC, early 1952, *As Ever*

163 'semi-pedantic' JK to Carolyn Cassady, March 1953; quoted in *Off the Road*. Two years later, he wrote to Cowley: 'I hardly deserve your friendship and help', 4 July 1955

164 'You are right' Cowley to AG, 14 July 1953, Malcolm Cowley Archives, Newberry Library, Chicago [MCA]

164 The Viking memos are housed in the MCA

165 'John Kerouac' Cowley's remarks about JK were reprinted in his book, *The Literary Situation*, NY 1954

166 'Rejected' etc JK to Sterling Lord, 23 Jan. 1955

166 'okay with me', title of *OR*, and 'bashful' JK to Cowley, 20 Sept. 1955

168 AG's description of Snyder is quoted in *Scenes Along the Road*, compiled by Ann Charters, NY 1970

168 'Down valley' Gary Snyder, 'Mid-August at Sourdough Mountain Lookout', in *Riprap*, Dorchester, Mass., 1959

168 'The world' Snyder, 'Riprap', in *Riprap*

169 'Perturb' JK to Robert Lax, 26 Oct. 1954

170 'clear eyes' AG, 'Dream Record: June 8, 1955', *Collected*

170 'I decided' AG, *Composed on the Tongue*

170 Solomon laid claim to certain images in 'Howl' in an interview with John Tytell, in *Emergency Messages*

170 Various drafts of 'Howl', with commentary, are presented in *HO*

171 'the original' JK sent the typescript to JCH on 30 Aug. 1955; it resurfaced among the latter's papers in 1980

171 'Saturday' JK to Lord, 23 Jan. 1955

172 'here's the trick' JK to AG, 18 Jan. 1955

173 'Thinking' 'How to Meditate'; composed in 1954, this poem was first published in *Pomes all sizes*, SF 1992

173 'since life' 'The Last Word', *Escapade*, Oct. 1959

173 'aryan' 'The Yen for Zen', an interview with JK by Alfred G. Aronowitz, *Escapade*, Oct. 1960

173 'Buddha found' ibid.

174 'Your HOWL' JK to AG, 19 Aug. 1955

174 'Remember, Jack' 18 Aug. 1954

175 'smoke some' JK to AG, 10 June 1949

175 'Western girl' JK to NC, 7 May 1948

175 'I'd like' JK to Philip Whalen, 7 Feb. 1956

175 'Bill is sitting' AG's letter to NC is quoted in Miles, *Ginsberg*

176 'end–of–the–world'   WB to AG, 16 June 1954

176 'Weed'   WB to NC, 12 March 1954

177 'looking up'   WB to AG, 1 March 1954

177 'the way'   Paul Bowles to Gore Vidal, 24 April 1950, *In Touch: The letters of Paul Bowles*, edited by Jeffrey Miller, London 1994

177 'He invites'   WB to AG, 18 Aug. 1954

177 'rigidly conventional'   WB to AG, 3 Sept. 1954

178 'no job'   WB to AG, 3 July 1954. Eric the Unlucky became Lief the Unlucky, and appeared in *Naked Lunch*; the Portuguese Mooch also turns up there

178 'Buddha doesn't'   WB to JK, 3 Sept. 1954

178 The sources for the colloquy on the Six Gallery reading are as follows: Michael Schumacher, *Dharma Lion: A critical biography of Allen Ginsberg*, NY 1992; Kenneth Rexroth and James Laughlin, *Selected Letters*, edited by Lee Bartlett, NY 1991; JK, *The Dharma Bums*, NY 1958; 'The Literary Revolution in America' by AG and Gregory Corso, in *Litterair Paspoort* 100 (Amsterdam), Nov. 1957, AG, *HO*; AG to John Ryan, 9 Sept. 1955, and 8 Dec. 1955; GCU; Aronowitz, op. cit.; JK to Cowley, 20 Sept. 1955; Rebecca Solait, *Secret Exhibition: Six California artists of the Cold War era*, SF 1990; Michael McClure, *Scratching the Beat Surface*, NY 1982; AG, 'Howl'; Snyder, *Myths and Texts*, NY 1960

183 Ferlinghetti's message to AG has been reported in various places. This was, however, not the original acceptance of the poem. AG wrote to JK five weeks before the Six reading, on 30 Aug., that City Lights meant to issue 'Howl' as a booklet, 'just that one poem, nothing else' (letter reproduced in *HO*)

184 'It was obvious'   Rexroth, introduction to the bound reprint, *The Pocket Poets Series*, vol. 1, NY 1973

185 Ferlinghetti discusses the opening of City Lights in *Golden Gate: Interviews with Five San Francisco Poets*, edited by David Meltzer, Berkeley, CA, 1976

185 'a surgical'   Rexroth, introduction to *The Pocket Poets Series*

186 dedication to 'Howl': AG's recollection that JK had provided the title of the poem was mistaken, as AG later remembered (see *HO*)

186 'I wonder'   AG to Ferlinghetti, 9 Aug. 1956, GCU

187 Naomi Ginsberg's last letters to AG are reproduced in *HO*

188 'a quorum'   Eugene Brooks to AG, 11 June 1956, GCU

188 'To My Mother'   *NY Times*, 25 July 1956

188 AG spoke about his 'longing' during a television interview with Jeremy Isaacs, *Face to Face*, BBC, 1995

188 mimeograph   The poet Robert Creeley typed a draft of 'Howl', which was distributed in a mimeographed edition of fifty copies

188 'violence'   LG to AG, 29 Feb. 1956, GCU

189 'There seems'   AG to Trilling, May 1956, *HO*

189 'lucky'   'Bop lyrics', *Collected*

190 'I almost'   AG to LG, March 1956, *HO*

190 Carr's name was removed from the dedication in the second edition, which cost the author $25 in printer's fees

190 'I'm afraid'   Trilling to AG, 29 May 1956, *HO*

191 'You got'   Ezra Pound to WCW, June 1956, ibid.

191 'excellent'   Solomon to AG, 29 Dec. 1957, GSU

191 'no one'   this and the following complaints by Solomon are undated; GSU

192 'The Education of Carl Goy' is included in Carl Solomon, *Mishaps, Perhaps*, SF 1966

192 'compounded'   *Emergency Messages*

193 Ferlinghetti's article, 'Horn on "Howl" ', appeared in the *Evergreen Review*, no. 4, 1957

194 Snyder's response to Chinese art is quoted by Dan McLeod, as being from 'a draft of a work-in-progress', in *DLBII*. McLeod also quotes Snyder's early attempt at translating from the eighth-century Chinese poet Wang Wei ('Empty Mountains' etc)

195 'a mask'   JK, *The Dharma Bums* [*DB*]

195 The Governor's account of Han-shan is presented as a preface to Snyder, *Cold Mountain Poems*, first published in the *Evergreen Review*, no. 6, 1958; later published as a single volume with *Riprap*, Bolinas, CA, 1969

195 Whalen's poem, 'Sourdough Mtn Lookout', is contained in *The Portable Beat Reader*, edited by Ann Charters, NY 1992 (issued in the UK as *The Penguin Book of the Beats*, 1993)

196 It required   JK describes his term on Desolation Peak in *DB*, in *Lonesome Traveler*, NY 1960; and in *Desolation Angels* [*DA*], NY 1964

197 'When I get'   *DA*

197 'ole Hateful'   *DA*

197 'Night'   *DB*

198 'What's the difference'   *Escapade*, Oct. 1959

198 The cat   Alan Watts, *Beat Zen, Square Zen, and Zen*, SF 1959

198 Paul Bowles, 'Burroughs in Tangiers', *Big Table* 2, 1959

198 'Lee's Journals', in *Interzone*

199 'I'm shitting'   *DA*

199 'I can't'   WB to AG, 23 Jan. 1957

200 'Money all over'   WB, 'WORD', in *Interzone*
200 'the harder job'   AG to Carr, n.d., circa spring 1957, GCU
200 'Take no thought'   Mark 13: 11
201 'That's a fine'   Cowley to JK, 16 July 1957. Adam Gussow, 'Bohemia Revisited: Malcolm Cowley, Jack Kerouac, and On the Road', *Georgia Review*, Summer 1984, gives a good account of the relationship between editor and author
201 'A good'   Gussow, op. cit.
201 'revised well'   Barry Gifford and Lawrence Lee, *Jack's Book*, NY 1978
201 'essentials'   JK's list, 'Belief and Technique for Modern Prose: List of essentials', written in San Francisco in the mid-1950s, is often called 'Essentials of Spontaneous Prose'. However, this title was also given to a separate list, written earlier in New York. Both manifestos are contained in *The Portable Beat Reader*
202 'I told him'   Cowley to Lord, 8 Sept. 1957; see Gussow, op. cit.
202 'I agree'   17 Sept. 1957, MCA
204 'as the phone'   Joyce Johnson, *Minor Characters*, NY 1983
205 'Buddha . . . preaches'   *Escapade*, Oct. 1960
205 'Drunk'   JK to NC, Oct. 1957; published in Arthur and Kit Knight, *The Beat Vision: A primary sourcebook*, NY 1987
206 JK on Mike Wallace Show, CBS TV, 1958; a transcript of the interview was published in the *NY Post*, 1 Dec. 1958
206 'in his own'   Rexroth, 'Disengagement: The art of the Beat Generation', *New World Writing* 11, 1957
206 'guttersnipes'   Solomon, 'Pilgrim State Hospital', in *Emergency Messages*
207 'real danger'   WB, 'Ginsberg Notes', in *Interzone*
207 'What is'   Rexroth, 'Disengagement'
208 The Natalie Jackson affair is related in *Off the Road*
208 Ganser Syndrome *Time*, 16 Sept. 1957
208 Norman Podhoretz, 'The Know-Nothing Bohemians', *Partisan Review*, Spring 1958
209 'Kerouac's shoes'   Baldwin, 'The Black Boy Looks at the White Boy', in *Nobody Knows My Name*, NY 1961
209 'Suzuki'   ibid.
209 black faces   for an account of LeRoi Jones among the Beats, see Hettie Jones, *How I Came to Be Hettie Jones*, NY 1990
210 Jones's reply to Podhoretz was published in *Partisan Review*, Summer 1958
210 toilet paper   Hettie Jones, op. cit.
211 'Johnson', 'Raskolnikov' etc   JK to George Apostolos, 7 April 1943

212 'just like Dostoevsky' 'The Origins of the Beat Generation', *Playboy*, June 1959

212 'third part' ibid.

212 'probably the greatest' JK to JCH, June 1952, in Arthur and Kit Knight, op. cit.

212 'prose Melville' AG to John Ryan, 28 Aug. 1955, GCU

212 'Charlie Parker' AG, *Allen Verbatim*

212 'Jazz Critic' JK to AG, 14 July 1955

212 Corso to Keats *Paris Review* interview with AG

212 Kerouac said Carolyn Gaiser, 'Gregory Corso: A poet, the beat way', in *A Casebook on the Beat*, edited by Thomas Parkinson, NY 1961

212 Huncke AG, introduction to *Huncke's Journal*, NY 1965

212 JK is quoted comparing WB to Swift on the jacket of WB, *The Burroughs File*, SF 1984

212 'better than Hemingway' Ted Berrigan, *Paris Review* interview with JK

212 'Joyce' JK to NC, 15 April 1955

212 'the muscular' JK to NC, 27 Dec. 1950

213 'the best' JK to JCH, June 1952, Arthur and Kit Knight, op. cit.

213 'modern Proust' JK to NC, mid-April 1955

213 'the greatest' ibid.

214 'natural ignu' 'Ignu', *Collected*

214 'Rimbaud the child' Corso, 'Paris 1960', in *Elegiac Feelings American*, NY 1970

214 AG's meeting with Auden is reconstructed from the following: AG to LG, 1 Sept. 1957, GCU; AG, *Journals*; AG, 'Transcription of Organ Music', *Collected*; Barry Miles, *Ginsberg: A biography*, NY 1989; Michael Schumacher, *Dharma Lion: A critical biography of Allen Ginsberg*, NY 1992

216 'The plague' AG to Eugene Brooks, 1 Jan. 1958, GCU

216 'Genet is' Corso to AG, n.d., GCU

217 'asking Picasso' GC to AG, 27 May 1957, GCU

217 'With Peter' AG, *Journals*

217 'stealing books' AG, 'At Apollinaire's Grave', *Collected*

218 Ezra Pound related in George Plimpton, *et al.*, 'The *Paris Review* Sketchbook', *Paris Review* 79, 1981

218 AG's visit to Céline is described in Miles, *Ginsberg*

218 'Mer ... de ... aux' was part of a Futurist bulletin, *L'Antitradition futuriste*, Paris 1913

219 An excellent account of Apollinaire's life and writing is to be found in Francis Steegmuller, *Apollinaire: Poet among the painters*, London 1963

219 'Moon Prevention' is included in AG, *Journals*

221 Genet's *Oeuvres* for more about the Olympia Press, and about the Paris life of Chester Himes, see James Campbell, *Paris Interzone: Richard Wright, Lolita, Boris Vian and others on the Left Bank, 1946–60*, London 1994

221 'one bed' AG to Carr, 11 Dec. 1957, GCU

222 'black cloak' AG, 'At Apollinaire's Grave'

222 'stepped out' AG to LG, May 1957, GCU

222 Poor Lucien JK to AG, Oct. 1944

223 'In a room' WB, Foreword to Harold Norse, *Beat Hotel*, San Diego 1983

223 'had no use' Brion Gysin, Foreword to Harold Chapman, *The Beat Hotel*, Montpellier 1984

223 Burroughs: 'Madame' Norse, op. cit.

223 Gysin: 'William' Chapman, op. cit.

226 'Question of' Ferlinghetti to AG, 17 Sept. 1957, GSU

226 The Apollinaire novels were translated for the Olympia Press by Alexander Trocchi and Richard Seaver; see Campbell, op. cit.; see also Patrick Kearney, *The Paris Olympia Press: An annotated bibliography*, London 1987

228 'Who are you?' *Chicago Review*, vol. 12, Spring 1958

228 *Evergreen Review*, no. 2, 1957: 'The San Francisco Scene'

230 AG's letter to Paul Carroll was published in the *Chicago Review*, Autumn 1958

231 WB's appearance in the *Chicago Review* in 1958 marked the first substantial publication of anything from *Naked Lunch* [NL]. *The Black Mountain Review*, no. 7, 1957, had published 'From *Naked Lunch*, Book III: In search of Yage', which is a letter to AG (10 July 1953), later included in *The Yage Letters*, and used in 'The Market' section of *NL*

232 'Wot about' Carroll to AG, 3 Feb. 1959, GSU

232 '*On the Road* is' NC to Carolyn Cassady, 20 Aug. 1958; Neal Cassady, *Grace Beats Karma: Letters from prison 1958–60*, NY 1993

232 'at a party' NC to Carolyn Cassady, quoted in CC's foreword, ibid.

232 'jail problem' *OR*

233 'People keep' AG to LG, 30 Nov. 1957, GCU

234 'I read' WB to AG, July 1958

235 'everybody ate' Barry Gifford and Lawrence Lee, ed., *Jack's Book*, NY 1978

235 The reunion of JK and Edie is related in Gerald Nicosia, *Memory Babe: A critical biography of Jack Kerouac*, NY 1983

235 'wasn't me' Joyce Johnson, *Minor Characters*, NY 1983

235 'I keep falling' *Mexico City Blues*, 149th Chorus

236 'hears Blake's' AG, 'Ignu'

236 'Poet is priest' 'Death to Van Gogh's Ear', *Collected*. When AG included the poem in the book *Kaddish*, it was with the remark that it was first published, 'strangely', in the *TLS*

236 'Widen' the motto is placed at the front of *Kaddish*

236 'poetry that' 'Death to Van Gogh's Ear'

236 'flow of organized' AG to LG, 2 March 1958, GCU

238 The circumstances of AG's completion of 'Kaddish' are given in Miles, *Ginsberg*

239 Jack Mabley, 'Filthy writing on the Midway', *Chicago Daily News*, 25 Oct. 1958

239 'innocuous' Rosenthal to AG, 5 Nov. 1958, GSU

240 'Dear Irving' Corso's letter was published in *Big Table* 1, Spring 1959

241 'Burrough's trip' interview with Ferlinghetti in *Le Monde*, 27 Feb. 1998

241 'Well well' Snyder to AG, 2 Feb. 1959, GSU

242 'Naked Lunch served' WB and Brion Gysin, *The Third Mind*, NY 1960

243 'make Massa' ibid.

243 'Unless I can' WB to AG, 10 Oct. 1958

244 'the whole' ibid.

245 'King of the Beatniks' interview with JK, published over three successive issues of *Athanor*, 1971–2

246 ' "beatnik" of mad' *NYTBR*, 11 May 1959

246 'big bunch' *DA*

246 'a vision' 'The Origins of the Beat Generation', *Playboy*, June 1959

248 *MAD* magazine, September 1960

249 'an intense' *NYHT*, 1 May 1960

249 The phrase 'fabled damned' occurs in a letter from AG to LG, 30 Nov. 1957, GCU

250 Corso's poem 'Hair' was included in his collection, *The Happy Birthday of Death*, NY 1960

250 'At length' *Time*, 6 Feb. 1959

251 'Not for nothing' AG to Max Gartenberg, 1 Jan. 1959, Berg Collection, New York Public Library

251 'Divine' from an ad for a reading at City Lights, Berg Collection

251 'the world'   AG to Max Gartenberg, as above

252 'America is having'   AG, 'Poetry, Violence, and the Trembling Lambs', *San Francisco Chronicle*, 26 July 1959

252 skull and crossbones   AG to Max Gartenberg, 9 Dec. 1959, Berg Collection

254 AG's anger at Diana Trilling, and Eugene's reaction, as described in a letter from Eugene Brooks to AG, 16 May 1959, GCU

254 'Various wrathful'   Joyce Glassman (later, Johnson) to AG, 13 May 1959, GSU. *Partisan Review* had intended to publish sections from *NL* at this time, as is made clear in letters from Phillips to AG. In a letter of 19 Oct. 1959, Phillips also asked AG, 'Whether you might have some poems we could use.' Nothing came of either project, GSU

254 'Will you'   Rosenthal to AG and JK, Dec. 1958, GSU

255 'San Francisco gang'   WCW to Joseph Renard, 24 March 1958, GSU. WCW also made negative comments about AG and the Beats to the journalist Alfred G. Aronowitz, which the latter included in his series in the *NY Post*

256 'The most noise'   Philip Whalen, *Off the Wall: Interviews with Philip Whalen*, edited by Donbald Allen, Bolinas, CA, n.d. (1978?)

257 'Jack got on'   Newman to AG, 11 June 1956, GSU

257 'My contract'   JK to Ed White, 29 March 1949

257 The film of *The Subterraneans* (1959) was directed by Ranald MacDougall; a copy of the script by Robert Thom is housed in the NYPL

259 JK, *Pull My Daisy*, NY 1961; the original incident involving the bishop is described in *Off the Road*

261 JK, *The Scripture of the Golden Eternity*, NY 1960

261 'I read'   radio interview with Charles Jarvis, WCAP, Lowell, Mass., 8 Oct. 1962.

263 'sophomoric'   Rexroth to AG, 19 Oct. 1959

263 Rexroth's review of *OR* appeared in the *SF Chronicle*, 1 Sept. 1957; his review of *The Subterraneans* was published in the same paper on 15 Feb. 1958

264 'don't expect'   Rexroth to AG, 19 Oct. 1959, GSU

264 Eberhart to AG, 19 Oct. 1959, GCU

265 'this magazine'   quoted in Edward de Grazia, *Girls Lean Back Everywhere: The law of obscenity and the assault on genius*, NY 1992. The book contains a full account of the *Big Table* case. De Grazia later defended *NL* in court

266 'innocuous'   Chancellor Kimpton protested to the *Saturday Review* that he had never issued this instruction to Rosenthal; in the issue of 1

Aug. 1959, Ciardi published a retraction of the remarks attributed to Kimpton in his earlier essay

267 Judge Hoffman's ruling was published in *Big Table* 5, Summer 1960. In 1969, Judge Hoffman presided over the Chicago Seven trial, during which the Black Panther leader Bobby Seale was ordered to be gagged as he stood in the dock. In a later dramatization of the trial, WB took the part of Judge Hoffman

268 'naturally' Aronowitz to AG, 13 Dec. 1959, GSU

268 Paul O'Neil, 'The Only Rebellion Around', *Life*, 30 Nov. 1959

269 Mr Luce's private' Ted Morgan, *Literary Outlaw: The life and times of William S. Burroughs*, NY 1988

270 'To protect' Gysin, 'First Cut-ups', in Sinclair Beiles, William Burroughs, Brion Gysin, Gregory Corso, *Minutes to Go*, Paris 1960

270 'someone else's WB to AG, 29 Oct. 1959

274 'dissatisfied' etc WB letters to AG, 10 Oct. 1958; 21 April 1959; 7 Oct. 1959

276 'Girodias thinks' WB to AG, 24 Aug. 1959

276 Girodias owned up to his larceny in his autobiography, *Une Journée sur la terre*, vol. II, Paris 1990. WB's forgiveness is stated in Morgan, *Literary Outlaw*

276 'Eight am' WB to AG, late July 1959

277 'Témoignage: à propos d'une maladie', *NRF*, 1 Jan. 1960

278 *The Soft Machine* was published by Olympia in 1961; a French translation of *NL*, *Le Festin nu*, was published by Gallimard in 1964

279 'I have been' WB to AG, late July, 1959

279 'STAND' ibid.

279 'Karmic' quoted in *Off the Road*

280 'beat parties' JCH to JK, 26 Feb. 1958, Arthur and Kit Knight, ed., *The Beat Vision: A primary sourcebook*, NY 1987

280 Rexroth's review of the *The Horn* was published in the *Saturday Review of Literature*, 2 Aug. 1958

280 'All the religions' Robert Palmer, interview with WB and Gysin, *Rolling Stone*, 11 May 1972

281 'I think of words' WB, 'The Literary Techniques of Lady Sutton-Smith', *TLS*, 6 Aug. 1964

282 'everything seems' *Rolling Stone* interview with Gysin and Burroughs

282 'I mean machines' WB and Gysin, *The Third Mind*

283 'Burroughs lay awake' Bryan Morgan, *Total to Date – The Evolution of the Adding Machine: The story of Burroughs*, London 1953

284 'Accuracy' ibid.

284 'My advice'   'Techniques of Lady Sutton-Smith'
285 Girodias said   Victor Bockris, *With William Burroughs: A report from the Bunker*, NY 1981
285 Orlovsky said   quoted in Barry Miles, *Ginsberg: A biography*, NY 1992

Grateful acknowledgement is made to the Estate of Allen Ginsberg, Barry Gifford, Carolyn Cassady, Steve Turner, Topham Picture Library, and Anthony Balch for photographic material. All quotations herein are used for critical purposes only, and the words quoted remain the copyright of the individual copyright holders. Grateful acknowledgement is made to the following:

Jack Kerouac: *Selected Letters: 1940–1956*, edited by Ann Charters, copyright the Estate of Stella Kerouac, John Sampas, Literary Representative 1995. *Vanity of Duluoz*, copyright Jack Kerouac 1967, 1968. *On the Road*, copyright Jack Kerouac 1955, 1957, renewed 1985 by Stella Kerouac and Jan Kerouac. *The Dharma Bums*, copyright Jack Kerouac, 1958, renewed 1986 by Stella Kerouac and Jan Kerouac. All these works published by Viking Penguin. *Mexico City Blues*, copyright Jack Kerouac 1959, renewed 1987 by Jan Kerouac. *The Subterraneans*, copyright Jack Kerouac 1958, renewed 1986 by Jan Kerouac. Both published by Grove Press, a division of Grove Weidenfeld. *Desolation Angels*, copyright Jack Kerouac 1960, 1963, 1965. *The Town and the City*, copyright Jack Kerouac 1950, renewed 1978 by Stella Kerouac. *Old Angel Midnight*, copyright 1959, 1961, 1964, 1993 by John Sampas, Literary Representative.

Alan Ginsberg: 'Dakar Doldrums', 'In Society', 'The Green Automobile', 'Song', 'Sakyamuni Coming Down from the Mountain', 'America', 'Love Poem on a Theme by Whitman', 'A Supermarket in California', 'A Strange New Cottage in Berkeley', 'Howl', 'Transcription of Organ Music', 'Kaddish', 'Death to Van Gogh's Ear'; from *Collected Poems 1947–1985*, copyright Allen Ginsberg 1984, 1995, published by HarperCollins and Penguin Books. *Journals Mid-Fifties: 1954–1958*, edited by Gordon Ball, copyright Allen Ginsberg 1995, published by Viking Penguin. Interview with Allen Ginsberg by Tom Clark for the *Paris Review*, copyright the *Paris Review*, Inc. Excerpts from Allen Ginsberg's letters are copyright the Estate of Allen Ginsberg.

William Burroughs: *The Letters of William S. Burroughs, 1945–1959*, edited by Oliver Harris, copyright William S. Burroughs 1993, published by Viking Penguin and Picador. *Naked Lunch*, copyright William S. Burroughs

Index

310